Despair and Deliverance

SUNY Series in Israeli Studies

Russell Stone, Editor

Despair and Deliverance

Private Salvation in Contemporary Israel

Benjamin Beit-Hallahmi

STATE UNIVERSITY OF NEW YORK PRESS

Production by Ruth Fisher
Marketing by Dana E. Yanulavich

Published by
State University of New York Press, Albany

Printed in the United States of America

For information, address the State University of New York Press, State University Plaza, Àlbany, NY 12246

Library of Congress Cataloging-in-Publication Data
Beit-Hallahmi, Benjamin.
Despair and deliverance : private salvation in contemporary Israel : Benjamin Beit-Hallahmi.
p. cm. — (SUNY series in Israeli studies)
Includes bibliographical references and index.
ISBN 0-7914-0999-6 (alk. paper). — ISBN 0-7914-1000-5 (pbk. : alk. paper)
1. Israel—Religion—20th century. 2. Cults—Israel. 3. Jews—Return to Orthodox Judaism. 4. Occultism—Israel—Religious aspects. 5. Self-realization—Religious aspects. 6. Conversion. 7. Jews—Psychology. I. Title. II. Series.
BL1650.B45 1992
306.6'9142'095694—dc20 91-16392
CIP

10 9 8 7 6 5 4 3 2 1

Contents

Acknowledgments

I want to acknowledge my debts to many friends and colleagues, who have helped with data, encouragement, criticism, and support during the years of work on this book. Among them were: Netta Amir, Hanni Amit-Kochavi, Issachar Arbel, Myron J. Aronoff, Sara Avni, Victor Azarya, Nitza Ben-Arie, Nachman Ben-Yehuda, Nehama Berlinski, Yoram Bilu, Netanel Blasblag, Noam Chomsky, Erik Cohen, Jean-Pierre Deconchy, Gordon Fellman, Danielle Friedlander, Daniel Friedmann, Mordechai Frischtick, Pnina Galpaz, Claude Gandelmann, Daniel Gat, Angela Greenson, Mira Halperin, Heather Kernoff, Ruth Kimchi, Simha F. Landau, Vera-Margrethe Levin, Etan Levine, Michael Löwy, Dina Merhav, David Navon, Baruch Nevo, Bernard Och, Lew Rambo, Nurit Ramon, Sam Rakover, Amiram Raviv, Dolly Ronen, Erella Rotem, Israel Shahak, Talya Shay, Michal Sherbak, Sammy Smooha, Zvi Sobel, Madeleine Tress, Jim Uleman, Gabriel Weimann, Eugene Wiener, Moshe Zeidner, and Robert A. Zucker. The original idea for writing this book came from Uri Eisenzweig.

I would like also to acknowledge the support given by the Research Committee on Social Science and the Research Authority at the University of Haifa, the Department of Religion at Columbia University, the Department of Psychology at New York University, and the Center for the Documentation of Israeli Society at the Hebrew University.

While all these friends and organizations have contributed immensely to my work, I alone am responsible for its faults and oversights.

Prologue: Miracles of Self-Transformation

The man sitting across the table from me was unusually handsome, confident in his manner, and articulate. Like many Israelis, he was a chain-smoker, and looked more like an athlete than like the scientist that he was, holding a faculty position at a leading university. He was telling me the story of his individual salvation, his conversion from great misery to great happiness, a metamorphosis that happens to only a few among us. His life was transformed in an instant of revelation, and he was telling me about that instant. Ten years before our meeting, in October 1973, he was a sergeant in an artillery unit fighting on the Syrian front. He was wounded in battle, and his injuries, while not serious, left him handicapped psychologically and physically. He simply could not do anything, could not study or work. He was staying home, preoccupied with his narrowing world, considering ways of getting out of his predicament, including suicide. Then, one day, in one instant of revelation, he realized that there was an answer. It was in turning to the spiritual world, which existed, invisible, above and beyond our obvious material world on earth. This world is only an illusion. It is the spirit world that determines what happens here, in the material one, through positive and negative energies. Death just means that the soul moves on. In that instant, his physical and psychological sufferings ended. He became committed to relations with the spiritual creatures inhabiting the invisible world and later formally joined one of the new religions.

Now, K. was no longer a member of that group but held a combination of Hindu and Jewish beliefs. The other dimension of living, that of the eternal soul, colored his perceptions of others and of his own experiences. He related to people on the basis of their "spirituality." Some people were recognized as having "spiritual connections" with the invisible world. Others were judged inferior, lacking in spirituality. Events in this world were determined by spiritual forces and energies. Political and ideological changes were the result of positive and negative energies, which could be stored and used over time. Thus, there have been negative political developments in Israel since the 1967 War, which were caused by the release of enormous negative energies, stored for centuries around the Wailing Wall in Jerusalem. These negative energies, left there by successive generations of praying and mourning Jews, who came to the Wall to bewail their bitter fate, were let loose when structures around the Wall were torn down in June 1967 by the Israeli government. It will take time until the negative energies dissipate. On the whole, however, things in the Middle East were moving in a positive direction, as positive energies were taking over.

K. believed that death was not such a terrible thing because it meant a liberation of the soul from its material shackles, but suffering, which often precedes death, is a problem. His attitude toward war was ambivalent, therefore, because it brought liberation to some souls but suffering to others. While he was no longer a member of a recognized group or a movement, he met regularly with spiritual teachers, whose identities had to be kept secret. Occult knowledge was an important part of his life, but it was not shared with his academic colleagues. Such knowledge could be shared only with the saved and the enlightened. What he told me was more in the way of a personal odyssey, a miraculous transformation, but he was not sure whether I could appreciate the fine points of his occult observations of people and events.

Not all salvation stories involve the world of the spirits. D., a successful, married professional woman and the mother of three, offered her salvation testimonial in an uninterrupted and uninterruptable monologue. She spoke with conviction and clarity. The story she told was of a life marked by all the external indications of success and by internal doubt and quiet desperation. She graduated from professional school with honors, got married, gave birth to her children and, together with the rest of the family, presented to the outside world a picture of the perfect Israeli family: two cars, big house, tennis lessons for the children, travel abroad, and a growing professional reputation for both husband and wife. But beneath all this was another reality. One of strain and conflict, between husband and wife and between parents and children, one of fatigue and meaninglessness, a feeling of always being on the verge of breakdown, always being on the edge of a cliff. Like most people in that situation, D. and her family accepted their situation with resignation, not being able to imagine that things could be different or better.

The change in D.'s life came by accident. Somebody told her about an experiential kind of learning to change, something conducted in English, even though all the participants were Israelis, some of whom could understand nothing but Hebrew. That something, conducted by trainers sent all the way from San Francisco, was est training. D., together with 250 others spent two weekends in the training. She came out of it a changed person. She persuaded her husband and her children to take the training as well, and so they became an est family. Today, the whole family is markedly changed and improved. Its members have not lost any of the external markings of success. Quite the contrary. Materially, they are more prosperous than ever, but the real change is psychological. According to D., all the family conflicts have completely disappeared. Both parents and children have been in perfect communion since taking the est training. D. herself has been able to get by on less than four hours of sleep per night, with improved productivity in every sphere. In addition to the inner peace that D. has acquired, she now has a new goal in life; making est available to more people. She now spends most of her free time trying to induce others to take the est training. She is always willing to share with them her personal story of total transformation and happiness.

Significant and dramatic changes in human beings are rare and unusual, because human beings do not easily change their beliefs or behaviors. The natural human tendency, so it seems, would be to carry on both individual and collective traditions. Constraints on human flexibility and reactivity, whether internal or external, make total transformation in individuals unlikely (Skinner, 1971; Etzioni, 1972). The first message of the salvation testimonial is that transformation is possible, and the road is open for us to follow and experience it ourselves.

Private salvation testimonials tell us of a miraculous transformation, from darkness to a great light, from being lost to being found. There is a sharp contrast between earlier suffering and current improvements. The salvation story always includes a wide gap between the past and the present, corruption and redemption. The power of transformation through enlightenment is proven through this gap. In some cases the change is fleeting and brief, and the tale is soon forgotten. In others it is lasting, and the improvements real. New ideas are not only roads to personal salvation but also paths to liberation from oppressive and oppressing past lives and past identities. These private salvations are also private revolutions, which turn an individual biography upside down, while not touching the world around it.

This miracle of rebirth through conversion has been described in another context: "The true believer who becomes a Muslim casts off at last his old self and takes on a new identity. He changes his name, his religion, his homeland, his 'natural' language, his moral and cultural values, his very purpose in living. He is no longer a Negro, so long despised by the white man that he has come almost to despise himself. Now he is a Black Man—divine, ruler of the universe, different only in degree from Allah himself. He is no longer discontent and baffled, harried by social obloquy and a gnawing sense of personal inadequacy. Now he is a Muslim, bearing in himself the power of the Black Nation and its glorious destiny" (Lincoln, 1961, pp. 108–9).

When we consider these dramatic transformations of individual lives, we find ourselves before a mystery. At some level, we admire and envy those people who had the courage to make a clean break with their situation and to really change themselves. These transformations often entail what we consider great hardships, and we cannot stop wondering about the price some individuals are ready to pay for (what they describe as) their peace of mind. These cases of rebirth must command our most serious attention, because what they represent, at least in some cases, are indeed immensely positive transformations, which are impossible under any other conditions. The lame do not start walking, and the blind do not enjoy the sweet light of day; these miracles do not often happen. But the psychologically lame, the self-destructive, and desperate sometimes emerge from darkness and belie everything that happened earlier in their lives. These transformation do not only arouse curiosity but envy as well.

The key to understanding the phenomena of salvation movements is first really listening to those who have been saved. Let us hear their personal testimonies, and testimonials, and let us take them seriously. What they tell us is absolutely true. The stories are full of suffering, confusion, and despair, and then everything changes into the clear light of salvation, which transforms life, either permanently or temporarily. The personal transformations are real miracles, and nobody can disregard them. Even if the happiness is temporary and, to us, based on pure illusion, who would slight the splendor brought into lives previously devoid of anything except misery and emptiness?

These true stories tell us everything we need to know about the psychological, sociological, and historical background of the saved, the saviors, and the damned. We should listen closely and carefully when people tell us of the meaninglessness and emptiness in their lives, about their despair and about the metamorphosis that filled the dark void of their souls with light and peace.

I am using the term *salvation* here deliberately, and I believe that its use is appropriate. The experience of personal salvation is the one element common to the various self-transformations we are describing here. A profound experience of change is the *sine qua non* for the definition of salvation. What these individuals have told us sounds just like a phenomenon William James wrote about more than ninety years ago: "To be converted, to be regenerated, to receive grace, to experience religion, to gain an assurance, are so many phrases which denote the process, gradual or sudden, by which a self hitherto divided, consciously wrong, inferior and unhappy, becomes unified and consciously right, superior and happy" (James, 1902/1961, p. 160). This is indeed what has happened to our saved individuals. They have been converted and regenerated, their divided and inferior selves happy and unified. James's words still ring as the truest description of such a transformation, be it religious or secular. The conversion experience, as described by William James and by the saved individuals I met, leads to a subjective sense of power. It also leads to an objective growth in energy and activity, and to better adjustment. What these individuals experience is surrender. "Surrender in the sense of experiencing a happening does two things. One, it shuts out the noise of the world, at least momentarily. Two, it stops the "doer and shaker" from pushing ahead with his or her ambitions often at a time of high stress or crisis. It invites play of the passive imagination and attending to novel visual and verbal images that present themselves as though offered by another power" (Poewe, 1989, p. 368).

In all conversion stories a past of doubt and error is transformed into a present of wholeness in one great moment of insight and certainty. This is a new birth, leading to a new life. And the new birth often follows reaching the lowest depths of despair and consists of "an unexpected life succeeding upon death . . . the deathlike termination of certain mental processes . . . that run to failure, and in some individuals . . . eventuate in despair" (James, 1943, p. 303). The new birth creates a wider belief in "a world in which all is well, in *spite* of certain forms of death, indeed *because* of certain forms of death—death of hope, death of strength" (James, 1943, p. 305). The salvation discourse is a complex of beliefs and explanations of change. Salvation testimonials include examples of physical and psychological change, telepathy, cures of minor and major ailments, and of the experience of enlightenment—a sudden reorientation of one's faculties, personality, and identity and a reordering of needs and aims. From the observer's point of view, all these are but rationalizations of an overwhelming subjective upheaval.

Ever since William James and E. D. Starbuck, cases of individual religious conversion have been the focus of interest in the psychological study of religion and with good reason. Such cases are the exception, rather than the rule, among religious individuals. They reflect a high level of ego involvement (Sherif and Cantril, 1947) and an opportunity to observe the psychological dynamics of faith as if projected on a large screen right before our eyes. Over the past two decades, interest in the development of new religions has reawakened the study of the individual conversion experience, and this book looks at conversions to both old and new religions, together with secular ones.

In this book, we are going to look into the varieties of religious and secular salvation that have appeared in Israeli society over a fairly recent period, since 1973. This is a story of miracles and transformations. Our focus here will be on the incidence and prevalence of individual salvation, cases where we encounter a private experience through reports of profound change. What we are singling out are those individuals who present to us both a self-reported, but easily observed, identity change, represented by a break with past histories, and a self-reported personality transformation.

My focus here is on the experience of private salvation, that is, the profound transformation of the self in the wake of restructuring of personal life-space. Private salvation is not solitary salvation. It is experienced in social settings and can occur within primary social attachments or within secondary groups. It can occur within religious or secular settings.

> But to find religion is only one out of many ways of reaching unity; and the process of remedying inner incompleteness and reducing inner discord is a general psychological process, which may take place with any sort of mental material, and need not necessarily assume the religious form. In judging of the religious types of regeneration which we are about to study, it is important to recognize that they are only one species of a genus that contains other types as well. For example, the new birth may be away from religion into incredulity, or it may be produced by the eruption into the individual's life of some new stimulus or passion, such as love, ambition, cupidity, revenge, or patriotic devotion. In all these instances we have precisely the same psychological form of event—a firmness, stability, and equilibrium succeeding a period of storm and stress and inconsistency. In these nonreligious cases the new person may also be born either gradually or suddenly. (James, 1902/1961, p. 150).

Here I focus on personal salvation within secondary groups, religious and secular organizations. I began with the individual experience of radical transformation and then looked at its forms, context, and possible antecedents.

Every religion tells us stories of miracles and transformations. For most people, they remain stories about events that happened long ago and far away. For others, they become part of their own personal history, which they are ready to share with us. When such individual stories are being told more often, especially where such stories had been totally unknown until recently, we may seek an explanation for this cultural innovation. We should ask questions about it especially when this epidemic of private happiness seems to coincide with a serious collective crisis. Until recent years, hearing such stories and encountering their protagonists in Israel was quite uncommon. By the early 1980s, one was approached quite often, either personally or in the mass media, by members of religious and secular salvation movements, inviting all and one to share in their miracles and joys. There is new discourse of private salvation, which did not exist in Israel in 1970 or 1960, but was very much in evidence in 1980. This new discourse is expressed in salvation testimonials, individual stories of dramatic and total transformation. The paradox of this new discourse is that it appears in the midst of visible despair and desolation.

It is vital to keep in mind that these individuals represent small minorities, and clearly deviant ones, in their own society, but their deviance is a symptom of a universal malaise. The phenomena we are dealing with are minority movements and similar groupings representing protest, rebellion, and despair, are in most times and places minority phenomena by their very nature. Nevertheless, these minorities and their actions are significant and often influential beyond their numbers. This is because they represent tensions and sentiments likely to be prevalent in less extreme forms among the majority in their respective societies. To use the psychoanalytic metaphor, these movements represent an acting out of hidden and suppressed impulses, which push for direct expression below the surface of majority social life.

A Note on Method and Scope

The materials collected for the understanding and analysis of the phenomena discussed here include countless conversations with those who have found salvation in a variety of modes and with those still seeking it. Our most immediate data are individual experiences of those individuals in whom a miracle of transformation has occurred. In addition to being a researcher I have also been an eyewitness. My basic research approach has been to observe and to absorb whatever was going on around me in the various salvation movements. For about ten years I collected every kind of relevant information, from posters announcing lectures on Judaism or "Kabbalistic astrology" to personal stories and scriptures of old and new religions.

Much of my primary data collection has taken the form of ethnographic fieldwork. I have attended lectures on astrology, scientology, Unification Church theology, est guest seminars, and Gurdjieff seminars listening to the message and observing the scene. I have met hundreds of true believers in anything from Krishna to est and palmreading. I have talked to hundreds of individuals informally about their knowledge and feelings in regard to salvation movements. I have read many publications of the groups themselves, seeking to understand their belief systems. I have done some formal, conventional psychological research, administering questionnaires and interviews to seekers, converts, and others, together with colleagues and students.

I have also relied heavily on media reports, many of which are quoted in the text, because of the special role of mass media in Israel. The community of 3.5 million Israelis, which is the focus of this book, has been served by one television channel, four radio channels, and four daily newspapers which are read by 90 percent of the population. Thus, we have here a centralized and uniform system of information, which plays a special cultural role. The mass media do not only reflect (faithfully or not) what is happening in society. They also affect developments in the following ways:

1. Status conferral—what is reported in the media is considered significant or important.
2. Agenda setting—what is reported in the media deserves to be discussed and decided upon.
3. Creating opinions—media reporting creates a group feeling, sometimes by just reporting such a feeling.

This study deals only with the Jewish population of Israel, which in 1989 included about 82 percent of its residents, i.e., 3.5 million individuals. I use the term *Israelis* to designate those individuals who will apply this label to themselves without reservation. As Arian (1985) reports, Israeliness is central to the identity of 90 percent of Jews in Israel, according to 1974 poll data. This excludes, on the one hand, Arabs living in Israel and, on the other hand, those Orthodox Jews who would oppose Zionism and the Israeli State. The majority of those living in Israel accepts this label, and this majority is likely to be made up of "secular" Israelis, who are the consumers for the four salvation movements described below. My research focuses exclusively on Israeli natives. Although Israel is known as a nation of immigrants, close to 60 percent of the population, as of 1990, was native-born. My analysis is tied to a crisis of Israeli identity, and I decided to exclude immigrants, who represent unique and different biographies and cultural histories. In this, my study differs from several other works, such as those of Aviad (1983) and Shaffir (1991).

A salvation movement, or a road to salvation, as referred to in this book, denotes a complex of beliefs that serves as the context for cases of private salvation. We will cover four such roads as they have developed in Israel since 1973:

1. The occult, the most superficial movement, which serves as a broad base for other phenomena.
2. The new religions in Israel, which have led to many cases of profound personal transformation and constitute the most radical road in the context of Israeli society.
3. The return to Judaism, which is the most popular road to personal salvation and constitutes at the same time a radical rebellion and a conformist solution.
4. Secular psychotherapy, a movement that leads to personal change within a world view radically different from those of all of the other ones.

Following the presentation of the four movements, an analysis will be offered for their astounding appearance and growth in Israel over a space of only a few years.

I first started studying the phenomena discussed here in 1979 when a considerable change could be noticed in the status of both psychotherapy and the occult in Israel. Twelve years later, as this book is ready for publication, we have enough of a perspective on the processes involved. There has been an epidemic of intense personal happiness in Israel, which is a relatively recent development, and must be tied to other developments in Israeli society. The happiness epidemic is not, of course, the only significant change in Israeli society during recent years. Reactions to a continuous crisis can take the form of stress-related diseases, self-destructive behaviors, or self-constructive activities. This book focuses on private salvation, which can be self-constructive, but it also surveys other reactions to stress.

The theoretical question may be referred to as the epidemiology of happiness (and despair), or how different personal philosophies and world views become acceptable under certain social conditions. There are two levels of possible analysis and explanation. The first is that of cultural innovation and resistance to innovation, as new cultural expressions are created, opposed, and accepted. The second is that of psychological dynamics and individual psychopathology.

The two approaches are inevitably linked. When observing these phenomena, one cannot ignore their social and historical context. At the same time, while observing the individuals involved and listening to them, one cannot ignore the psychological (and psychopathological) context. This is a story of heterogeneity and change in Israeli society. The cultural change created a new inventory of ways of viewing the self and, in some cases, redemptive actions.

Private salvation experiences start with private salvation dreams. Salvation stories appear in response to salvation dreams, dreams of a new self, a new society, a new world. What did the saved dream of while seeking their private Lourdes? And how did the dream match an external source of salvation? Most of the phenomena would be described by some as escapist, and indeed they are, but at the same time, these escapist salvations are expressions of protest. What Karl Marx wrote about religion in general applies to these newer movements: "Religious suffering is at the same time an expression of real suffering and a protest against real suffering. Religion is the sigh of the oppressed creature, the heart of a heartless world, and the soul of soulless conditions" (Marx, 1844/1964, pp. 43–44). The comfort provided by salvation may be illusory, but the suffering that leads people to seek this comfort is very real.

This book may be regarded as a contribution to social history, the study of "the culture of each age as it arose out of these general conditions of life, and took ever changing forms in religion, literature and music, architecture, learning and thought" (Trevelyan, 1944, pp. vii–viii). But Trevelyan also wrote that "Social history might be defined negatively as the history of people with the politics left out" (p. vii). In the following study, as will become clear later on, the politics are left in.

1

Beyond the Pale
New Religions in Israel

In February 1982, an interdepartmental government commission was appointed by the Education Minister, to investigate and report on "Eastern cults." The appointment of this commission was in itself an indication of the growth of new religions in Israel. It was a result of pressure from parents' groups, religious orthodox groups, and the media. It was then estimated that about 3000 individuals were involved as active members in all of these groups. By 1990, there were six communal settlements in Israel created and maintained by followers of new religious movements. They included two settlements devoted to the teachings of G. I. Gurdjieff, two devoted to Transcendental Meditation, and one each for Emin and Anthroposophy.

The new religions that have appeared in Israel since the early 1970s are the same new religions that have appeared in the West since the 1950s. Their message when they come to Israel is the same as elsewhere. Only their audience is radically different and so is the reception they are likely to get. New religions are belief minorities in constant opposition to the world around them, which is challenging the plausibility of their beliefs. The challenge and the opposition are going to be particularly fierce in the case of Israel. What is unique about the advent of these groups in Israel is not the specific content of their beliefs and activities but their history in Israel. Their beliefs and practices were well-known and predictable. What was totally unforeseeable was their development and growth within Israeli society. The appearance and growth of new religious movements in Israel since 1973 has included not only well-known new religions that appeared in the West since 1950, but also movements such as anthroposophy, theosophy, and Jehovah's Witnesses dating to the late nineteenth century.

New religions only partly fit the ideal type of religious sect, as formulated by Troeltsch (1961), which included voluntariness, selectness, egalitarianism, cooperativeness, intimacy, and opposition to the world. Sectarian religion means a total personal commitment, a frequent emotional expression of ecstasy, a total departure from the rest of society. Every religious sect, by definition, is in open rebellion against the ways of the world, and against the views of the majority (see Beit-Hallahmi, 1992). Religious sects overstep the boundaries of the area assigned to religion in secular society, and this is what is annoying and threatening. The sectarian rebellion against the majority is invisible in most cases, since sects tend to withdraw from the wider society or keep to their original environment. A few sects are visible and annoying, and attract much attention when their members perform deviant acts, but the more remarkable fact is that most of the time sect membership leads to very conventional behavior. Still, sect membership itself, which involves a total commitment, and a total personal involvement (e.g., living with other sect members, donating income) is deviant.

Glock and Stark (1965) define cults as "religious movements which draw their inspiration from other than the primary religion of the culture," whereas sects are "schismatic movements . . . whose concern is with preserving a purer form of the traditional faith" (p. 24). By this definition, all new religions in Israel are cults, since they draw their inspiration from non-Jewish traditions. Within their own frame of reference, some of the new religions can be regarded as sects, since they proclaim their own goal of preserving a purer form of Hinduism (ISKCON) or of Christianity (the Unification Church). One reason in favor of using the term *new religions* is its affective neutrality. Unlike sects or cults, which are often used to derogate, *new religions* is neutral.

The concept of new religions can be traced back to Needleman

(1970), who first made it popular. Following Needleman, we may define the new religions by three main characteristics:

1. They were founded after 1950.
2. They display "modern," often businesslike methods of organization and recruitment.
3. They all have a conscious psychotherapeutic component in their belief systems and practices.

We are looking at groups whose formal organization, if not their belief system, is of relatively recent origin. Some of the groups promote beliefs and practices that seem beyond the traditional scope of religion, especially in the two areas of occultism and self-improvement. This may be one of the characteristics of the new religions, as opposed to the old ones. Nevertheless, what the old and new religious movements always share is the *supernatural premise,* the belief in the invisible world or a spiritual world, which the believers have to relate to (Wallace, 1966). The existence and centrality of occult practices and beliefs and of various psychotherapy techniques indeed vary among the new religions, but what unites them is still traditional religious beliefs about the immortal soul and about gods, and other unseen cosmic forces.

There are organizational differences, related as well to the newness of the new religions. They are young in terms of organizational life cycle, and they are also very much belief minorities. Since the new religions do not enjoy the privileged status of the old ones and have to compete with them, their problem is the problem of every cultural innovation: how to create openness to ideas that are new and different. Plausibility for deviant beliefs is hard to gain. The problem new religions have to solve is that of gaining plausibility in the eyes of potential members and the public.

In many of the new religions, the member is offered a system of psychological (and sometimes physical) exercises such as meditation, individual psychotherapy, and group therapy aimed at self-improvement and psychological well-being. This may be one of the differences between the old religions and the new ones, and it reflects the historical process of the psychologization of religion (see Beit-Hallahmi, 1989). The technology offered by the group, whether meditation, chanting, or psychotherapy, creates support for weak egos. This psychotherapeutic aid naturally attracts and can potentially help individuals with a range of personal problems, from mild neurosis to active psychosis. Some of the groups take a gnostic stance, claiming esoteric knowledge that is available only to group members. Sharing in this knowledge creates an understandable feeling of superiority. The insiders feel naturally superior to the unenlightened majority, and this feeling may exert a powerful attraction.

The resocializing effects of membership in new religions, which often lead members to stop self-destructive behaviors and to reenter the work world have been widely recognized (Kiev, 1969; Robbins, 1969; Robbins and Anthony, 1972). Only rarely has the claim been made that membership in new religions can have negative consequences in terms of psychological functioning (Kiev, 1964).

New religions, as opposed to old ones, are close to what Judah (1967) has called "modern metaphysical movements." Especially prominent in these groups are two characteristics listed by Judah: first, the identification of religion and science as mutually supportive and continuous, and the psychotherapeutic approach to individual well-being. Members of new religions who have experienced profound private salvation are likely to enjoy considerable therapeutic effects as a result of their entry into the group and their membership. The effects depend on their preconversion psychological state and on the nature of the social network in the group. The new religious group becomes a highly supportive structure, which provides exactly what is missing for the vulnerable individual. According to the classification offered by O'Dea (1968), the new religions in Israel can be classified as either "introversionist," i.e., seeking to withdraw from the world in order to cultivate its inner spirituality, or "gnostic," i.e., offering some special esoteric knowledge. The eschatology of the new religions covers two realms. There is the promise of radical change in the individual, in the direction of self-improvement, perfect health, longevity, and even immortality. There are also, in some groups, the expectation of a cosmic catastrophe, which only the faithful will survive.

The analysis of new religions in Israel has to be informed by the nature of Israeli society, by the Israeli-Jewish identity and its problems, and by the crisis of Zionism. What is remarkable about the new religions in Israel is their phenomenal growth during a very short period of time. In attempting to assess the existence and growth of new religions in Israel since 1973 we are fortunate to have a survey published in 1972 by two researchers at the Hebrew University (Cohen and Grunau, 1972). This detailed survey of ethnic and religious minorities in Israel at the time also included a section on cults. Using informants, official statistics, published research, and media reports, it gives us what we can call our baseline. What it shows is that the situation in Israel as of 1972 with regard to new religions was strikingly different from that in Western Europe or the United States. The only groups listed were theosophy, anthroposophy, "yoga according to Vente Kesananda," transcendental meditation (TM), ISKCON, Subud, Zen, Krishnamurti, Rosicrucians, and "Spiritualists." The total number of members was at most 250. Most of the groups that became prominent later, such as Scientology and the Divine Light Mission, were simply unknown. The number of TM practitioners was estimated at less than ten.

In defining new religions in Israel we have another source of help. In Israel, where there is no constitution, no separation of religion and state, and a Ministry for Religious Affairs, there is a clear legal definition of new religions. They include all the religious communities not recognized by the state. According to Israel law, all residents must belong to some religious community, whose rules they then must follow with regard to marriage, divorce, and burial. The Israeli system of religious divisions uses the *millet*, the religious community, as a basic unit. This notion is taken from Turkish law (Cahnman, 1944). Under the *millet* system, the Israeli government recognizes certain established religious groups, whose leaders are accorded special status, even when they represent tiny minorities. These religious communities are also entitled to government financial support for keeping their churches or mosques, for maintaining their separate legal systems, and for paying the salaries of clergy. They have an official standing, their leaders are treated as dignitaries, and they are eligible for financial support and tax exemptions. All other groups, ranging from Reform Jews to ISKCON, are not recognized.

Conversions from one *millet* to another are possible under the system but have to be registered with the State to be legally valid. This according to a British order, based on the legal authority of the British Mandate of 1922. All these orders have been kept in force by the Israeli government since 1948. The British Mandate government recognized ten religious groups, namely Jews and nine Christian denominations. The Israeli government since 1948 has recognized the Druze (in 1957), the Evangelical Episcopal Church in Israel (in 1970), and Baha'ism (in 1971). Muslims have not been officially recognized, but their religious courts have been, and they have been empowered by two Israeli laws (1953 and 1961). Cases of conversion from one recognized group to another number under 300 a year, and most of them are conversions from one Christian church to another. About five cases of Jews converting to Christianity and about ten cases of Jews converting to Islam are officially registered every year.

As Pfeffer (1974) correctly points out, in Israel legitimation of a marginal religion is accorded by the government, and he chooses the good example of non-Orthodox Jews, who in Israel are members of a marginal religion and are not accorded legitimacy by the State. The boundaries of religious legitimacy and religious experimentation in Israel of the 1950s are faithfully described by Weiner (1961). The boundaries of religious legitimacy in Israel in the 1970s are delineated in Israel Pocket Library's *Religious Life and Communities* (1974), which contains material taken from the *Encyclopaedia Judaica*. The religious communities described are Jews, Muslims, Christians, Samaritans, Karaites, Druze, and Baha'is.

The common division of Jews in the United States into three denominations, Orthodox, Conservative, and Reform (Lazerwitz and Harrison, 1979) has little bearing on religious life in Israel. Reform Judaism and Conservative Judaism, imported from the United States, could be counted among the other new religions. They are subject to either opposition (from the Orthodox establishment) or indifference (from most Israelis) and have shown little success in attracting members. As Liebman and Don-Yehiya (1984) state: "The institutional monopoly of the Orthodox (Conservative and Reform rabbis are not recognized as rabbis in Israel . . .) is not a major political issue. There are no more than two or three thousand members of non-Orthodox synagogues" (p. 19). As of 1986, there were seventeen Reform and thirty Conservative synagogues in Israel (Bitzur, 1986). Their histories in Israel are similar to those of other new religious movements. They were imported by foreigners, who have been trying to convert the native-born to their viewpoint with limited success. Most members of these Jewish movements have been immigrants from English-speaking countries. As of 1990, there are probably fewer than 3000 Israeli adults in both.

In a sense, Reform Judaism has a harder task "selling" itself to Israelis than ISKCON. The former tries to present itself as an authentic form of Judaism, while the latter is clearly an alternative and an opposition to Judaism. Most Israelis have not responded to the Reform and Conservative messages apparently because they do not feel the need for another Judaism in addition to the Orthodox version readily available. The Reform and Conservative movements also express quite strongly values characteristic of U.S. culture, such as anti-authoritarianism and feminism, and which are quite foreign to Israeli experience and culture. The opposition to Reform Judaism in Israel comes from the Orthodox, as it threatens their dominance and monopoly. The opposition to new religions is almost universal because they threaten the unity provided by the Jewish identity common to secular and religious Israelis.

To appreciate the reality of new religious movements in Israel, we are now going to examine in detail the least known among them, the Emin Society, and in some detail the situation of Messianic Jews and Jehovah's Witnesses in Israel.

The Emin Society

The village of Maale Tzvia, in the hills of the Western Upper Galilee, appears to be just another struggling settlement surrounded by a barren, rocky scenery. Its nondescript houses, where only thirty families make their home, are not likely to attract much notice. The inhabitants seem to most observers to be busy, industrious young Israeli families, devoting their energies to work and family life, just like their neighbors in other villages. Little would lead the observer to guess that one of those light gray buildings houses a temple of worship, a hidden sanctum that is off-limits to the impure and uninitiated. Maale Tzvia is a settlement of the Emin Society, and its inhabitants' beliefs about the world, themselves, and others make them as unique as one could be in Western Galilee.

The Emin Society Israel, the Israeli branch of an occult group started by a London truck driver, is an impressive success story by any measure. In a few years it has grown from two emissaries to several hundred committed members, who are investing personal energies, money, and identities in this unlikely venture. And the members are by no means the downtrodden or visibly desperate. Many are young, handsome, neatly dressed, many of them officers in the Israeli armed forces.

History of the Emin Society

The only publication which is referred to explicitly as the Emin Bible, is *The Poem of The Church of Emin Coils* (Armin, 1978), which presents its history, rules, and sacraments. The *Poem* describes the growth of the organization from an inauspicious beginning of just five into a membership of 1000. This early membership, known as "the family," consisted of:

1. Mr. Raymond Armin, known as LEO (British)
2. Mrs. V. A. C. Armin, known as RUTH (British)
3. Mr. John Armin, known as PELLI (British)

4. Mr. Stephen Armin, known as PETER (British)
5. Ms. Deborah McKay, known as ETHRA (American) adopted family member, by agreement. (Armin, 1978, p. 1)

According to the *Poem*, "The Emin story begins at 3:20 A.M. on the 27th of July 1924 with the emergence from the small world into the large world of earth by Raymond Armin, who by the age of 12 years had become deeply religiously inclined at the cost of his early general academic qualities" (Armin, 1978, p. 1). Raymond married Ruth in 1945 and begat John Armin (Pelli) in 1958 and Stephen Armin (Peter) in 1964. On 3 December 1971, nine other people joined the church. One of them was Ms. Deborah McKay, who was adopted in February 1972 by Leo and Ruth. The "healing capacity" of "the Essence" (Leo, Ruth, and Ethra) appeared as a "marked emanation" in 1973. In 1974, according to the *Poem*, the membership reached 250. During that year Leo stopped working at his previous job and has been kept since then by "small donations" from members.

"During these formative years, choirs, herbal groups, tarot groups, Bible study classes, poetry groups, mumming groups, theatrical groups, bands, vocal groups, music composition, dancing troups, healers, astrology groups, palmistry, graphology, phrenology and other detection groups" (Armin, 1978, p. 3) were developed.

By 1977, according to the *Poem*, the Emin Society had 800 members, with 600 academic degrees, including eighty Americans residing in Britain. There was also "the retrieving and saving of some 450 persons from drugs (many hard-line), as well as the many successes in healing, of terminal conditions in both young and old, and of many other conditions, such as fibroids of the womb, arthritis and others." (p. 3). In 1978, there were groups in Israel, Canada, Australia, and the United States, in addition to the group in London. In November 1978, the Essence (Leo, Ruth, and Ethra) with Emin's executive officer (Pelli) traveled to the United States to start the Church of the Emin Coils. By that time, according to the *Poem*, membership reached 1000.

From various publications (e.g., *Private Eye*, May 23, 1983) it can be gathered that Emin was first known as the Eminent Way and that the current name Emin, is simply an abbreviation of the old one. The name Emin is pronounced *EE-men*, and various esoteric interpretations are offered to the members as to its derivation. The Church claims to have collected as of late 1978 (Armin, 1978) 14 million written words and 40 million spoken words on audio and video tapes, which are known as the Archives and serve as the source of all authority and knowledge. The prolific Mr. Armin thus resembles another founder of a well-known new religion, L. Ron Hubbard.

The roving ambassador for Leo is Mathew, who has resided in Israel as Leo's personal emissary, to oversee the activities of the Israeli branch. Mathew has also traveled to the United States to organize Emin activities there and to lecture. According to an Emin Foundation leaflet distributed in New York City, Mathew spoke on WMCA radio on October 15, 1982. The Church of Emin Coils is the Florida branch of the Emin Society, organized in 1978 by Leo and his emissaries.

Private Eye, London's muckraking satirical weekly, has devoted four articles to the Emin organization (Halloran, 1980a, 1980b, 1980c, 1980d), causing Mr. Armin to go to court and ask for injunctions against any more publications. These attempts have failed. *Private Eye* reported that Mr. Armin's real name was Schertenlieb and that he was the son of a British hotel waiter. As a child, he was often disturbed by "voices" and "past reincarnations." During World War II he was stationed in India and later employed as a house painter. In the early 1960s, he was an area manager for the *Encyclopaedia Britannica* sales organization in Britain but in 1965 was declared bankrupt in Nottingham at his own request. He then moved to London and worked as a truck driver. Then started his career as Leo.

The Emin organization in Britain operates through six registered companies, all owned and directed by members of the Armin family. Only one of the companies has ever filed annual income returns, as required by British law. The income for that company, Esoteric and Occult Lectures, Ltd., was rather impressive (193,000 British pounds for 1977) but most of it was paid to the directors in fees and salaries. *Private Eye* estimated that the Emin group of companies was making about 10,000 British pounds a week, from 2000 dues-paying members worldwide. In addition to the request for a court injunction, the *Private Eye*'s first article drew 135 letters from Emin members, some of which included rather explicit threats (Wallis and Curran, 1981).

The history of Emin in Israel starts in London in 1974, when Rafi and Erez, two young former commandoes, were serving as security men at the Israeli Embassy there. They chanced upon the developing Emin organization and became members. After what they call three years of study, they returned to Israel in 1977 and for the next two years held meetings with groups ranging from ten to thirty people. In 1979 Mathew, Leo's personal emissary was sent to Israel to oversee the development of the Israeli branch. In 1980, when membership reached 200, a former movie theater was rented in a lower-class neighborhood near Tel-Aviv and was then turned into the Emin center. According to Emin leaflets, from which the above information was taken, membership reached 350 in 1982, with an equal number of candidates for membership. In letters written to the Government

Commission of Inquiry on cults in Israel in 1983, membership was reported to be 550 or 600, and the number of candidates was not mentioned. Leo has visited Israel several times since 1983 to see for himself the development of the Israeli branch and direct its future course.

Emin Beliefs

Many of the beliefs and practices in the Emin lore are similar to those advocated by other modern occult groups, especially the Rosicrucian, Gurdjieff-Ouspensky, and Rudolf Steiner traditions. The basic beliefs and practices of the Emin Society are presented in *The Journey* (Armin, 1979) and in *Cobwebs and Tears* (Armin, 1982).

The following passages, written by Leo in 1972, give the flavor of much of the writings:

> From the foundations of the world, the Queen of the Galaxy has been nurtured and maintained by the three forces that are the breath of life throughout the universe, herself being a tripod and crucible in which the magical and mysterious blending never ceases. (Armin, 1972, p. 30)

> The Church of Emin Coils deems human life with its present possibility to have begun approximately nine thousand years ago, which is the measurement of the last evolutionary upgrading in the joint planetary and human story of trace. Therefore it is viewed that all ensuing evidence constitutes the current dignity and character of human existence, and stems from the King Scorpian dynasty of Egypt . . . from which all attested religions of the twentieth century are subsequent and derivative. (Armin, 1978, p. 8)

> [There are] two universal processes (blue and red) within the confines of the Blue Planet, Earth; the crossing of the three universes in the galaxy (blue, red and white) and the crossing of the five universes within the confines of middle space, which extends to the disc of the Milky Way (the colors of which are green, yellow, blue, red and white). (Armin 1978, p. 9)

The Emin view of other religions is accepting and eclectic: "Abraham is admitted to; Jesus Christ is admitted to (the Silver Chalice); Mohammed and the Blue Princes of Islam is [*sic*] admitted to (the Silver Beacon); Guatama the Buddah is admitted to (the Gold Road); the Platinum Triangle of Lords Brahma, Wishnu, [*sic*] Shiva is admitted to" (1978, p. 11.

The Emin Society does have some peculiar beliefs about human anatomy, especially the nervous system. These include the belief in the existence of three brains. "Yes, three, originally. Now two. Simply, the human used to have an equivalent tail in which was seated the third brain. For many reasons the third brain broke up and became widely dispersed throughout the diaphragm and stomach" (Armin, 1979, p. 54).

The practices of the Emin Society include reading auras and diagnosing individuals on the basis of aura colors, according to charts developed by Leo, Ruth, and Ethra. There is a rite of exorcism, which "arrests any hostile, degenerative or unreasonable essence, practice, mind or mental projection; which stands against anything which tries to prevent the given right of human life to become enhanced over its planatary station. . . . It is processed and dealt with entirely in the occult, electrical and electro-magnetic fields of human precincts, dwelling precincts, location precincts and all concentrated ground or dimensions" (Armin, 1978, p. 118). Reincarnation is discussed extensively in Leo's various teachings (Armin 1979 and 1982).

Leo teaches that "True Tarot cards are representations in picture form, using symbol, colour, number, positions and so on, which constitute an encyclopaedia of knowledge concerning the purposes of God, the mechanics of creation and human life in relation to God and creation; and so, within any true tarot, there are clues to self-development" (Armin, 1982, p. 118).

According to interviews with ex-members and informants, Emin doctrine includes belief in a coming disaster, which will destroy the whole world, leaving behind only Emin members and their immediate environment. Such a disaster had been predicted for 1984 but was averted at the last moment because of the "positive energy" created by Emin members in their activities.

A major concern expressed in Emin writings is that about becoming electrically polluted, and the means to avoid or rectify this pollution. "Part of self development concerns taking care not to allow oneself to coarsen or become electrically poisoned or polluted below the level of one's aim or attainment" (Armin, 1982, p. 74).

> Electrical stumps travelling through the astral light can attach themselves, in the way of a barnacle or limpet, to the human aura. Understand that all sorts of electrical filth can be released

> by people which then moves through the astral light looking for a human host which is higher than itself upon whose aura it can attach itself, and from which it can electrically feed, and even grow. But there is worse to come, for at close quarters someone can stick upon you one of those electrical barnacles or limpets deliberately, through spite, malice, hatred, jealousy, sexual projection . . . Now, this can become even more serious, in that once an electrical barnacle or limpet has attached itself to a person's aura, it can then work like modern radar, acting as a beacon to that from which it came; and so it can receive further transmission from its source, and from any source of like kind and frequency . . . this indicates a very dangerous prospect should a 'branch office' be established on the very edge of your aura which is transmitted into on [*sic*] a long-term basis." (pp. 78–79)

The solution for this worrisome state, according to Emin writings, is cleansing your aura by wiping it with human hands.

Emin Activities

Before a group meeting, the floor of the room is mopped by the men, who then arrange the chairs in a U-shape. The women then move around with a bell and with incense, and decontaminate the room from undesirable electrical charges, which may interfere with the activities. The women also provide cut flowers for a vase, put on the table in front of the chairs. To mark the beginning of the meeting, the Usher plays the same musical record. The Usher is accompanied by Back Up Ladies, who provide tea (for the Usher) and positive electrical energy. Participation by group members is handled rather formally.

Group meetings are held twice a week, in addition to other special activities. Fees are charged for each meeting, in addition to monthly dues. The total expense per month for an active member may reach more than $150, which is about one quarter of the average monthly income of an Israeli family in 1986. The Emin organization is highly centralized, with a small number of Ushers and Monitors, who have reached "more advanced levels of knowledge," being in charge. Personal emissaries of Leo, or Leo himself, make all policy decisions.

According to the *Poem* (p. 58), the church has its own calendar, with nine holidays as of 1978, including The Day of Seven Gifts (March 21 approximately), The Celebration of the Significance of Birth and Regeneration (Easter Sunday), and The Celebration of the Silver

Chalice (Christmas). For members of Emin, personal time is measured by Emin years, which are nine months long. "A normal seasonal life cycle is . . . 72 Emin years; which then translates into 54 calendar years, which is, interestingly enough, the age at which Mohammed is recorded to have become divine. Any more birthdays or cycles after this time are considered to be grace of extension" (Armin, 1978, p. 63).

Standards of behavior in the *Poem* include rules about symbols and sexual behavior. "It is forbidden . . . to erect a pentagram or an aeneagram; and it is against God and creation to worship any symbol in an upside-down condition, or to practice a ceremony backwards. Any offender will be exorcised and excommunicated" (Armin, 1978, p. 150). This is, in part, because "the two symbols become portals or terminal points of the arrival and dispatch of inter-galactic electrical form" causing death by "spontaneous combustion, petrification, lack of energy (wasting) and electrical gangrene" (p. 152).

Regarding sex, "At no time will homosexuality, lesbianism, transvestism, nymphonic or any other unnatural condition or freak practice . . . be permitted" (p. 156). Masturbation is allowable, only once a week, and with "no mental associations or mental pictures. . . . The action should be entirely mechanical . . . excess is sinful, and astral deterioration will ensue, by the power of the church Essences. Therefore, use it with care" (p. 161).

In sum, the Emin system of beliefs and practices seems to be an amalgam of Western occult traditions diligently and eclectically collated, if not integrated. These traditions include alchemy, numerology, tarot cards, astrology, palm reading, aura reading and cleaning, beliefs in reincarnation, animal magnetism, and electromagnetic healing. The sources of Emin beliefs and practices can undoubtedly be traced to the personal experiences of the founder Mr. Armin, who has been exposed to all these old and new systems through extensive reading, personal contacts with theosophical and occult groups of various kinds, and possibly with Scientology. The sheer volume of Mr. Armin's writings is impressive. What emerges from them is a system that can be described as modern occultism, and thus, Emin can be classified (alliteratively) as a modern eclectic (electrical) occult cult.

Emin in Israel, the Media, and the Government

The first newspaper article about the Emin in Israel was published in the daily *Davar* on June 30, 1980, and was clearly initiated by the group itself. It sounds like a press release and emphasizes the positive and social nature of its activities. The subtitle of the article proclaims: "A brain surgeon and a construction worker find a common language in a club aimed at personal-creative development." The article does mention some of the esoteric knowledge but refers specifically only to astrology, which in Israel is not considered occult. At the end of the article, Rafi Eyal, one of the founders, expresses concern that the group not be perceived as something mystical, and that it has no "missionary intentions." The number of members is reported to be 100. The same article, in an abridged version, appeared seven months later in a local weekly. *Teva Ubriut*, the organ of the naturopathy movement in Israel, carried in its October 1981 issue a brief article by Avi Levy, identified as an Emin member, dealing with the "Five electrical centers in the human body" (Levy, 1981).

Emin was one of the targets in the general attack on new religions, conducted by the Israeli press in 1982–83. *Laisha*, a women's weekly which has the highest circulation of all Israeli weeklies, published an article (Avidan-Barir, 1983) about an artistic couple who got divorced after the husband became a member of Emin. Zohar (1982) wrote about Emin as part of a series of articles pointing to the danger of cults. A local newspaper in Haifa (*Kolbo*, 1982) reported on an Emin meeting in a Haifa suburb, protested by Parents Worried About Cults. Kaffman (1983), a psychiatrist in charge of the section for research and prevention team on cults in the Kibbutz Child and Family Guidance Clinic in Tel-Aviv, denounced Emin in a letter to the editor of *Hashavua Bakibbutz Hartzi* (a weekly distributed in eighty kibbutzim). Kisslev (1983) devoted an article to Emin in a series of articles on New Religions, published in Israel's leading daily. The tone in all of these ranged from negative to vitriolic.

The Commission of Inquiry, appointed by the Minister of Education in 1982, was set up to investigate all cults operating in Israel. The Emin Society Israel responded by actively trying to persuade the commission that it was not a cult or a sect. The Society leaders appeared before the commission, bombarded it with letters and memoranda, and had members and their families send letters in support.

The Emin policy in regard to media criticism and to the government Commission of Inquiry has been one of responding to every mention of its name in the same way, trying to persuade the public that it was not a religious group and that it was not breaking the law. While the second point cannot be disputed, the Emin Society attempts to persuade the public and the government that their beliefs and practices focused on "study and self-improvement" seemed rather naive, as shown by their absolute lack of success. Of all new religions active in Israel in the early 1980s, including Scientology, ISKCON, Divine Light Mission, Ananda Marga, and Transcendental

Meditation, only TM has tried to respond directly to media attacks. Most groups did not respond to any media or government reports or inquiries. Emin chose almost a frontal assault strategy, possibly because of directions from Leo.

Publications by the Israeli branch of Emin are very much concerned with conveying a favorable image to the public. They include advertisements in newspapers, brochures, letters to the editors (usually in response to newspaper articles about Emin), and letters to various government authorities. There were newspaper advertisements offering information to the public about Emin on at least four occasions (September 22, 1982, March 9, 1983, February 6, 1983, and December 6, 1984). These carried the distinct griffin logo of Emin, and included a post office box address. Five letters to the editor (one of those signed by fourteen individuals) appeared in *Al Hamishmar* on April 6, 1982, in response to an article about Emin published on March 19, 1982. All five letters express the same message: Disappointment with the article of March 19, demands for apologies and retractions, and information about the society. The writers emphasize that they are gainfully employed, have served in the military, are loyal to the State, and are not members of a religious cult. Moreover, they claim that Emin represents the original Israeli pioneering spirit. A letter to the editor of *Hashavua Hakibbutz Haartzi* (a weekly publication of one of the two kibbutz federations) of May 27, 1983, signed only by the "spokesman for the Emin Society," declares, in response to an earlier article, that Emin is not a cult but a legally registered nonprofit club, whose members are adults, serve in the military, and do not use drugs. A letter in *Davar*, February 4, 1983, denies beliefs attributed to the group in an earlier article. It states that the Emin Society is a group involved in promoting personal development through "the application of studies in human culture, the human system and the natural laws of the universe." These studies were carried out "by hundreds of people during 40 years of work." The letter is signed by Udi Ben-Dror, spokesman for the Emin Society.

A lecture dealing with the Emin during the annual meeting of the Israel Anthropological Society at the Hebrew University in Jerusalem on March 14, 1983, was interrupted by shouts and yelling from the audience, which included about thirty members of Emin. The lecture by a graduate student in sociology at the Hebrew University, developed into a shouting match after Emin representatives demanded time to present their views, and the speaker was not able to present the prepared text. Yigal Tumarkin, a well-known Israeli artist and journalist, writes in his weekly column in *Ha'ir* on September 16,

1983, that, following the mention of Emin among other cults in an earlier column, he received numerous angry and insulting letters from members claiming that the Emin Society was not a cult.

Udi Ben-Dror, spokesman for the Emin Society Israel claimed in a press interview (Be'er, 1983) that Emin members had been fired from their jobs, and that property belonging to them had been damaged as a result of adverse publicity. The author has been contacted by the Israel Association for Civil Rights after members of Emin complained to the Association of Harassment. The association appointed a team to investigate those allegations, but no substantial proof was ever found.

The Emin Society held an art exhibit at a city gallery in Jerusalem in December 1982. The paintings displayed were reminiscent of traditional occult works, such as tarot cards. According to a report (Beer, 1983), the exhibit was removed after three weeks by the deputy mayor of Jerusalem, who acted in response to what he regarded as "missionary activities." A leaflet distributed at the exhibit stated that it "is one of the many areas of work that are part of the whole fabric that we cover in our studies, researches, and practical activities. We are also open to give demonstrations in other areas, such as 'Sacred Dance,' Choir and the arts of human expressions" (The Emin Society Israel, December 1982, original in English).

In the summer of 1983, the Emin Society started offering the public a variety of open activities at various locations. These included cleanups of historical sites and evenings of Israeli folk dancing. Such an evening took place on Saturday, August 13, 1983, in the largest public park in Tel Aviv. In a letter to the Commission of Inquiry investigating cults, the Emin Society spokesman stated (August 15, 1983) that the society had been engaged in volunteer activities of this kind, in an attempt to promote the values of honesty, honor, altruism, and cleanliness. The letter also states that Emin members are a part of Israel and Judaism, and that they promote original Israeli dancing and songs.

A letter to local government authorities, reporting on the cleanup operation of a historical site in the Galilee (August 21, 1983), signed by the Emin spokesman, mentions that the site was the center of Judaism in the Galilee during ancient times and emphasizes the keeping of Jewish traditions. A letter dated August 25, 1983, and addressed to various public personalities lists community activities being carried out or being planned, including theater; lectures on "family life, child rearing, developing thinking and personality, human history, palm reading, astrology, natural healing, art and creativity, the structure of the human brain"; art exhibits; and parties for elderly.

Between September 22 and 29, 1983, the days of the Jewish festival of Sukkot, the Emin Society Israel carried out a major campaign of open activities, announced through newspaper advertisements, leaflets, and letters to government authorities. The activities included cleanups of nature preserves and archeological sites, an exhibit of a "quality sukkah," concerts and choir performances, lectures on "Values to live by," and refreshment stands near highway intersections.

The Emin doctrine specifies and requires respect for other religions, especially the major established religions, and also respect and loyalty or civil law and civil obligations in all countries where members may reside (Armin, 1978). This doctrinal prescription may be the basis for the way in which Israeli Emin members treat the Israeli state. They emphasize their absolute loyalty and commitment. A major, and convincing, argument used by Emin members to justify their claim of complete loyalty to the state is their distinction in military service. The Emin membership contains an extraordinary number of men who have served in combat units as officers and noncommissioned officers. It should be remembered that in Israeli military service (compulsory between the ages of 18 to 21, then active reserve duty until age 55) is a major test of adjustment for all Israeli men. Military service is compulsory, but becoming a pilot, a paratrooper, or a combat officer is a matter of choice and distinction. Those who choose this career (and this is a secondary career if the man is a reserve officer) are not society's outcasts or deviants. They are in the mainstream and embody the culture's self-defined virtues. Whatever they do cannot be dismissed as lunacy or deliberate evil. It has to be reckoned with.

The Emin Membership

There are more data available about the Emin membership in Israel than on any other new religion, and this is due to the Emin Society itself. During 1982 and 1983, in a response to media reports about the Emin Society, the society started a public relations campaign, which included disclosing information about the members. To disprove what they say were misconceptions or deliberate lies, Emin members went public in media interviews, letters to newspapers, and paid advertisements. The most unusual step taken by the Emin Society was to publish two paid advertisements, in one Hebrew and one

English newspaper, which included a list of members' names, occupations, university degrees, and military rank. These advertisements included a total of 263 names. From other published sources I was able to obtain some additional names, and I now have a sample of 283 names of Emin members, with additional information on some of them.

Even a list of names, with no added information, tells us something about the social background of the members. In Israel, even a first name tells you much about an individual's background. Because of changes in naming traditions among secular Israelis and a rejection of traditional Jewish names (Beit-Hallahmi, unpublished) one's first name tells us something about family background and his age. A name such as Idan Saar, an Emin member (*Idan* means "era," *Saar* means "storm") tells us that its bearer was born in Israel after 1950. Names also indicate ethnic background.

The first thing I looked at were non-Ashkenazi names. The Jewish population of Israel in 1984 was made up of about 45 percent Ashkenazi and about 55 percent non-Ashkenazi Jews. Among 283 Emin names, only twenty-one were clearly non-Ashkenazi Jews, such as Kahalani, Mualem, or Matzliah. In terms of given names, 165 were clearly Israeli names—such as Ofra, Anat, Yael, Hadas, and Irit for women and Amos, Ehud, Boaz, Ronen, Erez, Oded, and Aviad for men. These first names were never known among Jews outside of Israel. They were invented or adopted by Zionist Israelis as one form of defiance with regard to traditional Jewish culture. Anat, a common name for women, is the name of a Canaanite goddess. Erez means cedar, and reflects a "return to nature." Such names faithfully reflect contemporary secular Israeli culture and tell us something about the parents of Emin members.

Tables 1.1 and 1.2 tell us much about Emin members' socioeconomic status. Most of them would be described as lower middle class, without much formal education. The number of professionals is relatively small. It should be noted that of the 283 names we have, eighty-four are of forty-two married couples in which both spouses are members. Forty-eight of the men (35 percent) and twenty-two of the women (15 percent) are reserve officers. From all this information, one may gather the clear impression that what characterizes the membership is not success or education. Some of them seem to have been fairly successful in the military but not in any civilian career. This impression was reinforced during meetings with members and attendance of one formal meeting. It seemed that the special knowledge offered by Emin and the special status conferred by it were a compensation for lives of quiet frustration.

Table 1.1. Reported Occupation of Emin Members (Men).

OCCUPATION	NO.	OCCUPATION	NO.
Unreported	24	Mechanic	3
Computer programmer	11	Pilot	2
Student	11	Reflexologist*	2
Salesman	13	Flight controller	1
Office worker	5	Waiter	1
Agriculture	5	"Physicist" (M. Sc.)	1
Bookkeeper	3	Optometrist	1
Teacher	2	Economist	1
Musicians	2	Private investigator	1
Designer	2	"Biochemist" (B. Sc.)	1
Computer technician	2	Air steward	1
Computer operator	2	Architect	2
Soundman	3	Weaver	1
Picture framer	2	Painter	1
Photographer	2	Graphic designer	1
Dentist	2	Model designer	1
Business executive	4	Reception clerk	1
Plumber	2	Electrician	1
Carpenter	5	Producer	1
Advertising man	3	Engineer	1
Technician	4	Lawyer	1
Foreman	2	Total	137

Of the above, twenty-three report having university degrees; only three have advanced degrees beyond the B.A.
*Refloxology claims to cure illnesses by applying pressure to various parts of the foot, which controls various parts of the body.

The explanation to Emin's extraordinary success in Israel has to be anchored in three levels of discussion: first, the content of Emin beliefs and practices; second, the structure through which the content is expressed; and third, the historical context of Emin's appearance in Israel.

The Emin's secret of success in Israel seems to stem from a combination of the three elements in its message. First, the occult knowledge, which promises clear and absolute answers to all of life's mysteries, together with much hope for coping with illness (through healing) and death (through reincarnation). Second, its petty-bourgeois ideology of hard work, clean living, and neat personal appearance. Third, the explicit loyalty to state and nation, which avoids any conflicts with the demands of Israeli culture for absolute

Table 1.2. Reported Occupations of Emin Members (Women).

OCCUPATION	NO.
Unreported	42
Teacher	22
Secretary	27
Computer programmer	6
Student	6
Physical therapist	5
Housewife	5
Designer	4
Artist	3
Speech therapist	3
Typist	2
Stewardess	3
Actress	2
Photographer	2
Air controller	1
Nurse	2
Dental assistant	1
Architect	1
Copy editor	1
Cabinet maker	1
Opera singer	1
Reflexologist	1
Policewoman	1
Musician	1
Tourist guide	1
Draftperson	1
Saleswoman	1
Total	146

Of the above, thirty-seven report holding a university degree; only three have an advanced degree beyond the B.A.

loyalty to a nation constantly at war. This combination may also explain another unique feature of Emin among new religions, which is the significant number of middle-aged individuals among its members and the support from some parents of members. These parents point to the change in their children's behavior in the direction of hard work and neatness as reason for their approval.

Several testimonials by Emin members, offered to the media and government authorities and supported by outside observers, attest to positive changes in the behavior of individuals as a result of joining Emin. These changes include the ability to be gainfully employed and to perform adequately at work, giving up self-destructive drug use, and being better organized in everyday life. These changes seem indeed to be directly tied to Emin ideology.

From a psychological point of view, two aspects should be noted. First, Emin membership creates in both the individual and the group a feeling of superiority with regard to nonmembers. At the same time, the belief in "electrical barnacles" has a clear paranoid flavor, even paranoid psychosis. Such beliefs create a special way of looking at nonmembers and of interacting with them. The feeling of superiority and the supercilious attitude toward nonmembers, justified by the special secret knowledge open only to insiders, creates obvious resentment among outsiders. The prominence of pollution fears in the Emin belief system calls for an explanation. In individuals who are otherwise functioning, the acceptance of such paranoid psychotic ideas must serve a function. At the individual level, it is a projection of threat and insecurity, in a desperate attempt to defend the self. At the social level, it may be the breakdown of social systems which is denied and projected on individual enemies, on evil and dirty people, such as masturbators. Thus, Emin creates a safe, pure zone of security, a shelter from the storm, which is what all Israelis are seeking, a means of defending the self and saving it from terrible events outside.

Emin ideology with regard to societal norms is part of its attraction for the members. It emphasizes hard work and respect for the law. It is opposed to the use of drugs, other than nicotine and alcohol, and to sexual diversities. It is also strongly patriotic of any country in which members happen to reside. In terms of the weekly activities, there is an emphasis on punctuality, good manners, and formal dress. There is a penchant toward the esthetic, which goes beyond neatness. It is also part of the doctrine, which is obsessed with cleanliness in all its forms (including that of the electrically clean aura). Some of the Emin norms of behavior seem a bit out of place in Israel. Israelis are notorious for informality in dress and behavior and are often described as lacking in manners and even rude (Landau and Beit-Hallahmi, 1983). Emin members with their formal dress and manners stand out in the crowd anywhere in Israel. It should be noted that wearing a suit and tie in Israel is not a common occurrence. For an Israeli man, and especially a young man, this is a behavior that needs an explanation.

Recruitment to the Emin Society is highly selective, and it can clearly afford to be. There is a careful screening process, and candidates for membership are asked to leave, during the six-month probationary period if they stray from Emin norms. This reinforces the feelings of members that they are the elect and they alone hold the keys to the only real knowledge about the mysteries of the universe. Nonmembers are regarded as inferior in knowledge and, because they are also electrically unclean and may contaminate members, mixing with them is not advised. The feeling of sharing secret knowledge is a powerful bonding mechanism.

Much business during Emin meetings in Israel is conducted in English, while the members are, with rare exceptions, native speakers of Hebrew. This undoubtedly requires an effort on the part of members, hampers natural expressiveness, and makes for a stilted style of communication. On the other hand, it ties the members to the written teachings of Leo, which provide the materials for discussion and averts the need for translation of the scriptures into Hebrew, which would be an almost impossible task. The members are also required to adopt new names in English, which are symbolic of their desired, or actual, personal qualities, e.g., Joy, Peace, Stream, or Sea. Leaders are known by a single initial. Only these names are used during meetings, and often members do not know the real names of others in the meeting. These "underground cell" mannerisms heighten the atmosphere of secrecy and exclusivity. The social climate in the meetings is described, by Israelis, as very British, that is, cold and formal.

The content of Leo's teachings is presented systematically, organized by laws and axioms. There is nothing sentimental or mystical about the presentation that offers the teachings as a comprehensive counter-science, covering all aspects of natural science, psychology, and physiology. All different occult traditions can be integrated because they all obey the same universal laws. The assumption is that conventional science is right for the technological level but not for the level of really understanding the universe and especially not for knowing the truth about humanity and "human essence." This is, of course, a common claim among religionists today. The systematic style of presentation, with charts and "laws," and the claims of scientific evidence seem to attract hard-nosed, practical individuals. It should also be noted that in Israel today some occult traditions enjoy almost universal acceptance. The validity of astrology, for example, is taken for granted, and other occult ideas enjoy prestige and visibility in the mass media.

Central to the self-concept of the group and its members is the idea of the "arcana mundi," a hidden knowledge which enables the select few to conduct their lives with more power over destiny, or at least with the superiority feeling gained from sharing in such secret knowledge.

The arcane knowledge available only to Emin members serves to compensate for their actual lack of education and social status. There is also an actual improvement in personal functioning because of the norms imposed by the group, which call for working responsibility. The exorbitant membership dues also keep members gainfully employed and thus serve a positive function.

Messianic Jews in Israel

Historically, the Christian message has been rejected by Israelis, and missionary efforts since 1948 had led to negligible results, but changes in Israeli society since 1973 have eroded this last taboo. Christian groups, such as Jehovah's Witnesses and Messianic Jews, have demonstrated remarkable growth. Messianic Jews define themselves as Jews loyal to their people, who have accepted Jesus as the true Messiah. They proclaim a double loyalty, to Jewish identity and to Christianity, though they reject the use of the term *Christian*.

Messianic Jews in Israel belong to a variety of groups and denominations. Some are active proselytizers. Others hide their true faith. Israeli society treats these individuals as outcasts, and they have often been subjected to verbal and physical attacks. They have their own communities, where they follow a combination of Jewish and Christian worship traditions. Orthodox "anti-missionary" organizations and orthodox communities in general see them as fair game, and there are frequent newspaper reports of attacks against Messianic Jews, involving destruction of their property, public demonstrations against their activities, and warnings about their alleged missionary campaigns.

A "group of Messianic Jews in Israel" published an advertisement in *Haaretz* on May 12, 1978, in which they protested against a "campaign of defamation." They proclaimed their commitment to their faith and their right to follow their conscience and stated that many of them serve in the Israel Defense Forces, especially in combat units. The advertisement asks the readers to support the struggle for true democracy by writing to the Prime Minister and to political leaders and expressing their views.

In October 1977, a small commune of Messianic Jews in Rosh-Pina, in northern Israel was attacked by thirty Orthodox Jews, who caused severe damage to property (Yeffet, 1977). Handwerker (1980) reported on physical attacks against a Messianic group in Rehovot, a suburb of Tel-Aviv. A Messianic Jewish group in Tiberias was the target of physical attacks and arson (Hurvitz, 1983; Mansur, 1984).

The Messianic community in Jerusalem was also the target of arson (*Jerusalem Post*, 1984). Zur (1984) reports on a Messianic group in Ashdod, which was forced to stop its activities, following threats and incidents of violence. Eden (1984) reported a demonstration by thousands of Orthodox Jews against the group in Rehovot. Following the demonstration, the mayor of Rehovot went to court and obtained an injunction against the group to stop any public meetings or religious activities (Peretz, 1984). Yad-La'ahim, the orthodox anti-missionary organization, has made Messianic Jews a prime target and inspires many newspaper articles on the subject (Handwerker, 1980; Galili, 1982; Kfiri, 1984; Leibovitz, 1984).

The number of Messianic Jews in Israel and their growth over the years, are hard to ascertain. Mansur (1966), who called them "an underground," estimated their number at 600. Cohen and Grunau (1972) mentioned a community of Messianic Jews in Jerusalem, numbering twenty to thirty. The number of Messianic Jews in Israel in the 1980s has been variously estimated to be between 1500 and 3000 adults, and these figures reflect significant growth since 1973 (Shapiro, 1984). Leibovitz (1984) estimates their number at 2000. Zur (1984) quotes an active member who claimed that the number is 4000. An informant, D. L., an American missionary working with Messianic Jews, told me in 1984 that there were several hundred active members in the several congregations he was working with. They included a score of American "Jews for Jesus," who had come to Israel and now had Israeli citizenship.

One indication of the growth of the Messianic Judaism movement in Israel is the development of its ambitious publishing program. As of 1990 there were in print in Israel about 100 Hebrew books published by the movement. They included several classics of United States Evangelical Christianity, such as *Peace With God* by Billy Graham, *The Late Great Planet Earth* by Hal Lindsey, and *Mere Christianity* by C. S. Lewis. The market for such publications in Israel is limited, and it is clear that an enormous effort has been invested in such a publication program, which also includes some titles by Watchman Nee and *The Total Woman*.

Jehovah's Witnesses

This is the only Christian sect to have gained a foothold among Israeli Jews. It cannot be numbered among the new religions because it has a place of honor among nineteenth-century sects. According to Etgar (1983), activities of Jehovah Witnesses in Israel started in 1963 with the arrival from Britain of Eric Pearce, who has remained the group leader in Israel. He came, with his wife, as the sect's emissary and has started to recruit members. In 1976, according to Ozerman (1976) there were 260 Witnesses in Israel, including a dozen Arabs.

At the end of 1976 Jehovah's Witnesses gained, for the first time, public attention in Israel. Several members of the sect were in Israeli military prisons because of their refusal to obey orders to report for active duty in the army reserves. As it turned out (*Jerusalem Post*, 1975), sect members used to be exempted from military service, but after the 1973 War, the rules were changed by administrative action because of manpower shortages, and so those refusing orders were routinely sentenced to prison terms. The military judges, like most Israelis to this day, probably had never heard of Jehovah's Witnesses and were following routine military justice. After the matter was brought up in the Knesset and drew worldwide attention, the Witnesses were released from prison, some of them after serving more than a year (Wallfish, 1976).

By 1983 membership exceeded 500, according to Etgar (1983), and there were Kingdom Halls in Tel-Aviv, Jerusalem, and Haifa. The membership included mostly lower-class individuals and according to newspaper reports, a significant number came from Sephardi families. Witness publications used in recruitment and study have been coming out in Hebrew since the late 1960s. *Awake*, the international Jehovah's Witness biweekly, has been published in Hebrew since 1980.

Reactions to the New Religions: The "Anti-Cult" Lobby in Israel

The development and impact of new religions can be assessed by looking at the reactions they have brought about in various segments of society. We will look at reactions in the media, community and religious organizations, and government agencies, including the police. In response to the growth of new religions in Israel since the early 1970s, a countermovement has appeared in the form of an anti-cult movement and lobby, modeled after parallels in the United States in some ways. We will survey the history of the movement by looking at its various components, including the Israeli government, the National Police, and nongovernmental organizations. New religions in Israel had to contend with the hostility of the religious establishment, the public, families of members, and the media, which were guided by all the above. The threat and the deviance represented by the new religions in Israel could not pass without a strong reaction. The opposition started, naturally, with Jewish religious groups, then came from parents' organizations, and then involved the media, Israeli government, and the public (see Cavaglion, 1990).

Israeli society clearly exhibits a low tolerance for non-Jewish old religions and even for non-Orthodox branches of Judaism. New religions present a direct challenge to the religious establishment everywhere. In Israel this challenge is more serious because it is directed toward Jewish identity and Zionism and thus touches the ideological base of the State itself. Most new religions in Israel, as we have seen, have been imported from the outside. Not all of them have been treated in the same way by the Israeli establishment. Some have been singled out for harsher treatment, and they have been those that present a threat through their basic message and their mere existence.

In a 1984 survey of Israeli youth, only 11 percent of respondents regarded joining new religions positively, while 85.6 percent regarded it negatively. On the other hand, the return to Judaism was viewed positively by 61.5 percent, while 32 percent viewed it negatively (Shem-Tov, 1985). The danger of new religions was a major topic in a novel written for teenagers and published in 1987 (Ron-Feder, 1987). The book described various crises and problems in a teenager's life, including parental divorce and remarriage and the Bhagwan Rajneesh cult.

In a public opinion survey in 1984, Israelis were asked about whether they considered certain actions to be damaging to Israeli society. Among the acts listed was "converting away from Judaism." Among those between ages 20 and 24, 52 percent considered it as damaging society, while among those over the age of 24, the percentage was 66 percent (Hacohen, 1984).

Action has been taken against groups that challenged military service obligations (universal in Israel), loyalty to the state, or loyalty to Jewish identity. One can be a secular Jew, but still preserve a nominal Jewish identity. Joining a new religion means, for an Israeli Jew, a rejection of Jewish identity. The positive step of joining ISKCON or Ananda Marga is a religious conversion, leaving behind the conventional Jewish identity and the attachment to the Jewish collective. Any ideology offering an alternative identity will be subject to vigorous attack and persecution. The touchstone is an alternative to the standard Jewish identity. Where there is no real claim of an alternative identity, reactions to a new religion have been milder.

The attitude toward new religions can be compared with the attitude toward Neturei Karta, an Orthodox Jewish anti-Zionist group (Marmorstein, 1969). Neturei Karta is opposed and denounced for its anti-Zionist stance, but it is nevertheless tolerated as part of Jewish identity continuum. On the basis of that common identity it can be attacked and criticized, but certain basic rights of its members (such as the right to live in Israel) are not challenged.

Concerned Parents Against Cults

This organization, modeled after similar groups in the United States, was founded in 1980 in Haifa and became formally incorporated as a nonprofit organization in 1982. In July 1981, it had fifteen members, but by late 1981, membership grew to sixty families. The organization has been active in lobbying the media and the government. Its chairman, N. B., has made numerous media appearances, including appearances on television, in which his face and full identity were hidden from the cameras.

Concerned Parents Against Cults has published its own leaflets, containing information about various new religions. The leaflets refer to est as a cult; their general level of accuracy and sophistication is rather low. N. B. has also been active in addressing letters to newspapers whenever any neutral or favorable mention was made of any of the new religions. The organization has been instrumental in bringing to Israel the film "Ticket to Heaven," which drew much media attention, including television coverage. There can be little doubt that effective lobbying by Concerned Parents was instrumental in the creation of the government commission of inquiry in February 1982, and members of the organization appeared several times before the commission and maintained informal contact with its staff. Concerned Parents was effective in creating contacts with other government agencies, such as the Health Ministry.

On May 12, 1983, a day-long symposium was held in Tel-Aviv, titled "The Problems and Treatment of Cult Adepts." It was organized jointly by Concerned Parents Against Cults and by mental health division of the Health Ministry. It was addressed, among others, by the director of mental health division and the legal counsel for the Health Ministry. Other participants included psychologists, psychiatrists, and former cult members. "Cult exit counseling" and deprogramming were introduced by individuals who wanted them to be imported to Israel. The individuals presenting and advocating deprogramming were Americans, who were ready to discuss their own experiences in practicing it and offered their services. It should be emphasized that strong doubts were expressed about the legality of such procedures in Israel.

Materials distributed to the audience at the symposium consisted of articles published in the United States, such as the one by Singer (1979) and an annotated bibliography of books on cults. The overall solution offered at the symposium, which I personally attended, was the medicalization and psychologization of the new religions phenomenon.

Yad La'Ahim and the New Religions

Yad La'Ahim is a nonprofit organization with eight branches in Israel. Its members fight against abortions, the drafting of women into military service, autopsies, and other issues of concern to the Orthodox community. According to Avneri (1982), they also fight against mixed marriages between Jewish women and Arabs. Yad La'Ahim constitutes an "anti-missionary" lobby in Israel, active since the 1950s. The ideology of the organization clearly represents Orthodox Judaism, and members believe that anything incompatible with it should be eliminated from the State of Israel. Any group that presents a challenge to the loyalty of Jews to Orthodox Judaism (including other Jewish traditions) should be confronted and thwarted, in other words. There is no differentiation, in the ideology of Yad La'Ahim, between old and new religions. Their struggle against the new religions in the 1970s and 1980s is a continuation of their struggle since the 1950s against Christian missionary groups, which culminated in the passing of an anti-missionary law by the Knesset in 1977. The only way in which the new religions may be different, and more dangerous, for Yad La'Ahim is in that they do not carry the old cultural stigma attached to old religions and their competition with Judaism. Thus, they are not as easily recognized for what they are and may be able to attract Israelis. In fact, this is exactly what has happened.

Yad La'Ahim activities include media relations, publications, and actual harassment of new religions. The most obvious and noticeable activity is that of initiating newspaper articles about new religions. Some of the articles sound like press releases and include wild claims about the success of new religions. Thus, Fisher (1979) claims, "Hundreds of young people in the Haifa area have fallen prey to mysterious cults from the East." Lior (1981) claims that there were 100 cults operating in Israel, with more than 50,000 members.

Yad La'Ahim publishes a monthly bulletin of activities against "missions and cults," which includes information about alleged Christian missionaries, Messianic Jews, and new religions. It also publishes special reports and reprints articles appearing in the press. In 1982, a special booklet containing testimonies of former members of new religions, who were now Orthodox Jews, was published. It contained seven personal stories. A special report listing seventeen cults operating in Israel was also published in 1982. Yad La'Ahim submitted a memorandum to the Commission of Inquiry investigating cults that included twelve recommendations for actions against new religions, from close police surveillance to declaring Scientology's E-Meter illegal. In addition to this document, the organization also arranged for witnesses to appear before the commission.

The Kibbutzim and new Religions

Kibbutzim, communal settlements that invest much energy and concern in the education of their young people (Rabin and Beit-Hallahmi, 1982), make up less than 3 percent of the Israeli population. Nevertheless, they are much more visible in Israeli society and much more visible in the world of the new religions. It is hard to determine the exact representation of individuals born and raised in kibbutzim in the new religions, but they clearly make up more than 3 percent, perhaps 10 percent in some groups, and thus are clearly overrepresented. Joining a new religion usually means leaving the kibbutz, and kibbutzim, which are justifiably concerned about desertions, have reacted to this threat.

One large kibbutz reached an important policy decision in 1983 (*Davar*, 1983). Since kibbutz members usually do not have private funds, the kibbutz used to cover membership dues in any external organization. In the case of new religions, members who had joined them while still in the kibbutz applied to the kibbutz education committee, claiming that membership in TM or the Emin Society was an educational activity. Concern was shown by education committees when the training courses never ended and when more became known about new religions. The kibbutz in question decided to stop any such payments and thus to force the member to choose between the kibbutz and the outside group.

Kibbutzim have their own centralized educational organizations and their own psychotherapy clinics. The policy with regard to new religions has been formulated by educators, psychiatrists, and social workers. An anti-cult task force, created in 1982, has been active in organizing symposia and lectures to kibbutz educators and to kibbutz members (Tene, 1982). In addition, there are treatment groups for families whose children have joined new religions and lectures to high school students in the kibbutzim (Tene, 1983). Training courses for professionals have also been organized by the Kibbutz Child and

Family Clinic in Tel-Aviv, under the heading of "Mystical Cults—How to Prevent and Treat Them." Most of the 260 kibbutzim in Israel belong to two large federations. As of 1984, there was an anti-cult task force in each federation, staffed by educators and mental health professionals.

Media Coverage of New Religions

As we survey the Israeli press, it is hard to find references to specific new religions, or cults in general, before 1973. The only new religions whose existence in Israel can be gathered from the Israeli media before the 1973 War were ISKCON and Transcendental Meditation. The first wave of media attention to new religious groups follows the 1973 War. Press attention to TM was positive or neutral, and the first press campaign against new religions in the spring of 1974 singled out the Divine Light Mission. No similar campaign is to be found in the Israeli press until 1982 or 1983, when no group is singled out, and the topic is cults in general. This second wave of media coverage, totally negative in tone, coincides with the creation of the government commission of inquiry on cults, and the increased activity by Yad La'Ahim, the Orthodox anti-missionary organization. It also coincides with the formation of the Concerned Parents Against Cults organization, active since 1980. The articles range from news reports covering the new religions and their relations with the community and government authorities to interviews with professionals and academics and reports on lectures by professionals with different orientations. In many of the articles, the inspiring hand of Yad La'Ahim can be immediately recognized. In a few cases, it is the parents organization that initiated such articles.

The electronic media, which in Israel are owned and controlled by the government, have also entered the fray. Radio and television programs have discussed cults with illustrations taken from the activities of specific new religions. ISKCON, TM, and Emin have been singled out on these programs. Most major Israeli newspapers have carried not just major articles on cults, but also a series or two on cults in Israel. *Al Hamishmar* carried an eight-part series in March 1982, and *Davar* had two major articles in December. Apparently, 1983 was a banner year for newspaper articles about cults. In addition to hundreds of articles about specific groups, there was an eight-part series in *Haaretz*, Israel's leading daily. The confidential National Police Intelligence Report on cults (Soffrin and Yodfat, 1982) was leaked to the press as soon as it was ready, and excerpts were duly published (e.g., Frenkel, 1983).

The tenor of all newspaper articles was negative, and some of them were purely sensational. The only exceptions to the moral crusade in the newspapers were those articles in which the new religions were defended on the basis of general democratic principles (e.g., Geffen, 1982) and on the basis of their similarity to the Judaization movement (Tumarkin, 1983). While Zaretsky and Leone (1974) suggest that the U.S. media have given new religious movements an appearance of legitimacy, in Israel, for cultural and historical reasons, the situation is totally different. The media present new religions as definitely illegitimate and deviant. Salvation stories of members in new religions are treated differently from those of returnees to Judaism. While the latter are celebrated, the former are regarded as deviants.

There has been one notable exception, however. Thanks to its dynamic leader, Yeshaiahu Ben-Aharon, anthroposophy in Israel has gained, by 1990, the status of a respectable philosophical-scientific approach. Ben-Aharon was often invited to a variety of events and even academic symposia, and Rudolph Steiner's occult "discoveries" thus won a measure of legitimacy. Thus, a popular symposium held at Tel-Aviv University in the summer of 1990 on the question of academic success, included a presentation by Ben-Aharon, who presented Steiner's "educational philosophy." Ben-Aharon shared the podium with authors, psychologists, mathematicians, and philosophers. The audience was treated to a lecture on Rudolph Steiner's occultist philosophy of education and greeted it with serious attention. This presentation was reported in the media as another "scientific" point of view, albeit an "alternative" one. Ben-Aharon skillfully managed to avoid any mention of the group's beliefs in reincarnation or its ties to Christianity, which would have aroused a negative reaction in Israel, naturally.

The Interministerial Commission of Inquiry on Cults

This commission was appointed by Education and Culture Minister Zebulun Hammer on February 5, 1982. Miriam Glazer-Ta'asa, Deputy Minister for Education and Culture, was appointed to head the commission. The commission was assigned to investigate "Eastern cults" and its mandate was formulated as follows:

> Determining the extent of cult growth in Israel, their locations and dimensions.
>
> Locating the causes for this growth.

Obtaining information on the nature of the cults: modus operandi, significance of effects, actions, and aims.

Consequences of cult activities for the individual and for society.

Determining ways for coping, by the educational system, with the cults.

Recommending treatment modes (legal, public, educational, etc.). (Hammer, 1982)

The appointment of the commission of inquiry was the result of lobbying by Concerned Parents Against Cults, by individual parents whose children had joined the new religions, and Yad La'Ahim. This showed that the new religions had become a pressing reality for the Israeli establishment. In view of the media attacks on the new religions and public sentiment in some communities, the creation of the commission may have been seen by some members of the government and by its chairperson Mrs. Glazer-Ta'asa as an opportunity for gaining some popularity. It should be pointed out here that Mrs. Glazer-Ta'asa had, since her appointment as Deputy Minister for Education and Culture in July 1981, earned a certain notoriety. She had become the spokesperson for reactionary and nationalist views and had gained the enmity of intellectuals and liberals in Israel. She expressed views critical of nudity in the theater, explicit sexual references in poetry, and the lack of nationalist spirit in Israeli culture. Before becoming a Knesset member affiliated with the Herut right-wing party, she was a school teacher and principal.

The first indication of an interest by the Ministry of Education and Culture in new religions came on October 29, 1981, when newspapers (e.g., *Haaretz*, 1981) reported on a meeting at Mrs. Glazer-Ta'asa's office to discuss the "Guru Maharishi cult." The meeting was held following requests from Yad La'Ahim and Concerned Parents Against Cults. On January 14, 1982, the director-general of the ministry issued a special memorandum to all high schools in Israel, titled "Educational Measures in View of the Trend of Some Youth to Turn to Various Cults" (Shmueli, 1982). The memorandum, which was clearly inspired by the October 1981 meeting, alerts teachers to the existence of cults and recommends general measures of "reinforcing value education" and helping parents prevent their children from becoming involved in cults. It should be pointed out that most new religions in Israel do not recruit high school students in any case.

The first session of the commission took place on February 22, 1982, in Jerusalem, and about thirty sessions of the full commission were held. The commission heard representatives of Concerned Parents, Yad La'Ahim, the kibbutz task forces on new religions, ex-members of new religions, and parents of members and ex-members. In addition, the leadership of two new religions, Transcendental Meditation and Emin, volunteered to appear before the commission in order to persuade its members of the nonreligious nature of their activities. The commission was not convinced. The commission received written reports and memoranda from the National Police, Yad La'Ahim, Concerned Parents Against Cults, and several of its own members. Detailed reports submitted by members dealt with various new religions and with legal aspects of their activities.

Since the commission had been at work for five years without publishing a report, this aroused curiosity and several newspaper stories have dealt with the delay. Normally, such a commission is expected to release a report within a few months following its appointment. The "final draft" of the commission report was published in December 1982 by an eager journalist (Be'er, 1982), but a final report took four more years. Another "final report" was published in February 1983 (Shapira 1983a and 1983b). Abramovitz (1984) stated that the real reason that the report was not published was an internal dispute regarding the similarity between new religions in Israel and the Judaization movement. He stated that several members have insisted on dealing with the Judaization phenomenon, which led to the resignation of two members, including this author. Abramovitz speculates that the report would be published before the general elections, held in Israel on July 23, 1984. *Haolam Hazeh*, however, reported on July 18, 1984, that the report would be published after the elections, and the "last-minute delays" had to do with legal matters. Lior (1984) announced again the impending release of the commission report, which would lead to police action against new religions because of fraud and misrepresentation.

When the commission report was finally released in February 1987, it was a long and cumbersome document, holding 503 pages, including a seventy-four-page bibliography. It contained detailed background surveys on Scientology, Emin, est, Transcendental Meditation, Bhagwan Rajneesh, Ananda Marga, the Unification Church, ISKCON, Divine Light Mission, and Divine Intervention. The commission treats est as a religious cult despite the fact that there is nothing religious in its teachings or practices. The commission recommended more energetic enforcement of consumer protection laws, the laws governing not-for-profit organizations, tax laws, and immigration laws in Israel as ways of limiting the activities and influence of new religions. In addition, the commission recommended government activities in collecting and circulating information about new

Table 1.3. The Development of the Anti-Cult Movement in Israel

1974	(Spring) First hostile media campaign; main target, Divine Light Mission.
1974	Confidential police report on the Divine Light Mission.
1980	Concerned Parents Against Cults—first informal organization.
1981	Concerned Parents Against Cults—formal incorporation.
1982	(February) Commission of Inquiry appointed by Education Minister.
1982	Report by Yad La'Ahim on "cults in Israel."
1982	Confidential National Police report on "Cults in Israel."
1982	"Anti-cult" task forces created by kibbutz federations.
1982–83	Second media campaign against all new religions.
1987	Interministerial Commission of Inquiry report is published.

religions, educational activities, and help to former members, families of members, and "vulnerable populations." Following the publication of the Commission Report, the two groups that cooperated with the commission, Emin and Transcendental Meditation, published lengthy rebuttals. The Emin document was 63 pages long, and the TM report (titled "The Truth about TM Versus the Commission Report") was about 100 pages of documents, including a list of 355 "scientific studies" of TM.

Highlights of the anti-cult movement in Israel are summarized in Table 1.3.

Looking Back: New Religions and the Boundaries of Religious Legitimacy in Israel

Looking back at the development of new religions in Israel, we can reach the following conclusions:

1. There is a reverse relationship, not surprisingly, between the degree to which a group deviates from majority norms and its success in recruiting members in Israel. There is also a positive relationship, again, not surprisingly, between the degree of deviance and the degree of opposition to the group, regardless of its size. Thus, ISKCON, the Divine Light Mission, and Ananda Marga have achieved only limited success but have aroused much opposition.

2. The successful new religions are those that combine a medium degree of deviation from the majority with regard to be-

> liefs and life style and a medium degree of separation from the member's previous social attachments. Such groups include TM, Scientology, and Emin.

The appearance of new religions in Israel can be described in a most basic way as a cultural innovation. It is an innovation because it represents behaviors previously unknown in the culture, which within a relatively short time have become established as the norm for a significant minority. This innovation has appeared together with several others (e.g., return to Orthodox Judaism) and thus should be analyzed within a broader context. The appearance of new religions in Israel is significantly more radical in its implications than the growth of new religions in the United States.

New religions in Israel are based on imported beliefs, that is, their belief systems were created abroad and then introduced to Israelis who have accepted them. The necessary condition for the acceptance of those beliefs is an openness to religious ideas as an answer to one's distress. Without this openness, i.e., the basic legitimacy of the religious viewpoint, the new religions cannot recruit any members. Those who become members are ready to experiment with new beliefs or are engaged in an active search for meaning.

We may speculate that the style of activity of these groups, in both management and recruitment, gives rise to opposition and antipathy. In some of these groups, members remind outsiders of aggressive sales representatives, especially when the membership is growing rapidly. Other new religions, such as anthroposophy and Jehovah's Witnesses, do not arouse these reactions because of their gentle manners. Christian missionary groups, which have been active in Israel for a long time, are often referred to in the Israeli media as cults, but the way they are treated in practice is totally different. New religions have been clearly more successful than old-style Christian missionaries in recruiting young Israelis. One reason is that the new religions do not suffer from the cultural stigma attached to Christianity. Their lack of history, and lack of historical contact (and conflict) with Judaism works in their favor.

Once a critical mass of a new social phenomenon exists, it is going to bring about a reaction, especially if it presents a threat to established groups and authorities. In Israel, the new religions have been regarded as threatening cultural uniformity and, more seriously, because of the nature of Israeli identity, as threatening basic loyalties to the State. In terms of deviating from the central norms of the Israeli society, the new religions are the most dangerous among the roads to salvation. There is one cultural factor that determines the nature of reactions to new religions in Israel, and this factor is the cultural uniformity of Israeli society around the core of Jewish identity.

In most Western societies today, new religions are perceived as a threat, first by relatives (usually parents) of members, and then by various government authorities and professional groups. Parents' organizations, commissions of inquiry, and legal actions are indications of that. In Israel, in addition to threats to the family and to establishment professionals, the new religions pose a threat to the basic Jewish identity of the State of Israel and to the basic loyalty to the State. In the United States, opposition to the new religions have focused since 1970 on their posing a threat to the family, namely, parent—child relations. In Israel opposition to the new religions focuses not only on the apparent threat they pose to family authority, but also on the threat to loyalty to the State of Israel and to the Israeli identity.

Concern about losing Jews to other religions is as old as Judaism itself. Old Testament prophets thundered against pagan practices, and Diaspora Jews, living in the midst of another culture, always lost in the battle against the majority. In the modern State of Israel, there was always concern about Christian missionaries, and the term "mission" (pronounced *mee-see-yon*) has become part of the spoken language in Israel since the 1950s. Any Christian coming to live in Israel and any Christian organization active in Israel have been suspected of missionizing. The lessons of Jewish history have not been forgotten, and for Orthodox and non-Orthodox alike this became a battle cry. When Billy Graham visited Israel in the late 1950s, he was denied the use of a city auditorium in Tel Aviv and was allowed only an appearance in Nazareth before an audience of Christian Arabs.

The concept of Jewish unity is used by both religious and secular Jews in Israel. It is the basis for overall cultural and political unity. Jewish identity and specifically religious symbols and practices unify Jews from other ethnic origins and cultures, especially Jews from Arabs (Deshen, 1978; Liebman, 1975). The new religions are seen as a threat to the solidarity and uniformity of Israel society. They present the prospect of an alternative loyalty or at least a divided loyalty. We may observe here something that is part of Jewish tradition and precedes the state of Israel: The sentiment of community loyalty beyond the wide spectrum of differences in beliefs and individual behavior.

Giving up Jewish identity means undermining completely the Zionist claims to exclusive rights in Palestine and to privileges over the local Arabs, and also means giving up the tie with Jews in the Diaspora, who are Israel's main support in the world in many tangible ways. The reaction to new religions in Israel is indeed in accordance with the threat they present to the Israeli and Jewish identity. When we observe reactions to various new religions, it becomes clear that what creates an opposition is not the size of a group but its ideology. ISKCON with a score of members, who reject the Israeli identity, is more of a threat than Emin, with hundreds of members who still keep the Israeli identity, and the reaction develops accordingly.

The largest new religions, Emin, Scientology, and Transcendental Meditation, have been treated more leniently by Israeli society (and have thus become the largest) because they are more ambiguous in the challenge they pose to the traditional Israeli identity. These groups do not offer the members an exclusive new identity but still allow them to claim loyalty to the State of Israel (either wholeheartedly or not, this claim is explicit).

Members of new religions in Israel are reluctant to cooperate with researchers because they feel they are under a real threat. This perception is quite realistic in view of the lack of constitutional guarantees to the freedom of religion. Unlike other Western countries, Israel does not have a constitution or a bill of rights for citizens. In response to public condemnation, new religions in Israel can claim that its members still preserve their Jewish identity. In this way they remain within the pale, but not all new religions make this claim.

Many groups function as resocializing agencies and provide a positive environment for a population of individuals who are maladjusted or deviant before joining them. Usually, these individuals were in a state of crisis before joining. After joining they live in a milieu that is warm, accepting, and meaningful. They finally have a home or a community they can relate to. They are valued for their contribution and are reeducated to work hard and consume little. Members of new religions demonstrate, for the whole world to see, many of the virtues of the Protestant Ethic. They are hard-working, devoted, and frugal. They don't use illegal drugs, and they obey the law rather scrupulously because they want to appear respectable. As others have observed, the new religions offer their adherents a community, a sense of belonging, a belief system, and sometimes even individual psychotherapy.

If we ask members of the new religions, they are eager to tell us how good they feel and how well they function. They all report being calm, happy, and saved. The lifestyle of members in most new religions is extremely active. Moreover, many of the members work extremely long hours for the group. Their level of energy is amazing, given their objective difficulties and external reactions. This is, of course, exactly how these groups manage to survive.

Eister (1974) suggests that cults are likely to flourish in modern societies that are undergoing cultural crises in the form of "discolations in the communicational and orientational institutions" (p. 612). The historical period of the deepening of the crisis of Zionism gives rise to both the success of new religions in Israel and the crusade against them. The new religions can be regarded as breaking up the old monolithic ideology and pushing Israeli culture toward pluralism. The other part of the process has been the resistance to such a push.

The new religions are a symptom of social and personal distress. The boundaries of religious experimentation in Israel before 1973 can be assessed by relying on the evidence provided by Weiner (1961) and Cohen and Grunau (1972). These boundaries were fairly narrow and tied to the unchallenged centrality of orthodox Judaism. Religious mobility in Israel before the 1970s was nonexistent. The kind of religious mobility we have described here, involving a switch to new religions, is dramatic and traumatic, since it means a total alteration of beliefs, rituals, and religious interactions. It may mean a growth in religious pluralism, but joining a new religion will probably remain marginal. Actually, the appearance of new religions has not diminished the intolerance and the xenophobia directed at religious minorities in Israel. Indeed, there is more pluralism in Israeli culture today compared to twenty years ago because more identity options are available and private salvation possibilities are recognized and open. Israelis are now faced with a supermarket of identities and transformative experiences, but customers' readiness to purchase is naturally related to the cost. The ISKCON identity, which entails ostracism and a total change in life-style, is chosen by only a very few. Occultism, which demands little, is the universal favorite.

2

Back to the Fold:
The Return to Judaism

Religion, for Israelis, means Judaism, and more specifically, Orthodox Judaism. Eighty-five percent of the population in Israel is defined as Jewish, and this definition is legally made by the State. Laws respecting the establishment of religion have been made in Israel, and in this it is like many European countries. What is almost unique in Israel is the officially sanctioned relationship between religion, nationality, and political rights. Being Jewish in Israel accords certain privileges, defined by law, as Jews constitute not only a religious group but a national group as well. The boundaries of the Jewish group are kept by the system of religious courts, as well as by civil authorities, and marriage between Jews and non-Jews is rare. The question of membership in the privileged group is not easily settled in cases where individuals want to separate religion and nationality (e.g., by being a Catholic Jew). Israeli secular courts have ruled that you cannot be a Jew by nationality and a Catholic by religion. This unique historical feature of Judaism has been preserved in Israel.

The religious system in Israel today is a continuation of religious traditions in the two main areas of origin for Jewish immigration to Israel: Eastern Europe and the Arab world. In both areas, though separated by geography and history, Jews carried on similar (or identical) rabbinical traditions for hundreds of years. Several features of historical Judaism have left their mark on Jewish culture all over the world. One such feature is the existence of a religious consensus without the existence of a central authority. This paradoxical tradition may be related to intellectual independence and the lack of respect for authority for which Jews have become known. A lack of respect for authority together with a national consensus have been a feature of social and political life in Israel.

Ben-Meir and Kedem (1979) followed the basic Glock and Stark (1965) model, and have developed two reliable indices, for religious beliefs and for religious observance. The indices were based on a survey of a stratified random sample of the urban Jewish population in Israel. The belief scale includes six items, which meet the requirements of a Guttman scale, and the observance scale includes twenty items, similarly scalable. The belief scale starts with the belief in the immortality of the soul (29 percent agreement in the sample) and goes on to the belief in the coming of the Messiah (36 percent), then to belief in the Jewish people as chosen (57 percent) and to the final item, belief in God (64 percent). When it comes to the twenty items of the observance scale, a similar picture emerges. Only 11 percent (of the men) cover their head at all times, and 14 percent lay phylacteries every day. Only 22 percent do not drive on Saturday, and 44 percent report keeping to the dietary separation between meat and milk. Seventy-four percent claim to fast on the Day of Atonement, 88 percent light Hanukkah candles, and 99 percent take part in the Passover meal. There is undoubtedly an element of social desirability and conformity here, as becomes evident when we compare the two scales. Thus, only 64 percent believe in God, but 74 percent fast on the Day of Atonement. Nevertheless, the important finding here is that of the continuum of religious belief and observance, reflecting the social and historical realities of Judaism in Israel. The range of individual differences is much greater on religious practice than on religious beliefs, again in keeping with Jewish historical traditions. Judaism in Israel remains a religion of practice, rather than dogma. The varying levels of religiosity among Israelis are reflected in the following labels: *Haredi*, denoting the very Orthodox; *Dati* (literally "religious"), denoting Orthodox; *Mesorti* (literally "traditional"), denoting those who are partially observant; and *Hiloni* (literally "secular"), denoting the non-Orthodox majority. These Hebrew terms are in everyday use, in both spoken and written language. A survey of a representative sample of the adult Jewish population in Israel (1153 individuals), conducted in July 1983, found that the population could be divided in terms of observance into four groups: complete observance (14.3 percent), largely observant (19.5 percent), some observance (41.1 percent), and completely non-observant (24.5 percent) (Shye, 1983).

The Jewish population in Israel (i.e., those individuals whose government identity cards show them to be members of the Jewish people) is divided into an Orthodox minority, known in colloquial Hebrew simply as "religious" and a secular majority. Sizes of the respective groups and respective subcultures can be reliably estimated. The dividing line is the practice of orthodox Jewish prescriptions, specifically covering one's head at all times (for males). Only a minority of Israelis do that. The state school system in Israel for Jews (there is a separate system for Arabs) is divided into two parallel subsystems, one religious and the other "secular." Children of the religious subculture, raised according to Jewish Orthodox beliefs and practices, attend state religious schools. There is also an independent Orthodox system, which is state-financed but directed by super-Orthodox community. (It should be remembered that even the "secular" state schools teach their students large doses of Old Testament classes, Jewish history, and even Orthodox law).

Within the Jewish population there is a clear dividing line between two subcultures, the religious and the secular. The nature of Judaism as a religion of practice makes this division public and visible. While the two subcultures cannot be defined as castes, intimate contacts across the dividing line are rare. Members of the two groups can identify each other immediately by distinctive cues, such as dress, and expectations for public behavior are quite clear. The taboos concerning the sabbath in Orthodox Judaism can serve as the best example of behavioral divisions. Driving on a Saturday (except for a life-saving emergency) is out of the question for members of the religious subculture, as is watching television or using the telephone. Making decisions about public activities on the Sabbath is a complicated matter in Israel. By force of tradition, created through constant political struggles between the two subcultures, a curious set of rules governs such activities. Public transportation in Israel does not operate on Saturday (except for a skeleton bus service in Haifa), but soccer games are allowed. Some movie theaters are closed on Friday night, while government television and radio stations operate, for the benefit of those who are not religious. Raising pigs and selling pork are forbidden by law, representing a symbolic victory of Jewish dietary taboos, but the nonreligious can easily get around these limitations. These are just a few examples of the special role of religion in Israel public life.

Judaization is defined here as the process through which secular, nonobservant, young (and not so young) Israelis, who have grown up in Israel within the majority culture, have become practicing Orthodox Jews and have joined the minority subculture or Orthodoxy. "Israeli baalei teshuvah [returnees] are quite clear and forceful in defining themselves as having been secular, meaning that their life was not determined by the commandments of the Jewish Law and that their actual behavior violated aspects of it" (Aviad, 1983, p. 8). Such a transformation obviously means leaving behind a secular identity and a secular life style. The return to Judaism is known in Hebrew as *Hazara Bitshuva* or *Teshuva*, and the returnees as *Hozrim Bitshuva* or *Baalei Teshuva*. These terms, taken from the Orthodox Jewish language, used to be heard only in the Orthodox community. Since the 1970s they have become part of everyday language in Israel. Judaization in Israel since 1973 should be regarded as a personal and collective renewal movement. It does not involve a complete change of identity. Nominally speaking, all returnees used to be regarded as Jews even before their transformation. The question before them, and before the majority of Israelis, is the kind of Jewishness they wanted to espouse. Judaization means accepting the assumption that being Jewish means a close continuity with historical Judaism.

Unlike some of the other studies of the return to Judaism (e.g., Aviad, 1983), our discussion here will be limited to returnees who are Israeli born and raised. The phenomenon of Judaization among Diaspora Jews is, I believe, a separate issue with different parameters. The problem of Jewish identity in the United States or Great Britain, where Jews are a minority, is totally different from the problem of Jewish identity in Israel. Israeli-born returnees start their return to Judaism at a different point on the religious-secular continuum, not only with a different identity from that of Diaspora Jews (Israeli Jews as opposed to American Jews) but also at a different level of practice. All of them know Hebrew, which is their native language, and have been exposed to Orthodox Judaism in a variety of ways. Many of them know quite a bit about Judaism at a cognitive and intellectual level. This is not always the case with Diaspora Jews.

Individual Judaization

The Israeli media have been filled with exemplary tales of return. Like any salvation tale, it follows a stereotype: the returnee used to be secular/anti-religious/Marxist/criminal/suicidal, and now, following the Return, is devout/happy/productive/a rabbi. Almost without exceptions, portrayals of born-again Jews in the Israeli media are extremely positive. They follow the formula of search and salvation: a former life characterized by restlessness, confusion and failure and a new life filled with joy and peace.

Women's magazines are filled with touching stories of returnees from elite families, who found their happiness in Judaism, individually and collectively. Thus, Yotam Shoham, son of a physician who retired from Israeli Defense Forces (I.D.F.) with the rank of brigadier general, married Shahar Prihar, the daughter of a Haifa veterinarian. Both are young, attractive, returnees, and their wedding made headlines (e.g., Ben-Ari, 1986). Returnees usually get married to other returnees, because the strictly Orthodox will not intermarry with the newly observant.

The media have given prominence to cases in which the returnees are children of political leaders and famous personalities. General Rafael Eitan, chief of staff 1979–83 and later a member of the Knesset, General Rahavam Zeevi, a distinguished military man with organized crime connections and a member of the Knesset, General Abraham Tamir, director general of the Foreign Ministry in 1986–87 all have returnee children. Yigael Hurvitz, a former finance minister, has a returnee grandson.

A public opinion survey dealing with the return to Judaism was carried out in November 1978. The results showed that 68 percent believed that Israel needed a "strengthening of religious values," 51 percent believed that the return was the way to do it, 46 percent believed that Israel needed a "strengthening of religious values," 51 percent believed that the return was the way to do it, 46 percent believed that the return movement had a positive influence on Israeli society, and only 4 percent thought it had a negative effect. Fifty-eight percent thought that the returnees were happy, and only 7 percent thought they were unhappy; 53 percent thought they were psychologically balanced, and only 14 percent thought they were unbalanced; 48 percent thought they were courageous, and 14 percent felt they were weak (Aviad, 1983). This positive valuation of the return movement and the returnees is reflected in media reports and in everyday conversations.

There are two classes of stars among the returnees: those who have been artists before their return and those who have been I.D.F. combat officers and fighter pilots. Public appearances staged with the aim of gaining more returnees often feature either the former or the latter. Having members of I.D.F. elite units as returnees changes the image of the Orthodox as unmanly and as outsiders to the Israeli elite. The I.D.F. has several commando units, whose reputation is legendary. When a returnee states "I served in Unit X," his audience may gasp, especially when the speaker displays the typical Orthodox appearance of long beard and long, black clothing. Such returnees arouse understandable admiration among most secular Israelis. Another admired group are combat pilots. Colonel Noah Hertz is a former combat pilot, who lost a leg in action and was a prisoner of war in Syria in 1973. Colonel Hertz's search for meaning started in the Syrian prison and ended up in Orthodox Judaism. As of 1986, Noah Hertz is a returnee superstar, who appears in public to proselytize (Genossar, 1986). (Colonel Hertz has a brother who is a member of the Emin Society.)

Present and former fighter pilots have been the stars of mass rallies for Judaization, and are often quoted in the media. One air force colonel, a squadron leader, is quoted as saying: "I am a model of a returnee. Nothing traumatic has happened to me. I wasn't a prisoner of war. . . . Suddenly I saw the light . . . I started thinking and saw the light. I started thinking that the State of Israel is a passing episode. In the Declaration of Independence the Holy Name was not mentioned. The heart knows what the mouth will not dare to say" (Artizelli, 1984, p. 15).

Among the stars of pro-Judaization public events is Rabbi Amir Yakiel, "A former combat pilot." Another returnee star, whose name has been mentioned in the press, is Shmaria Harel, a reserve captain who had served in the most celebrated commando unit of the I.D.F. Mr. Harel was born in 1951 in Kibbutz Kissufim and went on to become the epitomy of the new Zionist man, a farmer and a fighter. Since his return to Judaism, he has been a member of the Lubavitcher movement, which supports Zionism and military service enthusiastically, and he has continued to serve as a reserve officer.

Nothing has symbolized the success of individual Judaization like the cases of famous artists who have become Orthodox. When the painter Ika Israeli returned to Judaism in 1971, he was a unique and rare case, greeted by disbelief. His conversion, at the age of thirty-nine, did not represent a movement, but by the late 1970s, the movement was there, and its stars were indeed the stage actors, directors, and painters who now appeared in front of their shocked audiences wearing long black coats, black hats, and long beards.

The Case of Uri Zohar

Uri Zohar is the clear hero of the Israeli Judaization movement, its prized possession, its beloved emblem. He symbolizes more than anything else the victory of old Orthodox Judaism over Zionism, and the abject defeat of the latter by history and tradition. There could not have been a better example of the prototypical *tzabar*, the Israeli-born individual, embodying the free spirit and the lack of respect for tradition that characterizes the new Jewish sovereignty in Israel. Uri Zohar was born in Tel Aviv, the first Hebrew-speaking modern city in Palestine, and he represents in every way the spirit and the experience of that city, the center of Israeli reality. What Uri Zohar embodies is the greatest victory of Orthodox Judaism over mainstream Israeli culture.

Zohar was born in Tel-Aviv in November 1934. In 1952 he graduated from high school and went into the military service, where he was a member of a military entertainment team. By 1956, he was a civilian comedy star. Zohar first attracted attention in the late 1950s as a stand-up comic. He was an idol to thousands quite early on. His first marriage to a budding singer, the daughter of Israel's greatest actress, ended in divorce. Later on in 1960, the popular comic surprised everybody with his serious approach to film criticism and turned to philosophy studies at the Hebrew University. He also gained publicity and stature by his active participation in political demonstrations in support of better treatment of Arabs. Zohar found his true calling in films and became the leading film director in Israel.

The early 1970s were a time of artistic flourish in Israel, and Uri Zohar was at the center directing television shows and films. Zohar was known as an exceptionally intelligent entertainer, an intellectual among actors, the great hope of Israeli cinema. He was the first person ever to be given the Israel Award, the highest civilian honor in Israel, in recognition of his work as a film director. When this happened in 1976, it was the first time that an Israeli contribution in cinema was deemed worthy of such attention. Uri Zohar, in characteristic fashion, turned down the Israel Award, an act reminiscent of Sartre's refusal of the Nobel Prize. This was the first time in Israel that anybody turned down such an honor, and it increased Zohar's standing as an independent artist and as an *enfant terrible*. Before winning the Israel Award he was convicted of marijuana possession and spent three months doing "community service".

At the age of forty, he started his search. Before that time, he had a "wave of faith" at age twelve. He had always believed in a God that created the world but did not believe in the giving of the Law at Mount Sinai. The process of Judaization for him meant examining and accepting Orthodox claims about the Law being the absolute and only truth. Once he became convinced of that, he had to start following the Orthodox life style.

He started his Judaization process as a television star in 1977. He was starring then in a popular game show, and the viewers were shocked one day to see him wearing a skullcap, the familiar badge of the Orthodox. This gesture was first dismissed as a passing phase, an experiment. But Zohar started looking more Orthodox on the screen and then dropped out of television altogether and moved to Jerusalem.

In 1977, Zohar also had his own radio program, a call-in broadcast after midnight. While his viewers on television were shocked to see him in his Orthodox garb, his listeners were surprised to hear him preach and urge them to join the Return to Judaism movement. Telling his own story (Zohar, 1983), Uri Zohar spoke of turning forty as the starting point for his quest. He was a successful artist but without any real belief or mission in life, "Socialist Zionism, humanism, and the flower children all turned to dust" (Zohar, 1983, p. 5). There was a feeling of emptiness and estrangement, which reached its climax during a trip to Scandinavia with his wife. He decided to stop the trip in the middle and returned home. During a visit to Jerusalem he ran into a former colleague, who was now a returnee to Judaism, and was struck by the dramatic change in the man, who used to be depressed and depressing, and now was glowing with an inner light.

Like all Israelis of his background, Zohar was filled with disdain toward the Orthodox and expressed it on many occasions. He considered them primitive and repelling, relics from the Middle Ages and the dark ghettos of the past. A chance encounter with an Orthodox man at a party led to the beginning of the return for Uri Zohar. That man claimed that the giving of the Law on Mount Sinai was a proven historical fact. He strongly impressed Zohar as a man who was not only intelligent and well-educated but also without visible personal flaws or deficiencies. His Orthodoxy could not be explained away as the result of some frustration or ignorance. He presented a challenge that could not be answered.

The search, from that point on, as described by Zohar, was mainly intellectual. The question to be examined was whether Judaism represented the Truth. Through reading the Old Testament and the rudiments of the oral law, Zohar reached the conclusion that the whole edifice of Jewish tradition, created over thousands of years, is based on divine revelation and divine election. "What have we gained? Actually only one thing: the knowledge, which is not based on any experience . . . that there is a purpose to our existence, and there is a reward to our actions" (Zohar, 1983, p. 111).

Stars and Criminals

Uri Zohar was not the only show-business personality to return to Judaism. Batya Lanzett, one of Israel's leading actresses in the 1950s, returned to Judaism in the late 1970s, when she was over fifty years old. In her new life, as an Orthodox woman in Jerusalem, she would not dream of entering a theater or even watching television. Rutti Navon was a rising singing star in the early 1970s in Israel. Today she is an Orthodox married woman, who sings only before female audiences. In a newspaper interview, she mentioned two events that pushed her toward the Return to Judaism. The first was a road accident in which she was injured and her driver was killed. "Then, after the accident, the Yom Kippur War broke out. I started asking, what's happening in this country? Such a tragedy. Why isn't the nation waking up? I felt that spirituality was missing in my life, that the pioneers who built this country did it without a spiritual foundation" (Quoted in Maimon, 1986, p. 20).

Irit Bulka was a rising entertainment star, singing, writing, and composing her own songs. Her name kept popping up in the gossip columns. She was married twice and divorced and started her search for meaning. She first discovered naturopathy and then Judaism. Today she is an Orthodox married woman, who appears only before audiences of Orthodox women like herself. (There have been several cases of artists who have become returnees only to go back to secular life-styles.)

Another category of returnee celebrities contains former star athletes. Several leading soccer players now grace yeshivot that specialize in returnees. Soccer players are in Israel heroes to young people, and when they return to Judaism, they become role models and are promoted by Judaization organizations.

The Judaization of former criminals is the source of exemplary tales of salvation. Since 1980, the media in Israel have reported hundreds of cases in which convicted criminals or defendants in criminal trials have turned Orthodox. The "change of heart" claim, common in criminal cases everywhere, has a special kind of evidence to support it here. The defense can point to real and dramatic changes in behavior: "He has been studying the Talmud 12 hours a day and keeps all prescriptions and proscriptions." Everybody in court can observe the changed external appearance of the person involved: a long beard, covered head, face stuck in a religious book throughout the proceedings. There is an obvious utilitarian aspect to this change of heart. Judges have been impressed quite often, and leniency has been the rule. In some cases, the defense has been tried more than once, since the born-again Jew has reverted to criminal behavior. In other cases, this religious rehabilitation has worked, and former criminals lead new lives, free of their former bondage and bonded to religion as their calling and vocation (Cromer, 1981 and 1988).

The Israel Prison Authority started sponsoring the Judaization of prisoners. In 1985, 300 inmates took part in what was called "religious rehabilitation" (*Haolam Hazeh*, 1986). There were three yeshivot in Israeli prisons, each with twenty students. In 1985, the Israeli Interior Minister, Yitzhak Peretz, a member of the ultra-Orthodox Shass party, proposed a general pardon to all convicted criminals who had returned to Judaism. This proposal was not adopted by the government (Rabi, 1985).

Crusade and Revival

The Orthodox crusade has the effect not only of gaining new members for the Orthodox minority. It also invigorates regular members, especially when they act as recruiters. Returnees have been recruited through widely advertised study meetings and mass rallies. In the mid-1980s, the organizations working to promote returnees started to distribute cassettes with sermons about the evils of secular life and the benefits of Judaism. The Judaizers raise directly the question of Jewish identity. If secular Israelis claim to be Jews, representatives of Orthodoxy can challenge them on their Jewishness and their Judaism. Individual "sponsors" of returnees show sincere concern, love, and care to the persons who come to them in a state of crisis. The environment of the Orthodox yeshiva (religious academy) is as supportive as that of other religious groups and does have a clear psychotherapeutic effect on the returnees joining it.

When Orthodox Jews in Israel speak of the emptiness, shallowness, and materialism of secular individuals, they may be right in many cases. This was brought home to me in a discussion with students in 1986 in a psychology of religion class. An architecture student, a woman of twenty-three, simply could not imagine, as she said, that there could be a secular meaning system that would offer significance to one's life. If there was such a system, she never heard of it.

For secular demoralized Israelis, whose lives are devoted to materialistic, hedonistic pursuits in the shadow of annihilation, the traditional Jewish community has much to recommend it. First, it is a *community*, with sincere concern and mutual support among the members. Most of its members are clearly nonmaterialists and lead simple, austere lives. They seem happy, enjoy stable families, and are characterized by gentleness and kindness toward those who seek an alternative. Compared with the emptiness and despair of secular Israelis, the religious community presents an oasis of purpose, meaning, and honesty. The returnee says farewell to consumerism, alienation, egoism, and sexual permissiveness. He (or she) can get rid of the permanent hangover after last night's party, which is followed only by the search for the next party.

A secular young Israeli, whose life is basically an empty search for material security, is offered a meaning for his individual existence that ties him to a cosmic journey. He becomes part of the Jewish people, ordained as the Chosen People, through a direct tie to the Almighty, to keep sacredness alive right here on earth. For the first time, life has a meaning, and serious one, within a supportive, coherent, and united community of faith. Compared with the demoralized emptiness of secular life in Israel, Orthodox Judaism offers real salvation. In conversations with numerous returnees, the 1973 War was mentioned as the starting point in the questioning process, which led to the eventual return to Judaism. Between 1967 and 1973, there were several yeshivot in Jerusalem catering to returnees, but the latter were all non-Israelis (Kramer, 1972). Machon Meir, a yeshiva whose mission is Judaizing secular Jews, was founded in the summer of 1974 in Jerusalem.

The return to Judaism is an admission that the Zionist attempt to create a secular Jewish identity has failed. Other roads to private salvation express the same admission. Many of the returnees have left Zionism behind as they became increasingly Orthodox. This has caused concern and criticism in public. As long as the Judaization movement was seen as revitalizing Zionism, no such concern was experienced or expressed. Once Judaism is recognized as a challenge to Zionism, which it may be to 50 percent of the returnees, then Orthodox Judaism becomes only slightly better than the new religions in terms of the State of Israel and its goals.

The rejection of Zionism by many of the returnees (Meislisch, 1984) and their return to pre-Zionist Orthodoxy is, on a political and family level, a dramatic rebellion. Zionism has failed, and on its ruins, old Judaism is being rebuilt. After all, as many of the returnees say, Judaism has a history of millennia, whereas Zionism may be only a passing historical episode. The returnees' parents, "normal" secular Israelis, have called themselves Jews but do not take Judaism seriously. Their children are exposing their hypocrisy by going "all the way," back to real Orthodox Judaism, and not to any of the modern non-Orthodox varieties. This is clearly a challenge and a rebellion.

Returnees denounce their parents by their mere actions. They consider their parents to be hypocrites, if they claim to be Jewish while not taking Judaism seriously, and in general show that they are serious about their declared ideals, unlike most of their parents. In terms of majority opinions, there is no doubt that switching to a non-

Zionist Jewish identity is seen as preferable to switching to a totally non-Jewish identity, such as that of ISKCON or Jehovah's Witnesses. The cultural continuity, if not closeness, and the overall common identity of Jewishness, which is accepted by most Israelis, override other factors in forming an attitude toward the returnees.

A clear indication of moving beyond Zionism is the refusal to serve in the Israel Defense Forces. While conscientious objectors are not recognized in Israel and face prison terms, Orthodox Jews can refuse to serve with immunity. Those who have returned to Judaism while in regular military service or under reserve obligations (all men under fifty-five) are released from duty if they ask for it. According to I.D.F. sources, the number of such cases (returnees who have left the service) was no more than thirty cases in 1985. The rejection of Zionism by returnees is part of the overall rejection of secular values. Zionism, a secular national movement, is regarded as an element of the failed secular experimentation of the Jews, a passing phase destined to be soon forgotten, as other non-Orthodox experiments in Jewish history (Meislisch, 1984). Zionism has failed or at most produced ambiguous results. The Orthodox are confident in their eternal truths. Among the moderately religious, the religious-Zionist camp, pressure is felt from two opposing directions: first, from the more Orthodox side and, second, from the secular side. What we can observe as a result of cross-pressures is two kinds of personal changes, greater Orthodoxy and individual secularization.

Meislisch (1984) estimates the number of Israeli returnees as 8200 individuals as of 1983, not including family members who have become returnees in some cases. Here we are not including those Jews from other countries who have become returnees, which Meislisch estimates to be about 5000. In a survey of returnees who were active students at yeshivot (Orthodox religious colleges), Meislisch counted 1460 students in 1983. There were either returnees in the early stages of their personal transformation, who are engaged in full-time study of rabbinical literature, or veteran returnees, who have made study their way of life and sole occupation. One can speak today of a Judaization industry, which includes 230 yeshivot, and in 1984 had 4400 returnees in them. As of 1984, there was a total of eighty organizations involved in recruiting returnees (Kisslev, 1984). Forty percent of the budget for these groups comes from the Israeli government.

The Habad movement, better known as the Lubavitcher hassidim, has been extremely active in the Judaization campaign. It has fifty-six branches in Israel, and its members are busy recruiting non-Orthodox Israelis into Orthodoxy. Because of their Zionist stance they have had no difficulties with the Israeli establishment and is a favorite with the media. Returnees who have joined Habad remain Zionists and espouse a worldly way of life, most of them continuing to be gainfully employed. They also continue in the military services. The Belsz hassidic movement started offering evening lectures and weekend retreats in 1979 and has reached thousands of Israelis.

Several of the Judaization groups have offered weekend retreats devoted to Jewish education and values. Participants are expected to pay, but the prices charged are heavily subsidized. Thousands of Israelis have taken part in these retreats, which are oriented toward the entire family. The Judaization organizations publish a variety of pamphlets and leaflets addressed to secular readers that try to reach them with references to common problems and the emptiness of secular life. Several publications and lectures attack the theory of evolution with claims familiar from similar sources in Western countries. Of course, the majority of participants in lectures, rallies, and retreats organized by various Judaization groups have not become Orthodox and should not be counted among the returnees.

An organization of Parents Against The Return to Judaism was started in 1984, and its members have been visible in the media. Activities of parents whose children had returned to Judaism started taking a more militant and bitter tone, renaming itself "Those Victimized by the Return to Judaism" and starting vigorous media campaigns in 1985. One of the main arguments used by the group was that the returnees had become non-Zionist and stopped serving in the military. The organization had 100 members as of 1986. Some of the parents decided to tell their personal stories in the media and started debates with their own children with rebuttals and counter-rebuttals. The parents' complaints were of two kinds: against the Judaization process, which was compared to brain-washing, and against the final product, described as return to the ghetto (Meller, 1985).

The question of a tradition of interest in religious experimentation or in Jewish mysticism in Israel before 1973 is often raised. Isn't it possible that the recent wave of Judaization grew out of a broad base of general but more muted interest? The evidence shows that there was no such broad base, and that religious experimentation was quite limited. Weiner (1961 and 1969), who went searching for it, shows us that those "9.5 mystics" (1969) were indeed the last saving remnant of a great tradition with no prospect of a great awakening in sight.

It is vital to recall that the process of individual and collective secularization in Israel is still going on, and there is still an Orthodox minority and a secular majority. Apostasy continues to be a major problem for Israel's Orthodox community. The process of personal secularization, through which the Orthodox minority in Israel has been losing members, has been continuing despite the appearance of a movement in the opposite direction. It has been estimated that 10 percent of the moderately Orthodox (national-religious) youth leave the status of "observant" behind at age eighteen. This is marked by taking off the habitual skullcap (for men). What Liebman (1984) observes is that there has been an increasing overlap between Israeli and Jewish identity since 1973, "But whereas religious symbols play an increasingly important role in Israeli public or collective life . . . there is no evidence . . . that the level of religious observance has increased, that more people refrain from violating the Sabbath or eating bread on Passover, or that more people pray" (p. 6). Orthodox Jews are today, and have been at least for three generations, a minority among Jews all over the world and a minority among Israelis. This situation has not changed and is not likely to change in the future.

Collective Judaization

Orthodox Jewry has been in crisis since the rise of Zionism in Jewish communities. The decline and stagnation of political Zionism leads to a revitalization of Orthodoxy. Ever since the 1967 War, which brought vast new territories under Israeli control, a phenomenon that has become known as Judaization or a "turn to the right" has been noted in Israeli public life. What has happened is the Judaization of Israeli identity in the face of crisis. The process of Judaization in Israel since 1967 illustrates the paradoxical nature of Zionism as a secularized messianic movement. It can be seen as representing all the undercurrents and conflicts that have existed in Zionism since its inception.

Both public and private Judaization support the Jewish identity of the State of Israel and political claims based on this identity. These developments are beneficial, if not vital, for the State and so are going to be sanctioned. Judaization serves as a source of identity, justification, and hope for both individual and collectivity.

It is vital to understand that there is a basic gap and conflict between religion and nationalism, particularly between Judaism and Zionism. On the whole, the more Orthodox an individual is, the less likely he is to support Zionism. There is a clear negative relationship between religiosity and Zionism among Jews. The ultra-Orthodox, from Neturei Karta (Marmostein, 1969) to Agudat Israel, espouse separatism from the secular world, including Zionism. Supporters of Zionism are neo-Orthodox.

The creation of secular political Zionism meant a serious challenge to Jewish Orthodoxy. While the majority of Orthodox Jews have rejected Zionism, there was a minority that created religious Zionism. This religious Zionism deviated from traditional Jewish beliefs in advocating secular initiatives to bring about a redemption of the Jewish people, but it enjoyed the vitality of modern nationalism (Hertzberg, 1971).

It should be remembered that most non-Zionist religious groups in Israel recognize the State of Israel in practice. Most non-Zionist religious schools are happy to receive financial support from the state, and manipulate skillfully the political power structure (except for Neturei Karta). They challenge the Zionist ideology of the State of Israel but not its basic Jewish identity. "Jewish solidarity" is a theme common to secular Zionists and to most religious non-Zionists.

The Agudat Israel movement, despite its participation in coalition government since 1948, expresses on occasion its principled anti-Zionist stand. Thus, an Agudat Israel publication said in an editorial in 1986: "We demonstrate . . . against the whole Zionist enterprise. . . . We do not demonstrate just against a particular anti-religious act, we protest against the right of Zionists to rule over observant Jews. Those individuals . . . have no right to live here, much less to control us and manage our affairs. . . . The Jewish people has survived worse enemies than that" (quoted by Shragai, 1986). The complexity of the relationship between religiosity and nationalism in Israel is illustrated by the existence, even with the wave of individual and collective Judaization, of a visible nationalist-secular group. There are still those who are extremely nationalistic while at the same time proclaiming their atheism. Explaining why he has not become a returnee, an Israeli journalist writes: "Why? Because there is no God. The Holocaust is the scientific proof for that. The Holocaust is also theological proof for that. The Holocaust is God's way of punishing those who insisted on believing in Him. That's His way, blessed be He, to show us that there is no God" (Uziel, 1985, p. 23). Such a statement, published in a leading Tel Aviv daily, could not be published in most U.S. newspapers. It should be noted that the writer is both a rabid nationalist, and the grandson of a chief rabbi of Israel in the 1950s.

The Revival

Following a long period in which Judaism was in decline, and Zionism was full of vitality, religion is now capable of providing Zionism with justification and hope. Public return to Judaism stems from the declining fortunes of Zionism and the wars of 1967 and 1973—the first was the high point of Zionism, and the second its lowest. Defending Zionism against its detractors and against the mounting doubts about its morality and legitimacy even among its supporters has become increasingly difficult since 1967. Such defenses have become less rational and more emotional and authoritarian as time went on, and the frustration with Zionism has not diminished.

What religion does provide in the mounting crisis since the 1973 War is, first, a unifying idea for Israeli Jews, second, hope for the future, and third, a moral justification for Zionism. The religious argument becomes crucial when Israelis demand not just rights, but privileges over Palestinian Arabs. Judaism is simply the best answer for any challenges for the legitimacy of Zionism. It settles the doubts and the questions regarding the contradictions between Zionism and humanistic values. A collective return to Judaism can provide the best solution to the ideological crisis of Zionism, giving decisive answers to doubts about Zionism's morality. Religion becomes Zionism's last line of defense. Where doubts and difficulties are increasing, it can stem the tide by relying on divine authority. All questions and difficulties are removed once you accept the premise of a supernatural entity that is tied exclusively to the Jews and has given them a central role in history. The obvious injustice done to the Palestinians becomes irrelevant and pales in the light of God's promise to the Jews.

As Liebman and Don-Yehiya (1984) state, "religion also integrates the population and provides a vehicle for socialization and political legitimation" (p. viii). Religious rules are important to the basic definition of the State of Israel and to the basic definitions of citizenship. In Israel, by definition, Jews have more rights than non-Jews, and it becomes important to define who really belongs to the privileged group. The formal separation of religion and state in Israel destroys the religious basis of Zionist claims for exclusive rights in Palestine, and thus it may destroy the state itself. Since all other justifications of Zionism seem to be found wanting, Zionism cannot afford a divorce from religion, while Judaism can afford a divorce from Zionism.

The Judaization movement in Israeli public life is one of renewal and regeneration for both Judaism and Zionism. The creation of religious Zionism (or Zionist religion) provides new strength to both sides in the exchange. The exchange between Zionism and religion provides much needed support for both sides. For Zionism, an ideological shot in the arm together with a body of young idealists who are ready to carry on the fight. For the national-religious camp, the advantage of being in the mainstream with renewed confidence and self-respect.

The rise of right-wing nationalism has been correlated with strengthening of the religious minority allied with it and with the growing prestige of the religious point of view. Liebman and Don-Yehiya (1984) describe the development of religious nationalism as follows: "The awakening of ultranationalist sentiments among religious Zionists followed the Six-Day War and Yom Kippur War. These wars quickened messianic expectations among religious Zionists and strengthened commitments to notions of greater Israel" (p. 111). By joining forces with nationalism after 1967, the neo-Orthodox camp in Israel gained importance and vitality and overcame many years of marginality. The nationalist camp gained energy and legitimacy by aligning itself with the neo-Orthodox. Thus, we have witnessed a double revival.

Nationalism brings a new vitality to the religious subculture in Israel. In addition to unchanging traditions, which do not require any new energies, or dynamisms, the new goals of Jewish sovereignty and domination over the Palestinians create new structures and activities. This challenge has revitalized the religious minority in Israel, and has given it a position of superiority over the secular majority.

The secular majority in Israel is demoralized and confused, exhausted and pessimistic. Its problem is justifying Zionism in theory and ensuring its survival in practice, and it finds itself lacking on both accounts. The national-religious movement since 1973 has been the last and only source of faith and vitality for Zionism. Secular Zionists have been aware of this and have had to admit that they are in need of this revitalization movement. Secular labor party hawks were the first to admit that religiosity is the safest and most stable basis for nationalism.

Since most secular Israelis still claim a Jewish identity, they are in an initial position of inferiority before their Orthodox compatriots. Secular Israelis often claim that they represent a new but authentic kind of Judaism and that Judaism has always been pluralistic. They are thus trying to defend their historically new conception. Orthodox Jews have no such problem. They don't have to apologize because no one will ever doubt their Jewishness and their Judaism, which are historically authentic. If you claim to be Jewish, you cannot gainsay these representatives of Jewish history and historical Judaism. Thus, in any debate about Jewish identity, and there are many of those in Israel, the secular side is apologetic and apologizing. The Orthodox side is confident and secure.

For the Orthodox minority in Israel, the importance of the individual Judaization phenomenon is not in sheer numbers, which have not changed its minority status anyway, but merely in the trend. After 200 years of individual and collective secularization, the trend is being reversed. When leading personalities in the Israeli art world and family members of Israeli leaders return to Orthodox Judaism, the feeling in the religious camp is one of historical triumph.

The whole situation and status of the religious minority in Israel has changed dramatically since the 1950s and 1960s. Until 1967, the religious minority clearly accepted its status as a declining minority, outside the mainstream of Israeli public life. There was a tragic dimension to the existence of the Orthodox minority in those years, as the last remnant of a great tradition. Judaism was clearly disappearing from the face of the earth, and most Jews were thoroughly secular or followers of triumphant Zionism. Orthodox Jews were the last carriers of ancient traditions on their way out.

The religious-Zionist movement before 1948 was much weaker than secular Zionism and was the junior partner in political coalitions. After 1948, this tradition of being the weak partner continued until the late 1960s and 1970s. After 1948 and until 1967, religious Jews in Israel felt marginal and lacked in confidence. They were out of the mainstream of events in Israel, and there was a collective inferiority feeling (Meislisch, 1984).

One of the leaders of the National Religious Party and general secretary of its youth movement (30,000 members in 1985) expresses the transformation in the national-religious self-image after 1967: "I remember the frustration I felt before the Six-Day War while comparing our movement to others. We always followed the Zionist Labor movement . . . and suddenly, after 1967, the turning point came. We are no longer led, but the leaders" (quoted in Prister, 1985).

Before 1967, religious Zionists felt isolated and powerless.

> It reflected their marginal position in Israeli society and culture. Religious Zionists represented a small minority of the population; initiative and leadership of the nation were in the hands of secularists. . . . Religious Zionists played the role of satellites, and this status led them to a policy of defensiveness and separatism in order to defend their own particular values and principles, lest they be overwhelmed by secular Zionism. (p. 112)

Following the two wars, members of the younger generation of religious Zionism, now in positions of influence, were prepared to engage secular Zionism in ideological confrontation and to extend their activity to all areas of society. Their weapons

> included the expansionist philosophy . . . which reinterpreted Zionist ideology in the terminology of traditional Judaism, and their newly acquired status as standard bearers of Jewish settlement on the West Bank and examples of Zionism's pioneering spirit. To their surprise, they found the battlefield empty. . . . Following the Six-Day War, religious Zionists found that they were the segment in Israeli society that offered the most consistent support for a policy of retaining Israeli sovereignty over the occupied territories. Furthermore, they had an ideology that legitimated that policy. Among the secular Zionists they found hesitation, weakness and ideological confusion. For the first time since the beginning of modern Zionism, religious Zionists became the central force in settlement of the land. (Liebman and Don-Yehiya, 1984, p. 113.)

The regeneration of the Orthodox minority in Israel since 1973 has been remarkable. Still a minority but confident and well-organized, it has been at the mainstream of national issues and national events. The increased self-confidence of the Orthodox minority has caused it to become more assertive in cases of political disputes. It should be remembered that the overall picture has not changed. Less than 10 percent of Jews in the world are Orthodox, but Zionism is in decline, and the Orthodox minority in Israel and abroad is more confident and resilient than ever.

Among the Orthodox, the non-Zionist camp is confident in its tradition, buoyed up by Zionism's apparent decline and fall. The religious-Zionist camp gains its vitality from a messianic interpretation of Judaism and revitalizes nationalism through religious faith. The religious minority, in its two sectors, the nationalist and the non-nationalist, offers clear visions. One is that of a Greater Israel, triumphant and imperial, ruling over the Middle East and its backward natives, buttressed by a messianic certainty. The other is that of traditional Jewish Orthodoxy with a community of believers sustained in its life of sacred ritual by the weight of two thousand years of a coherent and proven Jewish culture. The nonreligious majority has only been saying no to these visions without much energy or conviction of its own. Since 1973, the religious and the nationalist have been filled with passionate intensity, while for the majority of Israelis the center no longer holds. Only a few secular Israelis offer positive visions, but those may be too unsettling for their compatriots.

Parallel to the Judaization movement which has been turning secular Israelis into Orthodox ones, there is within the Orthodox minority a process of Orthodoxization in which the Zionist-Orthodox camp is losing ground to the non-Zionist ultra-Orthodox. Zionist-Orthodox youth are becoming more Orthodox and less Zionist thanks to the influence of ultra-Orthodox teachers and the overall rise of the non-Zionist position among the religious minority. Among the Zionist-Orthodox camp, now on the defensive, there have been attempts to counter this trend but to little avail (Nuriel, 1986).

The Weakening of Secularism

Liebman and Don-Yehiya (1984) state that there has been "a weakening of secular ideology and antireligious sentiment," which paralleled "the growing penetration of religious symbols into Israeli culture" (p. 27). In the 1950s, one could have observed fairly militant secularism in Israel with demands for civil marriages and divorces and violent antireligious demonstrations. The religious community was viewed as marginal and experienced itself this way. In the 1950s, there was a League Against Religious Coercion in Israel, which opposed religious legislation and demonstrated in cases of what it regarded as Orthodox provocations. It drew its strength from left-wing Zionism.

The socialist-Zionist leadership was quite thoroughly secular. The generation of founders adopted a life-style that simply had no room in it for religious symbols. In 1960, during the Israeli population census, David Ben-Gurion described himself as an atheist. Other prime ministers, such as Moshe Sharett, Levi Eshkol, and Golda Meir, were involved in religious rituals only during their funerals. When Israel Galili, a member of the old guard who served as Knesset Member for twenty-seven years and as a minister for twelve, was laid to rest, the only words heard were those of a popular poem. But Galili's funeral took place in February 1986 and signs of Judaization were in evidence. When the official secular ceremony was over, the words of the Kaddish, the Jewish prayer for the dead, were heard near the grave. They were said by Yoram Lukov, an artist and a returnee to Judaism, who is a nephew of the late Galili (Vardi, 1986).

In September 1963, 5000 secular Israelis organized by the League Against Religious Coercion, which was started ten years earlier, marched into the Orthodox neighborhoods of Jerusalem in a show of force, unopposed, during the Sabbath. Twenty years later, such a demonstration was inconceivable. The last national convention of the League took place in January 1968, and then it disappeared from the Israeli scene as the spirit of militant secularism waned (Sarna, 1985). Most Israelis after 1967 have not been absolutely secular but only relatively so. They have located themselves at various points along the secular-religious continuum, and only a few have wanted to commit themselves to the secular end of the spectrum.

In 1978 an attempt was made to recreate a secularist movement, and in 1980, the Israel Secular Humanist Association was founded. This group publishes a quarterly and holds periodical meetings, but its base of public support is extremely limited. The Israel Secular Humanist Association takes a stand in favor of separating religion and state, a constitution for the State of Israel, and peace with the Palestinians. These unpopular ideas are the clear reason for its tiny membership. The Israel Secular Humanist Association is energized by a few secularists, who also tend to be left-wing. Such a connection seems natural and understandable because secular ideas of democracy and inequality tend to undermine mainstream Israeli conceptions of what Israel should be like, i.e., a Jewish state.

Messianic Political Movements

While messianic interpretations of events in the Middle East started after the 1967 War, it was limited to a few fringe groups and individuals. This trickle became a large stream only after the 1973 War, with the founding of the religious-nationalist group Gush Emunim on January 30, 1974. There are those in Gush Emunim (and outside the group) who believe that the State of Israel is but a preparatory stage for the coming of the Kingdom of Israel very soon. These religious-nationalist activists, small in numbers (equal to the number of members in new religious), enjoy a large influence thanks to their political vision and political actions. They offer the demoralized majority hope and vitality.

Since 1973 there have been in Israel other religious-nationalist groups of a messianic nature. All of these groups share a messianic vision of the coming redemption of the Jewish people in Israel. While some individual members of these groups are returnees to Judaism, the groups themselves do not offer or promote private salvation, since they are political movements, whose goal is to change the world and not individuals. The genesis and development of these groups parallels exactly the salvation movements we are dealing with in this book, but their response to private distress is socio-political, not individualistic.

The creation of messianic Zionism in Israel after 1967, and its growth after 1973, are documented by Liebman and Don-Yehiya (1984). The crisis that led to the development of messianic movements is described by the son of a national-religious leader (not nationalist) and a labor party member as follows: "As the Zionist era is fading we realize that our hopes were not realized. The Jewish people has not changed. Society is not healthier, and the State of Israel only added new troubles to the old ones. So the messianics have replaced the Messiah of hope with the Messiah of despair" (Burg, 1984, p. 7).

Here and there, one could find over the past ten years small groups of individuals, who indeed represent a messianic faith. These groups and individuals are on the margins of the Judaization movement. Some dream of building the third Jewish Temple in Jerusalem, and others have engaged in practical activities to that effect. We may consider their ideas and their actions strange, but they are not involved in private salvation but rather what they consider a collective or even universal salvation. There are those have been weaving special clothing for the priests of the Third Temple and making exact plans for the altar on which regular daily sacrifices of two sheep are to be made. All those individuals believe that the building of the Temple, through divine intervention, or by human hands, is to occur shortly.

Looking at an Israeli Messianic Cult

Through informants, I have been able to locate a small messianic group led by one charismatic woman and run as a cult. The leader, H. R., is a woman in her mid-thirties, well educated and respected in her community, where she works as a teacher. She is intelligent, articulate, and relaxed. Around H. R. gathered a small group of adepts, which meets at least once a week. The meetings are wholly devoted to the teachings of H. R., which are presented as messages from two spirits, J. and G. These two spirits speak through H. R. only. The small group of followers range in age from nineteen to fifty-six. There is a majority of women, most of them are married but pursue this without their husbands. The teaching include "unconventional thinking," expressed through new definitions for familiar terms, such as "ambition" and "education," and the development of "spiritual consciousness."

The most important teachings, dictated by the two spirits, deal with the destiny of humankind, and the special role of the Children of Israel. Humankind is about to enter a New Age, in which human beings will change their behavior completely. The most important change to take place in the New Age has to do with the two sexes, which will become one. Physical ability will lose its meaning as humankind learns to use gravity and move objects by "telecosmic" means. The two cosmic elements, feminine and masculine, are separate and unequal in this world, but this will change. The feminine element creates harmony in nature, and correlations among nature's laws. The masculine element is expressed through cosmic creation, planning, and changing. The feminine element is the Shechina (a female entity in Jewish mystical lore) and the masculine element is God. The feminine element was subordinated to the masculine one because of the Garden of Eden affair, but this will change in the New Age.

The Children of Israel were created in order to show all of humanity the way to a correct utilization of all psychic and physical forces in harmony with humankind and nature. Israel's wars are ordained by God, who specifies exactly their dimensions and goals. These wars are always aimed at destroying evil and aggression emanating from other human groups. Pagan nations that were beyond redemption were destroyed by the Children of Israel, when no other choice was left. People who refuse to change their evil ways have to be destroyed, and the Children of Israel should not flinch from their duty to God to carry out this task. In most cases, however, other peoples in the Middle East have shown themselves ready to accept Judaism, and no war was mandated against them. Those who resist the true faith will be subjugated.

Wars between the Children of Israel and other peoples occur because of three reasons:

1. Other peoples cannot accept the existence of the Children of Israel, who remind the former of their inferiority.
2. Peoples in the Middle East want to prove that they are chosen by God, through their control over territory.
3. Humanity still fights against the need to become better and to accept cosmic laws through the Children of Israel. They still resist the divine order.

For these reasons, more trials and tribulations can be expected, and the 1973 War was but the first example. In addition to the teachings of the spirits, which are recorded and mimeographed, members of the group are supposed to read contemporary messianic and nationalist literature. An example of the former is a book published by a Jerusalem technician, who has been predicting the coming of complete redemption (i.e., the Messiah) since 1967. The first edition of his book predicted redemption in 1968. In several editions since then, the date has been moved forward.

H. R.'s interpretation of Jewish history, which may seem bizarre and chauvinistic to many, is actually not that uncommon among Israelis. We have seen that the idea of chosenness is adhered to among many Israelis (Kedem and Ben-Meir, 1979), secular as well as Orthodox. We have to keep in mind that in "secular" Israeli schools, starting in second grade, Old Testament stories are taught as history and are accepted as such by the vast majority of Israelis. Old Testament stories, such as the creation of the Jewish people with the Patriarchs, the exile in Egypt, the Exodus, and Joshua's wars, are treated by most Israelis as history, not mythology. Analogies are sometimes drawn between Joshua's conquest and contemporary events (see Zweig, 1969). Israeli archeology is guided by a desire to confirm this outline of ancient Jewish beginnings. Connecting the Old Testament Children of Israel and contemporary Jews is, of course, one of the cornerstones of Zionism.

Thus, H. R. is deviant because she claims to receive knowledge from two spirits and because of her ideas about masculinity and feminity in the New Age. These universalistic ideas are not often heard in Israel, and in this sense H. R. represents a new religion. Her historical-religious-political message, nationalistic as it may be, is not that much further from what one can read in the writings of leading Israeli nationalists after 1967 and 1973 and what can be read every day in most Israeli newspapers.

The tiny group around H. R. represents a classic collection of seekers. There is a 56-year-old respectable grandfather seeking peace of mind, and a 19-year-old soldier whose parents were separated. There is a 32-year-old former political activist who has been disheartened by the failure of the "peace movement." There are three divorced women, burdened with worries about finances and children. There are two married women who do not share their search with their husbands. There is a teacher who has been involved in a variety of groups and actually started his own at one point after the deterioration of his marriage. All of these individuals have found some meaning and support in H. R.'s group, which is quite secretive and elitist. Told by their leader that they are among the elect, this experience of belonging obviously does something for them. Membership in the group, unlike that in a new religion or returning to Judaism, requires very little in the way of investment, commitment, or change in lifestyle.

3

The Triumph of the Occult

In early 1986, the executive assistant to the chief of staff of the Israel Defense Forces (I.D.F.), General Alik Harmatz, went to Jerusalem to visit the home of a civilian and to receive personally a document prepared by that civilian. It does not happen very often that a general is sent personally to collect documents from civilians, but the mission was considered important enough, apparently. The civilian was Mr. Elituzr Kdoshi, who makes a living as an astrologer. The document, which General Harmatz received and read, was an astrological birth map for the Israel Defense Forces (Walter, 1986). The I.D.F., like human beings, animals, organizations, and structures, has a birth date, and so, according to astrological logic, should have a birth map from which diagnoses and predictions can be drawn. Indeed, such maps have been published quite often in Israel. This visit by a general to the home of an astrologer may appear bizarre in most places in the world, but in Israel it is merely one of many indications of triumph of occultism, which has become legitimized and absorbed to an impressive extent.

This story about a trip by a general from his office in Tel-Aviv to the home of an astrologer in Jerusalem in search of vital information may sound surrealistic, but as we are going to discover, it is not very deviant in terms of the Israeli mass culture of the 1980s. What may seem to be an unusual and illogical behavior seemed to General Harmatz to be nothing extraordinary. In the Israel of 1986, astrology was simply another way of understanding and predicting people and events. The culture contained a particular Israeli mix of occult practices that appear together and enjoy mass popularity. This mix includes astrology, graphology (which isn't really part of the tradition, but is used by occult practitioners), palm reading, and magical healing. The occult in Israel offers individuals a form of pop psychology, providing self-understanding and explanations of private destiny. At the same time, certain occult traditions, particularly astrology, are used as guides for thinking about collective issues, from the stock market to the future of the country. A subculture of the occult has been developed, containing beliefs, norms, members, and leaders. It has achieved legitimacy and stability. What is significant about the occult subculture in Israel is the degree to which it is taken seriously by the media and by the elite. While the occult in other countries is treated as déclassé, in Israel it is established and legitimized. Those who do not share the faith in the occult feel deviant and excluded. An electrical engineering student at the Israel Institute of Technology told me in 1986: "You are the first person I ever ran into who does not have faith in astrology or graphology. What's the matter with you?"

Occult Occupations and Careers

Divination is "the use of magical means to discover information inaccessible to normal inquiry (about the future, lost objects, hidden character-traits, etc.). . . . The diviner . . . role, however humble socially, is inevitably a priestly one, mediating between worldly concerns and mysterious but purposeful higher powers" (Lindop, 1984, pp. 109–10). This general definition fits perfectly the phenomenon of occult divination in Israeli society, as it has developed over the past two decades.

According to the Israel Criminal Code, article 417(a), anybody guilty of witchcraft, fortune telling, or magic for pay, will be sentenced to two years in prison. In practice, very few cases are brought before the courts, despite the fact that, according to one source, thousands make their living as soothsayers and "healers" (Ella, 1981). Despite legal prohibitions, soothsayers advertise openly in newspapers and magazines and appear in the classified telephone directories. Such advertisements are especially common in women's weeklies but can be found in all daily newspapers. The institutionalization of the occult in Israel has led to the appearance and growth of new occupations, which have become widely recognized in everyday life and everyday language.

"What do you want to do when you grow up?" Address this question to an Israeli youngster and you may sometimes hear "astrologer" or "chirologist." And indeed, when graduating high school students are interviewed about their present views and future plans, we find Yaniv, who plays the guitar and supports right-wing politics. His future plans include service in the Navy and then joining the secret security police. His long-range dream is to get rich, by starting an astrology business that will provide customers with life plans (Strier, 1982). A Briton or an American hearing about such occupations as chirologist, graphologist, or astrologer upon being introduced to somebody may raise eyebrows and ask for explanations. In Israel today, such occupations are widely known and recognized, and one is not surprised to hear somebody introduced as practicing them.

ORT is a worldwide system of vocational schools for Jewish children, founded originally in Czarist Russia in the nineteenth century. In Israel ORT has operated an excellent system of vocational high schools, in which tens of thousands study every year. In 1984 it announced a two-year vocational course for adults, designed to train astrologers producing "character maps, life maps, and future predictions. Since the late 1970s, one can regularly hear about astrologers, graphologists, chirologists, numerologists, and even generic "parapsychologists." Such occupations and such terms were totally unknown in the 1960s. What has happened in Israel is a change in the status of divination from a marginal and socially backward practice to something not only acceptable but prestigious.

The triumph of the occult has found its expression in several large-scale events putting together occultists of all stripes for public consumption. The elegant Dan Carmel Hotel in Haifa hosted on January 23, 1987, such an event, titled Mystic '87. It offered expert "futurologists" from all over the world prognosticating by palm reading, coffee grounds, cards, crystal balls, graphology, astrology, and numerology. It also offered "regression," reincarnation, psychokinesis, and "transformation." The nonsensology subculture has become acceptable as part of vacation activities, and several resorts now offer both weekend and week-long programs devoted to astrology, coffee readings, cartomancy, tarot, graphology, and numerology. *Telling the Future*, an original Israeli product, made the best-seller list for February 1982 in the category of "Documentation and scholarship," according to *Yediot Aharonot* (March 5, 1982). The book, by Orna Levy and Yehudit Zamir, contains information on fortune telling through coffee reading, cards, numerology, and astrology. It also revives the old science of phrenology. The chapter on phrenology from the book was published by *Maariv* on January 29, 1982.

A basic assumption and an article of faith for customers and practitioners of occult popular psychology is the ease with which questions regarding personal destiny can be answered. Secrets of the past and the future are uncovered with certainty. Dynamics of personal fortune and misfortune and the true nature of one's hidden personality become known. There is a body of information that provides this knowledge, and it is retrieved from storage through the personal expertise of practitioners. Personality diagnosis is done through signs (birth dates, lines in palms) and not actual behavior. The whole process is a miracle, but that miracle is readily accessible. External forces, which truly control our lives, can be interpreted for our benefit. If we do not gain control, at least we have gained understanding.

The occultist is a modernized shaman, using charisma and his or her clients' vulnerability to perform mini-miracles. It is the belief in the miraculous that is the main characteristic of the occult and the alternative medicine subcultures. The atmosphere around the astrologers, the homeopathic healers, the palm readers, and other miracle workers is thick with the certainty of miracles which would relieve all pains and would deliver us from this vale of tears through physical and mental shortcuts.

True believers in the occult are ready with their own miracle stories, which are not usually tales of transformation but rather prophecy and enlightenment. A woman tells me of a birth map, made for her daughter on the day of her birth, which turned out to predict correctly everything in her daughter's development. While occultist practices only rarely provide a complete metamorphosis, they do offer clients meaning, if not purpose. Occultism cannot supply relief but a world in which events are interconnected and miracles are possible.

The occult offers an explanation of personal (and sometimes collective) destiny through references to visible and invisible powers. The occult is the obverse of secular psychotherapy. It provides answers to the same questions of individual destiny as psychotherapy within a traditional external fate framework. Women appear to be the main customers of occult practitioners, as they are in regard to psychotherapy, and in Israel these two findings have been demonstrated (Hochstadt, 1981). Many of the practitioners offer multiple services using, for example, both graphology and astrology or a combination of palm reading and astrology.

Personal involvement in the occult expresses itself at three levels. The first one is that of reading a newspaper astrology column or listening to a radio program on astrology or graphology. The second is that of an active search for divination, through visiting a fortune teller or astrologer. The third is that of aspiring to become an active occultist through formal studies, which may lead to a new occupational identity in some cases or a hobbyist status in most. The first level is superficial and prevalent, and involves most of the Israeli population. It entails a basic acceptance of occult systems as valid and some knowledge of those, especially astrology. The second level is that of the devotee who spends time, money, and energy in becoming an occult expert and practitioner. "Astrology is a theory that has invaded all spheres of our life in recent years, so that even the great and the wise will seek its help and will not make a move without an astrological map" (Levinstein, 1986). This is one journalist's description of the status of astrology in Israel.

Mentioning the subject's birth sign has become *de rigueur* in any article dealing with a sports star or a show business personality. Reuveni (1985), one of Israel's leading writers, in an interview with Yehudit Ravitz, a leading singer, has to "exchange" birth signs with her. Avron (1985), an interviewer for another newspaper, reports that Ravitz is a Capricorn, without disclosing his birth sign. When the news magazine of the Israel Defense Forces publishes an article about a singers' team famous in Israel since the 1950s, one of them turns out to be "typical Leo," while the other is a Scorpio (Bar-On, 1986a). A sensational murder trial in 1986 involves two women, one of whom is married to a leading television personality. The other woman was known as an astrologer and a witch. The first defendant, Mrs. Yaari, said during her interrogation about the other one: "When a person has Mercury in an astrological map, he is a pathological liar. Ask any astrologer about this map" (*Haolam Hazeh*, 1986). The two defendants spent the last day before the verdict was announced in attempts to predict it through astrological maps. They were both expecting an acquittal but were found guilty of murder in the first degree, and sentenced to life in prison (Werther, 1986). Astrology has become so legitimate in Israel that when the weekly newsmagazine of the Israel Defense Forces presents an article on the latest statistical annual published by the government by saying "the annual is like a horoscope: read it if you want to know your chances to get married, to get divorced, or to reach the age of 73" (Rosenthal, 1986, p. 22).

David Avitan was an Israeli success story. In 1980 he became known as a leading expert on stock market predictions by astrology. His friends, like himself employees of a defense electronics plant in

Ashdod, gave him their savings and were guaranteed profits of 50 percent. His investment consulting office, run in addition to his work as an electronics technician, was doing well until 1982. Then, a stock market decline led to a disaster. Mr. Avitan declared that the decline had been diagnosed in time and that he would turn to another astrologer for help (Mor, 1982). Astrologers have become business advisers, and they regularly provide intelligence on such things as the stock market and other investments. In a business dispute that came before the district court in Tel-Aviv, it was disclosed that one partner in a contracting firm paid 2.5 million shekels to Miriam Tamir, one of Israel's leading astrologers for business advice (Adiram, 1984).

What can be observed in the 1980s is how Israeli business publications devote space regularly to astrological analysis and predictions of the business world in Israel and abroad. A general forecast for the economy in 1990 by an astrologer was published in the official publication of the Israel Manufacturers Association in December 1989. *Ksafim* ("money"), Israel's leading business weekly, carries an astrology column, which offers analysis of the U.S. economy based on the U.S. "birth map," and analyses of various corporations based again on their birth dates. In December 1989, *Ksafim* reported that stock exchange difficulties were being caused by the behavior of the planet Saturn and that the expected behavior of the planet Uranus in 1990 should prepare us for even more serious problems. A movie producer whose film ran for only three weeks says: "When we started filming, a friend who works in astrology told me we shouldn't, because all the stars were against us" (Salhuv, 1984, p. 12).

As in many other cultures, fortune tellers often come from a disadvantaged group, and their upper-class clients believe that somehow the downtrodden have special powers and special knowledge, even though this does not seem to help in worldly matters. Members of oppressed groups are able to demonstrate secret powers but unable to improve their conditions in the real world. In Israeli most fortune tellers come from the lower classes, while some well-connected astrologers and graphologists come from middle-class backgrounds. The typical occult practitioner in Israel is an obese woman with little or no education who resides in a poor neighborhood. Clients, on the other hand, come from all walks of life (Halevy, 1980).

Occultism has even managed to create bonds across national barriers between Israelis and Palestinians. Among popular fortune tellers and miracle workers one can find several Palestinians in the occupied West Bank who enjoy an Israeli clientele, which sometimes include officials and military officers. In the early 1980s, a Palestinian named Muhammad Aid Zakarna (born in 1946) from the village of

Kabatia, near Nablus on the West Bank, developed a growing clientele that included both Israelis and Palestinians. He seemed to be very successful, enjoying wine, women, and fast cars. There was another side to his career, however. He was reputed to be an informer for the Israeli occupation army, one of thousands that made up a network that enabled Israel to keep 1.5 million Palestinians under control. His neighbors in the village described him as responsible for hundreds of arrests over the years. He was allowed to carry a gun and had extremely useful connections in the military occupation bureaucracy.

When the Palestinian uprising started in December 1987, people like Zakarna felt isolated and threatened and rightly so. The uprising was directed not only against the Israeli army but also against its Palestinian collaborators, and hundreds of them were to die over the next years. On Thursday, February 25, 1988, Muhammad Aid Zakarna was lynched by his neighbors. His powers of telling the future failed him for the last time.

Astrology as Pop Psychology

Pop psychology, unlike the certified kind practiced by professionals, uses everyday language rather than professional jargon and gives clients what they are looking for: straight answers to pressing questions about personal destiny and personal difficulties. Clients get for their money natural-language personality descriptions. For many of my informants, demonstrating a knowledge of astrology was proof of sophistication, intelligence, and breadth of interest. It was indeed perceived as being in the same realm as psychology, except that the latter seemed complicated and imprecise compared with astrology, which was seen as an "exact science." Astrological typology, dividing humanity into twelve personality classifications, has become part of everyday language in Israel, and proof of that can be easily found in the many cases in which it is used in the press to characterize individuals. The following is a sampling of articles from the Israeli press in which astrological classifications are used in personality descriptions and for the understanding of personal destiny.

Item: Zvi Lidsky, a well-known criminal lawyer in Tel-Aviv, was married at age 49, for the second time, to a 32-year-old secretary. The inevitable consequence was an interview in *Haolam Hazeh,* with the inevitable reference to the astrological match. Both he and his new wife were Scorpios (Galzan, 1984), and they were divorced shortly thereafter.

Item: A female drug addict is described as a "libra—tall, attractive and struggling. She has a sharp tongue, well-groomed hands, sensitivity to small details and lucid phrases. She radiates joy and warmth, but can easily switch from laughter to tears" (Azolay, 1980, p. 10).

Item: A leading comedian explains the failure of his marriage and the success of his current affair. Both women involved are Aquarius, but the wife was atypical, while the new lover is typical (Shalev, 1981).

Item: A 30-year-old life prisoner, whose criminal career started at age 14, writes from his prison cell about recent experiences in a moving and impressive document. Among other events, he mentions a female social worker who was his counselor but stopped treatment because of astrological mismatching. "She believed in astrology, and there was a "verdict" against me, because I am a so-and-so, and she is a Gemini. In her warped mind, the two signs did not match, and she stopped treatment" (Elkayam, 1981, p. 55). The prisoner's story should not be doubted because it definitely reflects Israeli reality.

Item: Yehoshua Forer, former director general of the Trade Ministry who has gone into private business quickly becoming a millionaire, describes himself in a newspaper interview as "a classical Gemini," which explains his success in business.

Item: Lea Avni, fifty-seven years old, director of nursing at the Hadassah Hospital on Mount Scopus, Jerusalem, a mother of four and grandmother of seven, tells the world that her son Eitan, who was killed on June 6, 1982, in Lebanon, had to die. She gained this insight from an astrologer who told her that Eitan was a "special soul," who came into this world to fulfill a special task, and there was no need for mourning. A month after Eitan was killed in Lebanon, his death was celebrated by his mother and 150 friends on his birthday at a jazz piano concert (Roman, 1983).

Item: A war widow, whose husband was the first casualty of the 1967 War turns out to be a Scorpio, who organizes a Scorpio birthday party every year (Lev, 1984). Another war widow, whose adjustment is far from ideal, offers a public confession about her life and frustrations. She describes her dead husband: "On the one hand he was practical, businesslike. On the other hand he was a Sagittarius and always dreamed about touring faraway places" (Yishai, 1983, p. 61). A local newspaper in Haifa presents an Israeli success story, an insurance salesman who has become a millionaire, he turns out to be a typical Leo who cannot follow orders (Ettinger, 1984). And when a left-wing magazine publishes an article about a controversial poet, he is described as a Virgo (Eliom, 1984).

Item: When an 18-year-old political activist, a follower of Meir Kahane's nationalist party, is interviewed about what had led him to his political position, he replies: "I am a Libra. We believe in what we do, and we carry it through to the end" (quoted in Oren, 1984). Even a portrait of a 14-year-old Palestinian, sentenced to five years in prison for making five Molotov cocktails and using one on an Israeli bus, includes a reference to his birth sign (Sarna, 1985).

Astrology and Intellectuals

The presence of occult beliefs and practices in Israel can be felt not only in folklore but in the productions of the literary elite. David Avidan is one of Israel's leading poets and man of letters, whose fame dates back to the 1950s. His poetry has become part of the canon, the subject of graduate theses. In an article published in a weekend literary supplement to the leading Israeli daily, he discusses the phenomenon of fascism in literature, and, among other observations, lists Adolph Hitler as a "Taurus with Aries on the horizon, heading a nation under the sign of Pisces" (Avidan, 1986, p. 21). Dr. Hai Halevy, a Jerusalem psychoanalyst and member of the prestigious Jerusalem Institute for Psychoanalysis, is married to an astrologer and declared in an interview that "the testing of psychoanalytic hypotheses through astrological data shows a positive relationship . . . there is an important psychoanalytic phenomenon of fixation, which is central to the structure of personality. When we succeeded in translating it into astrological terms, we had the key in our hands" (quoted by Galili, 1984, p. 2).

When David Greenberg, a renowned filmmaker, is interviewed, he explains his tendency to accumulate collections through his birth sign—Scorpio (Shalit, 1984). When a reviewer for *Davar*, the labor party daily, writes about Vladmir Nabokov's *Laughter in the Dark*, she does not fail to mention that the hero is a typical Gemini (Eival, 1984). And when the curator for Israeli art at the Tel-Aviv Museum is asked about what led to her position, she says that she became interested in art only in high school, but "as a Virgo, being critical and inquisitive, I started exploring [art]" (quoted in Ben-Zakkai, 1981, p. 27). When Igael Yadin (chief of staff 1949–50, deputy prime minister 1977–81, and renowned archaeologist) celebrated his sixty-seventh birthday, the newspaper *Hadashot* gave him a present in the form an astrological personality diagnosis. Yadin reviewed it and agreed with it in part (*Hadashot*, 1984).

When Dvora Omer, Israel's leading children's writer, the author of scores of books and the winner of many awards, is interviewed for an intimate portrait, she does not miss the obligatory gesture of interest toward the occult. When she is asked what she would like to study, her answer is "design, architecture, astrology, graphology, and the occult" (Bartzky, 1986, p. 29).

Stars in the Media

If we had examined the media in Israel around 1970, we would have found very few references to the occult. Only a couple of daily newspapers and women's weeklies carried horoscopes. Other occult traditions were unknown. By the late 1970s, this has changed drastically. The space devoted to the occult included not only horoscopes, but advice columns and long discussions. Astrology columnists often refer to numerology, palm reading, and graphology in giving advice to their readers. The left-wing *Al Hamishmar*, which used to refer to Stalin in earlier years as "the rising sun," updated its star worship and thirty years after Stalin's death started publishing a weekly horoscope. Apparently, it could not resist demands from its readers, who are mostly kibbutz members. Thus, media reports in Israel on the occult both reflect historical developments and contribute to the same developments. Media discussions of the occult in Israel range from the respectful to the committed. Case studies of miraculous cures, diagnoses, and predictions abound.

A radio program known as "Five following One," combining graphology and astrology, was started in January 1981. In this program astrologers and graphologists are supposedly presented only with minimal information about famous personalities, usually entertainers and politicians. The information is birth date and birth place for astrologers, and a handwriting sample for graphologists. On the basis of such information, expert diagnosticians never fail to astound the audience in the studio and at home as well as the diagnosed individuals with their accuracy. Their complimentary character readings are often reported in gossip columns, at the inspiration of the persons involved.

Most depictions of occult practitioners in the media are extremely positive, despite the fact that their predictions are often of doom and destruction and they have become the vulgar prophets of despair and hopelessness. They are described as warm, charming, and intelligent. The wife of Knesset member Benjamin Ben-Eliezer (labor party), who is also a former army general, is portrayed in the media as a brilliant astrologer who graduated from an intensive astrology course at "the University of Berkeley, USA" (Levanon, 1986).

Testimonials, giving us detailed accounts of the miraculous

effects of occult divination can be found in the Israeli mass media without much effort. Thus, *Haaretz,* Israel's most respected daily, reports on a dramatic comeback by a popular singer and producer. The singer says: "My friend, Yossi Gil, who is an educator and astrologer, forecasts according to an astrological map that my 'comeback' [originally in English] will be through singing. . . . He said that people would vote for me with their feet" (Levinstein, 1988, p. 10). On page 12 of the same newspaper we find an advertisement by the same Yossi Gil, who offers "personal counselling, matching couples, family counselling, business advice and help in vocational choice."

The undisputed leader of Israeli astrology is Mr. Ilan Pecker of Jerusalem, who has his weekly astrology page in the weekend magazine of *Yediot Aharonot,* the leading Israeli daily, and his biweekly radio program on the A Network of state radio. Mr. Pecker is a practicing attorney in Jerusalem and an Orthodox Jew. He is also an Israeli cultural hero, whose name is almost universally known. With a whole page devoted to his writings every Friday in the most popular daily, *Yediot Aharonot,* read by 75 percent of Israelis, and with a personal biweekly radio program, this is no wonder.

Before Mr. Pecker started starring in his own program on the A Network of state radio, he was a regular guest on the astrology program of the B Network. On one of these occasions he predicted that the next world war would erupt in July 1978 (Avigal, 1977).

The Pecker weekly page of astrology in *Yediot Aharonot* is significantly different from most astrology columns found all over the world. In addition to the weekly prediction for the twelve birth signs, its main feature has to do with political events and political personalities. There are predictions of political crises, wars, and natural disasters, and there is always an analysis of a "Personality in the News." This personality may be an Israeli or foreign political leader, but it may also be a political party, an organization, or another collective entity. Pecker's astrology page does not only deal with private affairs of the heart and pocket but also covers the world economy, politics, and natural disasters. Among the political leaders that have starred on Mr. Pecker's page are most of Israel's government ministers, and prominent members of the Knesset.

On November 1, 1985, Pecker discussed Margaret Thatcher (Libra) of Great Britain (Aries). Pecker paints a hopeless picture for the former empire, with riots in the streets and the fall of Thatcher's government. On September 12, 1986, Mr. Pecker's "Personality in the News" was the United Nations organization itself, born under the sign of Scorpio on October 25, 1945. King Hassan II of Morocco, another Scorpio, was discussed on August 8, 1986.

The return of Halley's comet in 1986 caused a flurry of excitement among astronomy buffs and professional astronomers. Israel was one of the few places in the world where Halley's comet was not regarded as an astronomical event but rather as astrological one. On March 28, 1986, Halley's comet was the "Personality in the News" on Pecker's astrology page. "This star's approach, and three to six years following it, humanity, or part of it, experiences disasters and serious upheavals. Some of them are especially prominent: the destruction of the Second Temple five years after the star's appearance; its appearance in 1066, and then when Constantinople was conquered by the Turks in 1456. . . . During its current appearance in recent months we have witnessed natural disasters in Mexico and Colombia, aerial disasters unprecedented in scope and number, international terrorism, and personal violence of people against themselves (suicide) and others."

The Likud political bloc, which took over the government in 1977, is, according to Pecker on April 11, 1986, a Virgo (born in September 1973), whose leaders are likely to be born under the signs of Aries or Pisces. The fortunes of the Likud can be predicted from looking at its birth map, which with the moon (representing the people) under Pisces with negative radiation to the sun, spells stormy weather. Only a strong leader can save it from ultimate dissolution.

On May 9, 1986, the personality was the State of Israel, born on May 15, 1948, under the sign of Taurus. According to Pecker, Israel's birth map "points to a personality of an ambitious, tense, very aggressive state, in daily struggle for survival, both military and economic—social. . . . The astrologer Nostradamus predicted the rise and fall of the Soviet regime in Russia 450 years ago, noting that it would exist for 74 years (1917–91). If we use the Nostradamus system on Israel's celestial map, we will reach a surprising conclusion because the current regime in Israel has a life span of 40 years (1948–88). In light of this prediction, current political questions become dwarfed and insignificant." One cannot imagine too many nations in the world in which such visions of doom are published in the mass media.

On August 22, 1986, Mr. Pecker discussed the peace treaty between Israel and Egypt, born in Washington, D.C., under the sign of Virgo on September 17, 1978. Because of the growing closeness between Saturn and Uranus, starting in 1987, this peace treaty would become a passing episode in the history of the Middle East. The New York Stock Exchange drop of September 1986, writes Pecker on September 29, 1986, resulted from a struggle between Virgo and Saggitarius. The 1929 stock crash, was a Scorpio but resulted from a similar combination of stars, according to Pecker.

Astrology and Politics in Israel

Ronald Reagan's alleged readiness to consult horoscopes was sometimes used by detractors who wanted to prove that he is a man of extremely narrow horizons (Golden, 1985). The White House refused to admit such embarrassing practices. In Israel, hobnobbing with astrologers is the right thing to do for a politician who wants popularity, and gossip columns are filled with anecdotes and pictures showing astrologers among the high and the mighty.

Nothing indicates the acceptance and legitimacy that astrology has gained in Israel as much as its use for predicting political developments and fortunes. On the basis of media reports, we can point to hundreds of examples since 1975 in which astrological advice and predictions have been given prominence. The prognosticators have become familiar media figures, and their views have been taken very seriously. The term "political astrology," which gained much currency in the Israeli press in the early 1980s, can be counted among Israel's original contributions to the development of the occult. Any political crisis in Israel or around the world becomes an opportunity for the Israeli media to interview astrologers and ask for clarifications and predictions.

The extent to which astrology has achieved legitimacy in Israeli culture is illustrated by a story from an article summing up on the 1981 general election campaign:

> Last winter things looked different. In the Knesset cafeteria, excited supporters were surrounding Yigal Allon [1918–80; general, 1948-49, government minister, 1960–74, labor party leader], chatting about what the newspapers were reporting that day: astrologer Herzl Lifshitz predicted that Allon would be heading the Labor Party in the next general election. . . . Shimon Peres [1959–63 deputy defense minister, 1974–77, Defense Minister, 1984–86 prime minister] was quite depressed. His assistant Boaz Apelbaum decided to save the day and pump morale into his depressed leader. He invited a competing astrologer, Jerusalem attorney Ilan Pecker, so that he would present other predictions to Peres. Pecker sat with Peres in his office for three hours, and then Peres looked much better." (Dankner, 1981, p. 22)

Three years later there was a meeting between Mr. Peres and Herzl Lifshitz reported by the Israeli press. Mr. Peres, as Israel's new prime minister (despite all predictions) was on his way to a meeting with President Reagan. Mr. Lifshitz was on the same plane from Tel-Aviv to New York, and asked to meet with the prime minister. At the meeting, Mr. Lifshitz congratulated the new prime minister on the timing of his trip because the same voyage two weeks later would have led to catastrophe (Boshes, 1984).

During the 1981 election campaign, astropolitical predictions were unanimous in claiming that the date (June 30, 1981) was badly chosen, and spelled absolute disaster. The election outcome was said to be a tie or a combination that would lead to total instability (Binyamini, 1981). The actual outcome was a clear victory for the Likud. A young member of the Knesset, Micah Reisser of the Herut nationalist party, talks about his unexpected success in the elections: "I was sure that I would not be elected, but on election day, I ran into an astrologer who asked for my birth sign. I said 'Taurus' and he answered: 'You will win.'" Mr. Reisser indeed was elected, and astrology apparently won another follower. Closer to the election date, Miriam Binyamini, the resident astrologer of the radical weekly *Haolam Hazeh* offers her prognosis for the outcome of the campaign. Her prophecy is one of storm and stress: riots during election day itself, a serious decline for the Likud Party, complete chaos following the elections for months. The biggest problem, according to Binyamini, and other media stars, is that Shimon Peres could never be prime minister for more than a few weeks, because of a basic deficiency in his birth map. Despite the degree of agreement among soothsayers, there were no riots, the Likud did not lose much of its power, and Peres served as prime minister between September 1984 and October 1986.

Astrologers have been asked to predict not only election outcomes and the survival of governments as well as the outbreaks of wars. The following paragraph is the beginning of a chapter in a best-selling book on the 1982 invasion of Lebanon, authored by the political correspondent of Israel State Radio: "As 1982 started, astrologers were predicting a war with Syria during the course of the year. One astrologer, a friend of Defense Minister Ariel Sharon, told him that he would reach the zenith of his power, but added a warning: towards the end of the year the stars were indicating danger, and he would encounter serious distress" (Shiffer, 1984, p. 75). One of Israel's leading political commentators, when discussing the probability of a war with Syria during the 1984 election campaign, writes: "The astrologer Lifshitz, I think, claims that there will be one and we will even win, and then Yitzhak Shamir will become Prime Minister" (Abramovitz, 1984, p. 17).

References to astrological signs in discussions of political leaders have become common. Thus, a former personal assistant described Ariel Sharon, one of Israel's leading figures in both military and civilian life since the 1950s: "He is the most sensitive person I have ever met. He is a Pisces. Just like a real Pisces" (Ehrlich, 1988, p. 9). In summarizing the 1984 election campaign, Nahum Barnea, the editor of the left-of-center *Koteret Rashit*, discusses Yossi Sarid, a left-of-center member of the Knesset, and writes: "We are talking, among other things, about birth signs. Sarid was born on October 24, a Scorpio" (Barnea, 1984, p. 10). An economic columnist critical of a finance minister does not forget to mention that the minister is a Scorpio and that is the source of the problem with his policies (Kessler, 1984).

The prognostications are often of disasters, wars, and deaths. Herzl Lifshisz, one of the most quoted astrologers in the media, says in September 1981, "I still believe that Hussein [of Jordan] falls, as well as Khomeni, and even Brejnev in Russia. It's a matter of days, at most weeks. A Third World War is in the offing . . . following a Russian invasion of Poland" (quoted in Mazori, 1981, p. 16). *Maariv*'s resident astrologer, Ruth Eli, patiently explains, "Nations, like humans, are born, grow, change, and die . . . there is always a match between a people's character and its birth map. The USA, according to its most accurate horoscope (4.30.1789) is a combination of Taurus (money, comfort, and luxury) Virgo (industry and realism), Aries (dynamism, initiative, courage) and Cancer (patriotism)" (Eli, 1990, p. 44). Iran has been a focus of astropolitical predictions ever since the fall of the monarchy in 1979. Israeli astrologers were unanimous in forecasting the end of the Khomeini regime and the return of the Shah, and after his death in 1981, the return of his son to power. Israeli newspapers have been eager to report this good news (e.g., Gal, 1984).

The most important question before Israeli astrologers is their country's future. The most logical and most interesting idea to come out of Israeli astropolitics belongs to Ilan Pecker. Since fate is determined at the moment of birth, changing the moment of birth will change anybody's fate. The destiny of the State of Israel is determined by its birth, on May 14, 1948, at 4:30 P.M. (approximately). As it is evident that the State of Israel has been plagued by problems, and its future does look uncertain, astrology can offer a solution. Let there be a new State of Israel, whose Declaration of Independence will be delivered at an opportune moment, determined by a team of qualified astrologers. This simple, elegant, and easy solution to Israel's problems, proposed by Mr. Pecker in 1984, has so far been turned down by the people in charge (Michael, 1984).

On November 15, 1988, at 1:38 A.M. Algiers time, Yasir Arafat finished reading the official declaration creating the new state of Palestine. The inevitable result: a birth map of the new Palestinian entity, published in *Maariv* on December 9, 1988. The newspaper's resident astrologer concluded that the Palestinian state is, astrologically speaking, a perfect "negative" twin of the State of Israel, and so the two states cannot coexist.

When the Bush-Gorbachov summit meeting in Malta, in December 1989, was held in extremely stormy weather, Israeli newspapers turned to the astrologers, who predicted not only storms, but continuing problems in super-power relations due to the retreat of "Aries, Mercury and Venus." The dramatic changes in Eastern Europe in 1989 did not escape astrological scrutiny in the Israeli media. The fall of the Romanian dictator Nicolae Ceausescu, who was executed together with his wife, gave rise to several learned disputations of this kind. Eli (1990), the *Maariv* astrologer, claimed that Nicolae was basically a nice guy who was subverted by his wiley wife. Both of them, however, suffered from the basic incompatibility between their personal birth maps and the birth map on the People's Republic of Romania, born on December 30, 1947, which brought about their inevitable downfall.

The Gulf War of 1991 was an occasion for public expression of disappointment with the astrological soothsayers. Numerous media articles criticized astrologers, together with political leaders and Israeli military intelligence, for failing to predict the war (astrologers were unanimous in predicting a peaceful resolution of the Kuwait crisis) and the missile attacks against Israel.

Occultists as Psychotherapists

Occult divination in Israel is used either to obtain a general reading of one's character and future or to answer specific questions about future events, such as disasters and mishaps, or involving missing persons. Occult traditions offer what we should call, using the terminology of professional psychology, a personality diagnosis and sometimes a biographical reconstruction of the past and predictions about the future. This diagnostic information may have a therapeutic effect and is sometimes experiences as liberating or redeeming. The occult does not normally offer complete transformations, but it can offer mini-salvations. Thus, we read a report of a Tel-Aviv restauranteur, Rimon Ben-Yakir, whose life has been transformed by a change in the spelling of his first name. Mr. Ben-Yakir met in 1984 a numerologist, who told him that all his difficulties in life stemmed from the fact that he spelled his name RMON. In Hebrew, vowels are often not written, and until the age of thirty-one, Mr. Ben-Yakir followed the custom. Since the encounter with the numerologist and the new spelling, life is much more enjoyable, and many difficulties have been resolved.

A new pattern of using astrology has been developed in Israel: personal advice columns, in which the Israeli Dear Abby is an astrologer, offering advice not on the basis of personal knowledge or common sense, but on the celestial combinations. "I am 30 years old, divorced and the father of two. Since my divorce, a few years ago, I have been experiencing confusion, tension, and uncertainty. I go out with women and I have a good time, but it isn't it. I am trying to change, but I don't know how" (*Maariv*, February 9, 1990). The astrologer responds with good news. More than half the stars in this man's birth chart had been under attack by four evil stars for years, but this attack will soon end. Beyond the astrological information, she offers more reasonable advice along the lines of "new challenges," athletic activities, and more social contacts.

The highbrow woman's monthly *At* provides its readers with an information service reflecting the richness of occult practices in Israel. Readers can send in questions to be answered by astrology, I Ching, graphology, chirology, Tarot cards, or coffee grounds. In April 1984, one of the readers asked whether her decision to begin graduate studies at the university was correct. The resident chirologist states that she could expect success and self-actualization and that the right occupation for her was that of a literary critic. The resident Tarot expert tells A. D. from Haifa that her relationship with a married Christian man will hamper personal achievements.

In 1989, courses in astrology, numerology, chirology, and Tarot, offered by the Jerusalem Center for Astrology, were officially recognized by the Israel Ministry of Education as continuing education classes for teachers on sabbatical, which means that a teacher coming back from a sabbatical and graduating from these courses would be entitled to a tuition refund as well as a salary raise.

Cartomancy in its various forms is also part of the divination establishment (see Aphek and Tobin, 1981). On November 4, 1983, *Haaretz*, Israel's leading daily, introduced a weekly Tarot column devoted to answering readers' questions regarding difficulties, crises, and major life decisions. An anonymous reader who asked whether Bar-Ilan University would grant him a Ph.D. degree was told that his thesis was poorly organized and spreads over too many areas. Once the thesis is organized with much reworking, the degree will not be far behind (Ben-Dov, 1984).

Graphology and the Occult Subculture

When Brigadier General Avi Gluska was appointed to be the personal secretary and spokesman for the president of Israel in 1980, the final decision is made only after a graphological "test" (Tzimuki, 1986). And according to media reports, the president of Israel always enjoys the secret advice of a graphologist, who scrutinizes the handwriting of visiting dignitaries before their arrival so that he can be better prepared to meet them.

Graphology, the analysis of psychological attributes from an individual's handwriting (Allport and Vernon, 1933; Roman, 1952; Wolfson, 1949) is considered in most of the world to be a frivolous and marginal, if not a nonsensical, form of personality diagnosis. In Israel it is taken very seriously. Despite the fact, noted elsewhere, that Israel has the highest rate of professional psychologists per million of population, graphology is estimated to be in more widespread use than any psychological personality tests (Ben-Shakhar et al., 1986).

A survey of advertisements offering employment in four Israeli newspapers during two months in 1985 showed that 22 percent of them included a specific demand for a hand-written curriculum vitae, to be used in a graphological test (Nevo, 1986). Even advertisements for positions as bodyguards for businessmen in Europe and South America, something that Israelis have excelled in over the years, includes a reference for a "graphological test," for which those seeking the job have to pay. When a murder case, in which a man killed his mother, daughter, brother, and his wife as well as himself, occurred in Israel in October 1986, the police turned to the experts. Newspapers reported that the murderer's suicide note would be referred to graphologists for an analysis of the real motives (Sharon, 1986).

Israeli journalists have often turned to graphologists for an "in-depth" look at personalities. When Shimon Finkel, an 77-year-old retired leading actor, is interviewed and gives a piece of his mind to younger actors and directors, the resulting article is accompanied by a graphological portrait, telling us that he has got both acting talent and anger in him (Bar-Kadma, 1984). When Yaacov Levinson, former president of the General Labor Union Bank, committed suicide amid charges of mismanagement and corruption, his suicide letter (in meticulous handwriting and style) was the subject of interviews with graphologists in all newspapers (e.g., Avneri, 1984), and when Yigal Cohen-Orgad became Israel's finance minister in October 1983, the country's leading graphologist was asked to give her opinion of his personality and fitness for the job. She approved.

Yonah Avrushmi was arrested in 1984 for the murder of a left-wing activist during a political demonstration in Jerusalem in 1983. Avrushmi's handwriting has been the source of newspaper reports that dealt with his character and mood. One graphologist analyzed Avrushmi's character on the basis of his signature on a bounced check

(Ronen, 1984). The same newspaper published two separate diagnoses on Avrushmi, provided by two graphologists (Lior, 1984).

The attraction of graphology is similar to that of occult diagnosis. It is simple, cheap, and does not even require the physical presence of the subject under diagnosis. On the basis of very little information, graphologists are ready to provide judgments about personality and with recommendations for action (hiring or vocational choices). Graphology becomes a part of the occult complex because many practitioners offer graphology, astrology, and palm reading to their customers, and both customers and providers do not differentiate between graphology and other occult systems. Several Israeli newspapers and newsmagazines now have graphology columns, usually in the section devoted to the occult. Graphology courses, leading to unofficial certification, have been offered all over the country by scores of practitioners. Matchmaking through the use of graphology was displayed on Israeli television in the 1970s and on Israeli radio in the 1980s. The Israeli state radio matchmaking program, known as "A Mate From The Same Star" for its reliance on astrology, used graphology as well. Every potential mate is introduced through an astrological map, and a graphological diagnosis.

The Israel Defense Forces radio station has had a graphology program titled "Five-Finger-Exercise" since November of 1975. The format is the familiar one of diagnosing and recognizing a person through graphology. There is a team at the studio whose task is to identify the celebrity in question on the basis of the graphological character reading. The career section of *Maariv*, the Tel-Aviv daily, has been offering its readers a free service of personality diagnosis through graphology. Readers can send in a hand-written letter, and a lucky winner picked by a lottery gets to read his or her own life story analyzed and receives vocational advice. After *Maariv* started offering career counseling through graphology, another newspaper followed suit with a matchmaking service run jointly by a graphologist and a psychologist.

The use of graphology almost overshadows the use of legitimate psychological tests in industry and most public organizations. One is likely to encounter reports of actual or proposed graphological tests in the context of the selection of judges for district courts (recommended by some members of the Knesset), the selection of bank tellers (practiced by most banks), and the selection of employees at all levels. The wide use and acceptability of graphology in Israel brought about a reaction of established psychology, in the form of academic studies, most of which cast serious doubts on its validity (see Keinan, et al., 1984; Nevo, 1986). During the years 1975–85 Israeli academic psychologists carried out fourteen validation studies on graphology. These studies showed an overall validity coefficient of 0.15, which is quite low. Studies done in other countries have shown similar results. In a test of the graphologists' ability to predict success in real estate sales, the finding was that "no evidence for validity was detected" (Rafaeli and Klimoski, 1983, p. 212). The campaign started by a group of academic psychologists against graphology in the early 1980s erupted into the media, with confrontations being staged for the benefit of magazines and television (Caspi, 1984).

Graphology books have been best-sellers in Israel and are often published in new editions. There have been books published on "graphotherapy," i.e., psychotherapy through writing exercises (Yogev, 1980), and on the analysis of personality through signatures alone. Acceptance of candidates into membership in a kibbutz or in a collective village (*moshav*) is a serious decision. A vote for admission means, in most cases, that the candidate remains with the collective for life. The admissions commissions are under much pressure and anxiety and need support and advice. In most cases in Israel since the late 1970s, the decision is made by a graphologist. Israeli settlements in the occupied West Bank have attracted worldwide attention over the years. Some of them were started through night-time secret operations, with the settlers defying the Israeli government. Others were created with the full blessing of the authorities. What both the illegal and the official settlement have in common is that their inhabitants have been selected by graphologists (Goell, 1984). A report on employees' level of anxiety during the 1991 Gulf War quotes a graphologist, who has been called in as a consultant by numerous executives to assess individual cases of anxiety and offer solutions (Arad, 1991).

Graphology classes have been offered by several institutes, and courses last as long as eighteen months. Admission is based on a graphological test, of course. As of 1988, the Israeli Education Ministry officially recognized graphology courses as an appropriate subject for continuing education study for teachers on sabbaticals.

Palm Reading in Israel

An article about Israeli settlers in the northern Sinai who were forced to leave their homes in 1982 when the area was returned to Egyptian control, mentions one of them, who is now economically secure. He is Mr. Shalom Tass, an agronomist by training, has started working as a palm reader, and his economic worries are over (Oren, 1985). Leading the field of palm reading in Israel are two brothers, Meir and

Shalom Shaul. While Shalom practices chiromancy, which reads the past and future in palm lines, Meir practices chirology, which uses the palms to diagnose personality traits, and then offer practical advice. The latter includes vocational guidance and the choice of a life mate (Shaul, 1986). Palm readers in Israel usually call themselves chirologists and their field of endeavor chirology. In the Yellow Pages, on the other hand, they appear under "Counselors using the palm." Another class of palm readers has appeared in Israel, which claims to offer not just a "diagnostic instrument of personality characteristics and a way to deepen consciousness and personal identity" (*sic*) but also treatment. This group of practitioners utilizes not only palm reading but also astrological charts. According to advertisements, they deal with "stress situations . . . interpersonal dynamics, and vocational choice."

Leading politicians love to have their palms read in public. The powerful chairman of the Knesset finance committee, Abraham Shohat, volunteered to have his palms read by the resident astrologer *cum* palm reader of *Maariv* in June 1989. According to an Israeli financial weekly, Mr. Yitzhak Modai, who has served in various Israeli governments as industry minister, energy minister, finance minister, and justice minister, is also an expert on chiromancy and has amazed his friends and wife with his diagnoses and predictions. The same source claimed that Mrs. Ora Herzog, the wife of Israel's fifth president, is also an expert on chiromancy (*Ksafim*, 1984).

The degree of legitimacy and acceptance enjoyed by palm reading in Israel was demonstrated in 1981 when the Institute for Psychotherapy in Haifa offered its students an elective course in chirology. The Institute of Psychotherapy trains psychologists, social workers, and physicians in modern psychotherapy. Its faculty is made up of respectable professionals of all theoretical persuasions, most of whom have part-time university affiliations. The chirology seminar was offered to advanced students in psychotherapy, and was being given by a practitioner who is quite well known among mental health professionals. I myself have heard several psychologists and psychiatrists refer to her quite positively. The same practitioner was invited to speak at the International Interdisciplinary Congress On Women: The New Scholarship, which was held at the University of Haifa in December 1981. I heard her presentation, titled "Some feminine archetypal images in Chirology." It contained the expected Jungian terminology with a heavy dose of Greek mythology. The characteristics of various Greek goddesses were embedded in segments of the palm, according to the speaker. I personally could not really follow the argument, which probably had to do with my palm (or my birthday).

As of 1986, Mr. Arnold Holzman, a chirologist in Tel-Aviv who had been teaching chirology classes to the general public, started offering courses limited to members of the helping professions. There was sufficient demand so that Mr. Holzman was able to change his clientele and cater to psychologists and social workers. "Dr." Holzman, who earned his doctorate in 1989 from a U.S. diploma mill, was the subject of an adulatory article in the weekend edition of *Davar*, the labor party daily (Golan, 1991). The success of palm reading in Israel in the 1970s has led to a number of academic studies utilizing the behavior of palmists and other fortune tellers (Aphek and Tobin, 1981).

Foot Reading

A few years ago, while discussing various occult methods of diagnosis, I used to joke about foot reading as a supplement to palm reading. I didn't have to wait long. By 1989, newspapers in Israel were reporting on the new technique, designed to assess "personality, potentials and inclinations, relations with the social environment, family relations, emotional states, and more." Courses in foot reading were being held regularly in Haifa and Tel Aviv.

Numerology

References to numerology have been appearing in the media with greater frequency since the late 1970s, and its popularity has led to several books (e.g., Rosenfeld, 1984). According to a leading numerologist in Tel-Aviv, who doubles as a kindergarten teacher, numerology is much simpler than astrology, and the diagnosis takes only a few minutes. The data needed are: date of birth, first name, street address, and apartment number. Numerologists often suggest changing one's given name, and often do it themselves (Bloch, 1982). The high point in the history of numerology in Israel was reached in June 1981, on the eve of the Knesset elections. Yizhak Natani, the ruling star in the skies of Israeli numerology, was interviewed on television and asked to predict the election outcomes. Natani has been interviewed in the press since then and predicted the coming of the Messiah in 1998 (Oren, 1983; Shapira, 1983).

1984, The Year Of Destruction

The years in the Jewish calendar are designated by Hebrew letters, according to *gimatria*, which constitutes the rules for the numerical equivalence of letters. Numbers written by letters sometimes can be read as words, and Hebrew acronyms are often pronounced as words. From time to time, a particular year will spell a word that provokes strong associations. The Jewish year 5744, or tav-shin-mem-dalet, aroused associations tied to destruction, because of the root *shin-mem-dalet* ("destroy"). This magical connection has created a wave of reactions and fantasies in Israel, including expectations of the end of the world, and the resulting mass hysteria was instructive in demonstrating both magical thinking and a total insecurity about the future.

The 1984 panic started around 1980, and by the fall of 1981, it was felt all over the country. *Al Hamishmar*, the Zionist left-wing daily, had a report about the coming destruction, from which only Jerusalem may be saved, according to Nostradamus, a favorite source of soothsayers (Margalit, 1981). During 1982 and 1983, the idea of a catastrophe or even the end of the world during 1984 gained more and more currency. The idea of total destruction caught on. Visionaries were being interviewed by the media and reported their fantasies about the end of the world. Hundreds of reports in the press and on radio and television dealt with the coming year of destruction. "The 1984 craze has taken over the country, because those among us who had any dreams died or left the country, and all we have is the party of destruction" (Geffen, 1981, p. 11).

In January 1982, Yitzhak Or, a painter, had an exhibit in Tel-Aviv titled *1984*. Only one of the many paintings included a human being, supposedly the only person to survive the events of that year. The absurd claim that "Christian theologians" predicted the end of the world in 1984 also gained a following in Israel and was mentioned numerous times in the media (e.g., Rosen, 1984).

Professor S. G. Shoham, a renowned criminologist-philosopher at Tel-Aviv University joined the prophets of destruction. "It is no accident that the year 1984 and the Jewish year of 5744 (Tashmad) overlap," he stated. "I am convinced that this is no accident, there is a real possibility that Orwell, while living as a tramp, met a rabbi, a cabbalist, or a scholar that told him about it" (Ben-Zakkai, 1983). Here we see several absurd notions in action. First, the reference to George Orwell's novel *Nineteen Eighty-Four*, and the presumed connection between Orwell's choice of name and 5744. Second, the notion that some cabbalist tradition has mentioned 5744, which has no basis in reality, and then the presumed meeting between Orwell and a cabbalist.

One solution to the 1984 problem was proposed by Zevulum Hammer, serving as education minister in the government. Hammer proposed a magical solution to a magical problem. He suggested that the letters representing the number 5744 (actually 744) be written as *shin-dalet-mem-tav* (pronounced *shadmat*) rather than *tav-shin-mem-dalet* (pronounced *tashmad*) with its horrendous connotations. Hammer submitted his proposal officially to the government Commission on Symbols and Ceremonies, but it did not come to fruition, and Israelis continued to use the dreaded combination of *tashmad* (Hoffman, 1982).

The predictions about the catastrophe of 1984 were supported by leading astrologers. Ilan Pecker, when interviewed on Israeli television on January 26, 1982, stated that indeed all astrological calculations point to the end of the world in 1984, but there is one way of changing that. According to Mr. Pecker, who happens to be an Orthodox Jew, a return to Judaism in beliefs and practices would prevent the end of the world. The year 1984 has come and gone, and the world is still very much with us. The failures of all the doomsayers has not affected their followers and customers, and the legitimacy of occultism in Israel has not apparently suffered.

The Occult Subculture in Israel

The occult has been an established part of publications catering to the poor and uneducated in Western countries. Describing the anti-utopia of the future, George Orwell wrote of "separate departments dealing with proletarian literature, music, drama, and entertainment generally. Here were produced rubbishy newspapers containing almost nothing except sport, crime and astrology" (1949, p. 38). Such rubbishy newspapers can be found today in all Western countries and indeed make up the common reading material of the proletariat. One can point to a whole category of publications, that specialize in the occult, gossip, and miracle cures. In the United States, the best known of these is *The National Enquirer*, reputed to have the highest circulation of any U.S. periodical (around 7 million a week) and enjoying a host of competitors modeled after its successful format. A typical issue of the *Enquirer* contains stories of visits by ghosts and UFOs, gossip about television and movie stars, predictions by psychics ("Victoria Principal to become mother" or "Prince Andrew's ex-girlfriend will attempt suicide in front of Buckingham Palace"), and advertisements for get-rich-quick schemes, books by Nostradamus, and creams designed to give you "a beautiful bust in five weeks." *The National Enquirer* can be said to be a part of the U.S. nonsense industry, catering like the "rubbishy newspapers" of Orwell's *1984* to the proletariat.

Occultism also triumphed in Germany after the World War I.

> In postwar Germany hypnotists, clairvoyants and mind readers were suddenly able to fill huge concert halls. There was scarcely a single large music hall or cabaret that did not stage a telepathic act. Enormous placards and newspaper advertisements pompously proclaimed: "The Most Important Parapsychologist," "The Woman with a Thousand Eyes" (Madame Karoli at the Busch Circus), "The Great Enigma, an Outstanding Achievement in the Sphere of Occult Science," "The Lady who Tells You All", etc. Swindle or not, both public and press found it all fascinating (Wulff, 1973, p. 29).

The success of astrology in Germany was indeed astounding. There was an Association of Scientific Astrology, directed by Dr. Hubert Korsch, as a part of the German Astrological Center in Dusseldorf. The coming of the Nazis into power created problems for astrologers and other occultists, as the universalism of astrology was repugnant to racism. The answer was in creating Nazi horoscopes for different races and the founding of a National Socialist Community for Members of the Occult Profession. This did not satisfy Heinrich Himmler, who is purported to have stated, "In Berlin this mischievous business of telling people's fortunes on the basis of so-called horoscopes had assumed such proportions in 1934 that I was already thinking of prohibiting astrology then. Horoscope shops sprang up like mushrooms in every corner of Greater Berlin and in many other big cities as well. Provided they paid, the credulous masses could discover 'all that the future holds in store' " (Wulff, 1973, p. 113). Despite official Nazi efforts, interest in the occult did not decline.

Another witness to the triumph of the occult in Germany writes: "In almost no other country were so many 'miracles' performed, so many ghosts conjured, so many illnesses cured by magnetism, so many horoscopes read, between the two World Wars. A veritable mania of stupidity has seized the country, and all those who made a living by exploiting human stupidity thought the millennium had come" (quoted in Sklar, 1977, p. 3). Graphology was immensely popular. Nazi leaders, despite their ideological objections continued to consult astrologers, especially during the last years of the war, when defeat seemed certain. Goebbels and Hitler reportedly consulted secret horoscopes cast for Germany and the Fuhrer and based on the dates of November 9, 1918, the birth of the German Republic, and January 30, 1933. They did that during the last days of the war and were encouraged by the predictions (Sklar, 1977).

The correlation between a superstitious beliefs and fascist ideology was noted by Adorno and coworkers (1950), who stated that it "indicates a tendency to shift responsibility from the individual onto outside forces beyond his control; it indicates that the ego might already have 'given up', that is to say, renounced the idea that it might determine the individual's fate by overcoming external forces" (p. 236).

There is little question about the observation that right-wing political ideology is tied to a greater readiness to embrace religion, mysticism, and the occult (Adorno et al., 1950). "Conservatives, then, are inclined to be convinced of the efficacy of fortunes, horoscopes, and 'patent cures', and fearful of "omens" that are traditionally supposed to portend bad luck or doom" (Wilson, 1973, p. 9).

If indeed the occult holds a special fascination for the human psyche in all times and places, why was this fascination not in evidence in Israel in the 1950s and the 1960s? Interest in the occult, as in other explanatory systems, waxes and wanes with the times, and the Israeli case, presented here, proves it most clearly.

The Israeli occult subculture is not identical by any means with occult subcultures in Western countries. The occult subculture in Israel does not include such things as witchcraft, "Satanism," exorcism, communication with spirits, or the cultivation of trancelike states, which are integral parts of the occult subculture in Western countries. Certain staples of occultism, such as spiritualism, are totally absent in Israel and have not managed to gain popularity. Although spiritualism in Israel is almost unknown, references to it are found in occult writings and speeches. There has been an original Israeli contribution to the field, in the form of an electronic communication system with the dead, using tape recorders without microphones. The system was demonstrated on Israeli television in 1981 and is being promoted by the inventor in a book (Raviv, 1981).

Parapsychology, which has its origins in nineteenth-century spiritualism (Mauskopf and McVaugh, 1981) has shown so far a fairly limited presence in Israel. The wave of interest in near-death experiences, which struck the shores of the United States in the 1970s, has not reached Israel. In general, ghosts seem to avoid the Israeli population, and the feeling is mutual. Dowsing, an occult skill quite popular elsewhere, is totally unknown in Israel, possibly because water is hard to find there.

While it is clear that astrology survives all over the world as a part of popular culture (Truzzi, 1975), only in Israel has it achieved a legitimacy among the elite, as reflected in my evidence presented here. In other countries, astrology is only a part of mass culture, and the level of mass involvement is low.

The triumph of the occult in Israel since 1973 represents a triumph of fatalism. The basic fear behind it is of the future, of the end of Israel—the end of the world that seems so near. Psychologically speaking, magical thinking and magical actions represent an archaic level of functioning, but it is not as archaic as pure fantasy and withdrawal. Tiryakian has suggested that the pursuit of understanding through the occult reflects "a loss of confidence in established symbols and cognitive models of reality" (1972, p. 510). Using astrology to deal with political questions involves a collective destiny, not just private destinies, and indicates a feeling of extreme hopelessness about the collective future of the State of Israel.

In 1988, the Israeli government itself went into the amulet business in a big way. The Government Corporation for Medals, which manufactures special coins and medals for collectors mainly in connection with commemorative occasions and holidays, issued its "Safe Return" pendant. Its advertisements in all Israeli newspapers recommended that the pendant be bought by mothers for their sons who are entering compulsory military service at 18. The pendant carried the legend of "Safe Voyage and Safe Return." This development reflects both the growing concern over continuing warfare and the safety of young soldiers and the readiness to rely on magical means in order to ward off danger.

The basic miracle in occult divination is in the simplicity and accessibility of answers to complicated questions. Nonsensology is a collection of small miracles, rather than a dramatic, total salvation. The investment needed by clients is minimal, and the rewards match the cost, but nonsensology in Israel is the gateway to bigger and better miracles through the maintenance of a miracle-oriented worldview. The occult as a road to private salvation in Israel is obviously secondary. Occult involvement is superficial and usually does not entail individual transformation. At the same time, as part of the Israeli mass culture, it provides a wide ideological base and a climate that makes other more significant roads to private salvation more easily accessible. Occultism assumes and represents a world in which miracles are not just possible but common, and these include the miracles of self-transformation.

4

The Liberated Self:
Developing a Psychotherapy Subculture in Israel

An oft-quoted remark expresses the inherently problematic nature of psychotherapy: "Psychotherapy is an undefined technique applied to unspecified cases with unpredictable results. For this technique, rigorous training is required" (Raimy, 1950, p. 93). Meltzoff and Kornreich (1970) described psychotherapy as the application of procedures derived from established psychological principles by trained persons whose intent is to modify maladapative behaviors, feeling, values, and attitudes. Wolman (1970) defined psychotherapy as the psychological treatment of mental disorders. Frank (1974) described psychotherapy as a form of influence characterized by a trained, socially sanctioned healer, a sufferer seeking relief, and circumscribed contacts between the healer and the sufferer, when the former attempts to change the latter's emotional state through words, acts, and rituals. Frank (1974) refers also to what he calls more ambitious forms of psychotherapy. These are techniques whose "goal is to facilitate development or maturation of the patient's personality, to help him become less conflicted and better integrated, to help him become, in some sense, a better person" (p. 78).

The psychotherapy subculture exists in those societies where psychotherapy is used by a significant minority not only as a way of alleviating symptoms, but as a way of general self-improvement or self-liberation. Members of the subculture are likely to become habitual, or chronic, psychotherapy clients and are likely to use more than one mode or style of treatment. Psychotherapy as a way of life means not just having been a psychotherapy client but also continuing as one for some time. When a typical member of the psychotherapy subculture is in therapy, he or she is not a naive client. If this is not the second time in treatment, he or she has heard about it from friends, has read psychotherapy literature, or has practiced it on others. The mark of the committed member in the psychotherapy subculture is the fact of having experienced some form of psychological treatment more than once. The subculture of psychotherapy is, as the term implies, a minority phenomenon within any society, but this minority reflects much wider trends in the culture around it.

When I discuss the subculture of psychotherapy, I am not referring to the use of psychological treatment in response to recognized symptoms, syndromes, neuroses, or psychoses but rather the use of psychotherapy to facilitate "growth," self-understanding, and a generalized change in self-perceptions and functioning. Normally, psychotherapy clients are defined as seeking help, but members of the psychotherapy subculture may be seeking not just help for a difficulty but also meaning for their lives and understanding of their personal destinies. Secular psychotherapy, like occult divination, offers its clients an interpretation of personal destiny. Philosophically, of course, what psychotherapy has to offer is in strict opposition to any occult interpretations. A subculture of psychotherapy exists when a significant minority of individuals in any society are committed to secular psychotherapy as a way of finding meaning to their lives. This is shown by their commitment of time and money and the emotional investment involved. Around the core of the committed there is a wide circle of those less firmly so at various way stations on the road to complete socialization into the ideology of psychotherapy. The subculture of psychotherapy par excellence exists in the United States, or to be more precise, in certain large urban centers in the United States, such as New York, Chicago, Los Angeles, Boston, and Philadelphia. It can also be found in Paris and Buenos Aires.

This subculture is defined through the body of beliefs and values shared by its members. It encompasses the individuals who hold the belief, quite consciously, that undergoing some form of modern psychotherapy is essential to self-enrichment, self-actualization, or optimal functioning. Phrases such as "looking for myself" or "searching for the real me" are part of the conscious expression of the ideology. The subculture is sustained by a core of clients (and providers) of psychotherapy who have accepted the ideology of psychotherapy as an answer for their need for meaning and guidance in life, an answer that replaces, or supercedes, political, religious, or ethnic ideologies. For this hard core of true believers, psychotherapy becomes truly a way of life and a way of living.

The psychotherapy subculture can be observed only in a few societies today. Since it is actually so rare, we have to ask ourselves what are the forces and conditions that make it possible and make it even appear necessary and natural in those societies in which it already exists. We can glean the distinctive features of the psychotherapy subculture through cross-national and cross-cultural comparisons. We can intuitively note the differences between cultures that have well-developed psychotherapy and those that do not have them. We can intuitively understand why Ireland, Poland, or Iran do not have psychotherapy subcultures, and why the United States leads the world in the development and sophistication of its variant. The subculture of psychotherapy does not develop under forced conditions. Prisoners sent to psychological treatment are not members of the psychotherapy subculture, unless they have adopted its ideology. Normally, socialization into this ideology occurs in noninstitutionalized settings. The private-practice model is most common in the subculture. It involves a great deal of personal commitment and a personal relationship. France and the United States are two countries where two well-developed subcultures of psychotherapy can be found, though these are marked by significant differences, reflecting, of course, respective differences in national cultures.

Before the appearance of secular psychotherapy, there was a long and well-developed tradition of a religious "cure of souls" (McNeill, 1951), and the growth of secular psychotherapy is correlated with the historical decline of religion in the Western world (Beit-Hallahmi, 1989). The United States seemed most hospitable to new modes of secular psychotherapy since the nineteenth century (Hale, 1971), and it has a long history of openness to "mind cures" and "mental healing." The background against which secular psychotherapy has developed is that of the growth of industrial capitalism, characterized by the emergence of the bureaucratic state with centralized authority and power and the segregation of work from domesticity. This process of modernization led to the destruction of community and kinship relations. The realization of pervasive depersonalization, as a result of the above changes, has created a movement of liberal intellectuals, searching for ways of restoring human relatedness and community. The development of secular psychotherapy is a response to a felt need, a social class of potential clients, and an appropriate ideology presented at the right time. As Broughton (1981) put it, "The changing basis of state organization and the form of production with its proliferation of white-collar workers necessitated new forms of control mediated by social psychological science and technology rather than by religion and work ethics" (p. 404).

Secular psychotherapy has emerged in Europe and in the United States at the end of the nineteenth century, when the change in the economic structure and the growth in the number of white-collar workers made necessary the development of new methods of social control that would not rely on religious authority. Psychotherapy, like other theoretical and ideological developments of that time, "expressed and promoted a sincere desire to combat depersonalization and promote social integration. However, as is necessarily the case with all liberal remedies . . . [it] actually served to obscure the real causes of the alienation and fragmentation visible in civil society" (Broughton, 1981, p. 404).

There seem to be two necessary conditions for the development of a psychotherapy subculture in any society. First, there has to be a viable ideology of individualism, acceptable at least to some members of the society, and there has to be a recognition of frustration of that ideology of individual self-actualization and happiness. The necessary material conditions for the creation of a psychotherapy subculture include a general rise in living standards and the existence of an educated middle class (cf. Ellenberger, 1970). Ideological conditions include the awareness, on the part of this class, of contradictions and frustrations in its immediate experience, which cannot be resolved. The development of psychotherapy in its various forms and under a variant of labels in modern society can be related to what Foa and Donnerwerth (1971) have called "love poverty," the paucity of interpersonal communication expressing positive feelings and sympathy.

The first problem of a new subculture is recruiting members, and the second is establishing legitimacy. The professionals practicing psychotherapy belong to what Halmos (1970) has called the "personal service professions", defined as "professions whose principal function is to bring about changes in the body or personality of the client" (p. 22). These professions require "self-denial, matter-of-fact self-effacing care and . . . human warmth and kindly solicitousness" (p. 22). The constant growth and broadening of the psychotherapy perspective has led to such concepts as "counseling," "the helping professions," and "facilitators."

The classic (post–World War II) division of the role of the clinical psychologist included diagnosis and treatment, the former with the help of a special technology of testing, which was the psychologists' professional monopoly and served as a basis for differentiating clinical psychology as a profession (cf. Rosenwald, 1963). Since the 1960s the emphasis in the professional activities of the clinical psychologist has switched to treatment in various forms. The decline in the emphasis on diagnosis is tied to the decline in the importance of symptoms in seeking treatment. Since the client most often does not come in because of specific symptoms or neuroses, there is no need for an accurate diagnosis. The diagnostic role of the clinical psychologist is central in those places where individuals with well-defined symptoms do not seek treatment on their own but are most often referred against their will (e.g., hospitals, prisons, or school systems). What seems to be regarded as most desirable by most clinical psychologists today is a definition of their role as primarily therapists to a "neurotic" population, which seeks treatment voluntarily and is in search of a personal meaning system. This development leads to a widening of the gap between academic psychology, which searches for generalizations about universal psychological processes, and contemporary clinical psychology, which is busy supplying individual meanings.

The expansion of psychotherapy and the proliferation of its forms is described by Sedgwick (1982) as follows: "Primarily in the United States but also in many other countries of the advanced West, the years since 1950 have been those of a long growth-cycle of such forms of counter-neurotic technology as joy therapy, reality therapy, primal scream therapy, transcendental meditation, Gestalt therapy, marathon encounter groups, Reichian massage, co-counselling, psychodrama, Lacan's 'ten-minute psychoanalytic session,' re-birthing, 'transactional analysis,' bio-energetics, existential therapy, behaviour modification, rational-emotive therapy, postural integration (or 'rolfing') and psychosynthesis" (p. 189). Deliberate psychological education (DPE) is a variant of mass psychotherapy aimed a "healthy psychological growth," and has been promoted in American schools in the 1970s (Vriend and Dyer, 1976).

Klerman (1983) described the growth of professional psychotherapy as follows:

> The period from 1950 through 1980 represents a time of considerable expansion of psychotherapeutic endeavors in the United States. By whatever measure used, the field had expanded greatly. The types of practitioners—psychiatrists, psychologists, psychiatric social workers, psychiatric nurse practitioners, marriage and family counselors, and pastoral

> counselors—have multiplied. The number of techniques and schools has multiplied. (p. 929)

Parloff (1976) reported on 164 "brand names" in American psychotherapy.

The culmination of the development of the nonsymptomatic psychotherapy subculture in the United States seemed to arrive with the 1970s, which came to be known as the "Me Decade" (Wolfe, 1976). The "helping professions" have gained more public acceptance over the past thirty years, as studies show. Kulka and colleagues (1979) compared the results of two surveys of the U.S. population, conducted in 1957 and 1976, dealing with expressed readiness to seek professional help in cases of personal distress. The results show a doubling of the actual use of professionals over the years. There was a correlation between an individual's level of education and readiness to seek professional help, but this correlation was weaker in 1976 than in 1957. The last stage in the formation of a psychotherapy subculture is its legitimization by the mass media. As Albee (1977) reports, popular advice columnists, such as Ann Landers, are in the habit of recommending to their readers "professional help," i.e., psychotherapy. Psychotherpy in the electronic media has been a growing trend ("Dial Dr. Toni for therapy," 1980) since 1975 and provides a final proof of the acceptance of "professional help" by the masses.

The basic message of psychotherapy comes across most clearly in best-selling self-help books. One of those, serialized in one of the most popular daily newspapers in the United States, brings us the following set of beliefs: "Happiness is only a state of mind and, because it is a condition that merely describes emotion and feeling, it has no real substance. It cannot be touched, or seen, or physically measured, nor can it be obtained or purchased. It is within you, essentially a product of your imagination" (Becker, 1978).

The self-help movement is an advanced stage in the development of the psychotherapy subculture. Here, the knowledge of psychotherapy techniques is no longer considered esoteric and "professional," and thus overeaters, alcoholics, homosexuals, or drug abusers can be, at the same time, both healers and clients (Gartner and Riessman, 1984).

The mass market paperback best-seller list of the *New York Times* for November 27, 1977, included, as No. 2, *Your Erroneous Zones*, by Dyer (1976). Among trade paperbacks, No. 2 was *The Joy of Sex*, by Comfort (1972). Indeed, *Your Erroneous Zones* was No. 3 on the nonfiction best-seller list for the 1970s, with a total of almost 4.5 million copies sold (Walters, 1979).

Subculture Membership

The psychotherapy subculture is a community sharing language, mores, explicit values, and socioeconomic background. The subculture is maintained by a group of individuals sharing the same language and the same ideology, which are taken for granted by the membership. There is a special lingo, common to all members of the subculture, but there are also more limited dialects, stemming from specific psychotherapy theories, invoked by special groups. Membership of the psychotherapy subculture includes an overrepresentation of unmarried individuals, women, and the highly educated. The members are likely to interact with each other often, which is not surprising in view of how much they share, in addition to membership itself. The subculture includes both providers and clients, though one person may, and often does, play both roles at the same time.

Personal psychotherapy is almost the norm for members of the "helping professions." Wispe and Parloff (1965) reported that one-third of all the recipients of a Ph.D. in psychology between 1945 and 1951 had some kind of therapy (as clients). Compared with Ph.D. psychologists who had not had therapy, those who had undergone therapy were more likely to be practicing clinicians. Richards and Gottfredson (1978) found that psychologists, psychiatrists, and clinical social workers are distributed in strikingly similar ways in the United States. All three professions, which are also the major psychotherapy professions, are concentrated in urban areas and in large cities. A survey conducted by the American Psychiatric Association (Isensee, 1984) shows that psychiatrists tend to overconcentrated in suburban communities and university towns. The ten communities with the highest rate of psychiatrists per 100,000 residents are Ann Arbor, Mich., New Haven, Conn., Topeka, Kan., Poughkeepsie, N.Y., Raleigh-Durham, N.C., Boston, and New York.

Temerlin and Temerlin (1982) describe what may be regarded as the hard core of the psychotherapy subculture: an intermingling of roles and personalities in psychotherapy relations that are also personal and occupational. They describe "psychotherapy cults" which include "from 15 to 75 mental health professionals, held together by their idealization of a shared therapist and the activities which they conducted jointly: workshops, seminars, courses, business and professional ventures, and social life . . . proud to be members of their therapist's 'professional family' (p. 133). It should be noted that all members of the group are themselves in the "helping professions."

The subculture of psychotherapy recruits its members from the ranks of what Ehrenreich and Ehrenreich (1977) call the professional-managerial class, which is defined "as consisting of salaried mental workers who do not own the means of production and whose major function in the social division of labor may be described broadly as the reproduction of capitalist culture and capitalist class relations" (p. 13). It is quite clear that the subculture of psychotherapy is part of the reproduction of capitalist culture. This class includes such occupations as teaching, social work, psychology, advertising, engineering, and science and includes between 20 and 25 percent of American workers. The connection between the professional-managerial class (PMC) and the subculture of psychotherapy is analyzed by Ehrenreich and Ehrenreich (1977) as follows:

> As a result of the anxiety over class reproduction, (i.e., keeping the status achieved by the individual), all the ordinary experiences of life—growing up, giving birth, childraising—are freighted with an external significance unknown in other classes. Private life, thus, becomes too arduous to be lived in private; the inner life of the PMC must be continuously shaped, updated and revised by—of course—ever mounting numbers of experts: experts in childraising, family living, sexual fulfillment, self-realization, etc., etc. The very insecurity of the class, then, provides new ground for class expansion. By mid-century the PMC was successful enough to provide a new mass market for many of its own services—and unsuccessful enough to need them. (p. 29)

The Ideology of Psychotherapy

What defines a subculture are norms and roles, but what is most distinct, and makes both norms and roles plausible, is the underlying ideology. This ideology is what members of the subculture are committed to beyond their particular commitments to techniques or schools of psychotherapy. Psychotherapists and their clients share certain basic beliefs, which are often held to be self-evident regardless of sectarian commitments to the justice of a particular school or orientation. The subculture can be understood as a world of discourse, which has evolved organically, without deliberate, conscious planning, and whose rules are followed unconsciously by those committed to it. This ideology can best be recognized and examined when it is looked at from the outside. If this is hard to do when it has reached a high level of elaboration. It may be easier to do when it is in its early stages of development.

The healers are similar to their clients not only in terms of social background but possibly in personality and identity as well. Healers and clients share a language and a worldview, a way of perceiving objects, analyzing them, and categorizing them. This way of seeing the world focuses on the personal and private meaning of things and moves away from the public sphere. All forms of psychotherapy, regardless of their technical differences, share a common ideological core, which can be gleaned from observing them. While "pop" or new therapies introduced since 1960 may be differentiated in many ways from traditional, insight-oriented psychotherapy and may be denigrated by members of older schools, all types of psychotherapy share the same basic ideology that is identical regardless of the particular school or orientation espoused and regardless of whether the therapy involved is "old" or "new" (Appelbaum, 1979).

The ideology of psychotherapy shares something important with religious traditions: positive thinking (Meyer, 1980) and the reliance on will power. All psychotherapies, despite vehement denials, rely on free will and its exercise in the direction of morality, responsibility, and growth. (How many psychotherapists does it take to change a light bulb? Just one, but the light bulb has got to want to change.) The light-bulb joke contains the message heard by millions of seekers of happiness through psychotherapy. The exercise of free will in a positive way is the condition for any improvement, and as in the religious tradition, the choice is between good and evil. If you choose evil, you have only yourself to blame. Success in any particular case of psychotherapy is a triumph of individual will, and this experience of will power is often the essence of personal transformation during psychotherapy. The hallmark of the ideology of psychotherapy is, of course, individualism. Thus, it is the expression of a secular, modern worldview. The ideal of positive intimacy, both within and outside the psychotherapy relationship itself, is another component of the ideology of psychotherapy. The quest for meaning and quest for intimacy are the two cornerstones of secular psychotherapy.

In modern literature and film, psychotherapy is portrayed as a situation of self-confrontation or merely as a legitimate means of coping with the trials and tribulations of modern life. Not only has individual psychotherapy become a common occurrence in modern novels and films as part of the hero's or heroine's odyssey of self-discovery, but psychotherapy in itself has been a fictional theme (Sohl, 1967). Psychotherapy is the modern hero's way of finding oneself, of defining oneself, and of finding meaning in life. It is the place for baring and searching one's soul and of finding true intimacy in a world of loneliness and meaninglessness. *Portnoy's Complaint* (Roth, 1968) is the apotheosis of modern psychotherapy, being a novel composed only of a monologue before a psychotherapist. This psychotherapeutic soliloquy takes the place of Hamlet's monologues and Rousseau's confessions. The consulting office is the stage and the temple in which the lost self is found and then rehabilitated to be worshipped anew. In psychotherapy we can understand our destiny in a privatized, or even customized meaning system. The events of our intimate biography, our innermost experiences, are the only clues to giving our lives meaning. One's destiny is totally private, and a personal history is the only one that matters. What modern capitalism has evolved is a deliberate ideology of the self and its value. The ideology of modern psychotherapy can be viewed as a deliberate search for an authentic self, which is presumed to be somewhere inside every human being. The types of search expressed by the ideology of psychotherapy range from self-improvement to self-liberation. Modern psychotherapy aids the individual in establishing a viable identity, a viable core of self, capable of leading the person through the uncharted waters of alienated society.

What the psychotherapy process aims at creating in the client may be defined as self-love or, at least, self-acceptance and self-improvement. In response to the individual experiences of meaninglessness, emptiness, and identity diffusion, psychotherapy offers the ethic of self-fulfillment. Fairbairn (1955) stated that "what is sought by the patient who enlists psychotherapeutic aid, is not so much health as salvation from his past, from bondage to his (internal) bad objects, from the burden of guilt, and from spiritual death. His search thus corresponds in detail to the religious quest" (p. 155). Nelson (1963) suggested that psychotherapy clients were seeking "self-definition, social significance, meaning, influence, deference, income, salvation, health" (p. 279). There is a process of "psychologization" through which more individuals find meaning in life through the reliance of psychological theories. Albee (1977) called it "the glorification of self" (p. 159), and referred to "the new Religion called psychotherapy" (p. 161). A strong commitment to a political or religious ideology, especially of a conservative kind, is likely to rule out a commitment to the subculture of psychotherapy. Pastoral psychology, unlike secular psychotherapy, is nevertheless the product of modern society and modern secular psychologies (Beit-Hallahmi, 1989).

A major theme in the history of secular psychotherapy is that of catharsis, conceptualized as the removal of internal corruption, either physical or psychological (Finkel, 1976). Modern psychotherapy from its early days in the nineteenth century to the present in the late twentieth century has shifted from the treatment of syndromes and symptoms to the improvement of personal functioning (Ellenberger, 1970). And that improved functioning is defined more and more through a subjective feeling of happiness or, at least, satisfaction and through the adoption of a personal philosophy offered by the therapist. Rokeach (1968) differentiated between instrumental values, which refer to preferred modes of behavior, and terminal values, which refer to preferred end states of existence. Psychotherapists talk quite often about instrumental values such as being independent, ambitious, broad-minded, loving, and honest, but less often about terminal values, such as equality, pleasure, or wisdom (Vonnegut, 1965; Beit-Hallahmi, 1974). What is the real essence of the therapeutic message and of the therapeutic attitude? Indeed, is there a basic difference between Dale Carnegie's message of optimism and modern cognitive psychotherapy?

Parsons (1951) considered psychotherapy to be "the case in our society where those fundamental elements of the processes of social control have been most explicitly brought to light. For certain purposes it can serve as a prototype of the mechanisms of social control" (p. 301). This mechanism includes four sequential stages: permissiveness (allowing free expression), support (accepting the client as a human being despite his or her excessive demands and shortcomings), denial of reciprocity, and manipulation of rewards (reinforcing only adaptive behaviors). The social control function of psychological treatment was noted generations ago by Davis (1936) in his critique of the mental hygiene movement. He suggested that through its psychologistic position, mental hygiene enforces social standards under the guise of science.

The ideology of psychotherapy culminates in a reductionism that seeks to explain every social and political activity as a reflection of private psychological dynamics. Fine (1971) explicity regards psychotherapy as the royal road to social, and not just individual, metamorphosis: "The entire corpus of knowledge that we call psychology and psychiatry today leads to the momentous conclusion that it is essential to reorganize the total social structure along the lines of the analytic ideal. Hence, psychotherapy is inherently a means of social reform" (p. 168).

The ideology of modern secular psychotherapy has most often been detailed by those who are opposed to it and view psychotherapy as a conservative or reactionary social force (Albee, 1977; Beit-Hallahmi, 1974). Critics of modern psychotherapy have blamed it for being a method of social control and a rationalization for preserving the status quo (Schrag, 1978). They have charged that the ideology of psychotherapy covers up social realities and that its practice serves the function of pacification of the alienated.

One of the best known critiques of the ideology of psychotherapy is that by Berger (1965):

> The fundamental structuring force in modern society is industrialization. A modern society permits the differentiation between public and private institutional spheres. What is essential for the psychological reality of such a society is that its members experience this dichotomization as a fundamental ordering principle of their everyday life. Institutionalized psychologism (Psychoanalysis) straddles the dividing line between the public and private spheres, thus occupying an unusually strategic position in our society. In the private sphere, it appears as one of the agencies supplying a population of anxious consumers with a variety of services for the construction, maintenance and repair of identities. In the public sphere, it lends itself with equal success to the different economic and political bureaucracies in need of non-violent techniques of social control. . . . A psychological model that has as its crucial concept a notion of the unconscious may be related to a social situation in which there is such complexity in the fabric of roles and institutions that the individual is no longer capable of perceiving his society in its totality. . . . The theme of sexuality fits the requirements of the social situation in which the essential self is located in the private sphere. . . . Again, the theme of childhood serves to establish the primacy of the private sphere in the hierarchy of self-definitions. . . . The understanding of the self as an assemblage of psychological mechanisms allows the individual to deal with himself with the same technical, calculating and "objective" attitude that is the attitude par excellence of industrial production. Furthermore, the interpretation of culture as a drama between individual "needs" and social realities is a fairly accurate reflection of the ongoing balancing act between "fulfillment" and "frustration" in the everyday life of individuals in a high-level consumers' society. In consequence, psychologism provides a "scientific" legitimation to the adjustment technology without which such a society could hardly get along." (pp. 35–40)

Psychotherapists are not only agents of social control, they are also ethical guides, from the client's point of view. Clients still come to psychotherapists to confess their sins, not only transgressions against conventional morality but also sins against the ethic of self-actualization and achievement. What the client confesses to is a betrayal of the self. The psychotherapist offers universal forgiveness, so that the client can face the world with renewed energy and to pursue self-actualization more successfully. In secular psychotherapy, forgiveness is achieved without much suffering (save the suffering of confession itself), but salvation is not without effort. The client has to internalize a doctrine of salvation based on responsibility without limits and a limited and circumscribed happiness.

Secular psychotherapy offers an explanation of personal destiny through references to personal history and internal forces and representations. It also offers an opportunity for change through one's will to change and getting to know one's internal landscape. Psychotherapy emphasizes personal responsibility and the possibility of change, if you really want it. The philosophy of modern psychotherapy in its clearest form is summed up by Werner Erhard: "You and I possess within ourselves, at every moment of our lives, all under circumstances, the power to transform the quality of our lives." The individualistic philosophy of psychotherapy proclaims the uniqueness, autonomy, and freedom of the individual. At the same time, it insists on one's absolute responsibility for his or her destiny and salvation. Psychotherapy is a celebration of the self in it aloneness, once this aloneness has become a compelling reality.

The philosophy of secular psychotherapy represents what might be called a ritualized sacralization of the self. Freud referred to psychotherapy as an intervention in the civil war within the personality on the side of the ego. But the message to the client is that of understanding one's fate as lying wholly within one's personal history, one's body, and private experience. This also means a heavy responsibility that is being imposed on the self to control fate and future.

Halmos (1970a & b) sees in the ideology of individualistic psychotherapy a rejection of all political struggles because such struggles are "messy" and frustrating (cf. Riesman and Miller, 1964). The individualistic bias of psychotherapy has been seen as a mechanism that insures the diversion of personal energies from political issues to private preoccupations and "ego trips" (Beit-Hallahmi, 1974 and 1977a; Hurvitz, 1973 and 1974). Simon (1983) lists the "undesirable social side effects of psychotherapy, as follows: "(a) fostering adaptation to an inherently unhealthy environment, (b) stigmatizing legitimate dissent as personal maladjustment, and (c) focusing personal and societal attention on intrapsychic phenomena instead of upon social structures, all of which leads to (d) inhibiting socially beneficial change (Halleck, 1971; Hurvitz, 1973; Ryan, 1971; Talbott, 1974)" (p. 555).

Caplan and Nelson (1973) showed that the prevalent mode in which psychologists study social problems is one of a "'person-blame' causal attribution bias" (p. 199). This means that social problems are analyzed in terms of individual attributes. There is an exclusive definition of personal problems as personal, private, and unrelated to social and historical context. Poverty is explained through the psychological deficiencies of the poor (Hersch, 1968). The individualistic nature of psychotherapy, in the way it assumes that individual problems are to be understood in terms of individual and internal causation is evident even in the case of behavior modification (Holland, 1978). Even the behavioristic school, emphasizing how individuals are controlled by their environments (or "contingencies"), has created a system of psychological treatment that attempts to change individual behavior and not external contingencies.

Explicit statements about personal philosophies of therapists are rare, but those that have been published (e.g., Foulkes, 1974; Lynn, 1961; Schutz, 1974) demonstrate clearly the totally individualistic point of view used in treating clients and conveyed to them during the treatment process. Bart (1972) describes what she calls the quietism of psychotherapy, based on the exclusive attention paid to the self's private world as the source for all public behavior. If all problems stem from intrapsychic conflicts, then society becomes a mere epiphenomenon, and social change becomes predicated on individual psychological changes. The slogan seems to be "It's what's inside that counts," with the implication being that social and economic realities are irrelevant to the psychotherapeutic process and to changes in the client's self-perceptions and behavior.

Modern nonsymptomatic psychotherapy attempts to combat subjective feelings of isolation and meaninglessness by helping clients to achieve a sense of their own unique worth and to accept their own inner experiences. The modern psychotherapist is under pressure from two directions: the client and his or her expressed needs and the needs of societal institutions. However, as sincere as psychotherapists may be in their support for the client, they are still powerless in the face of social forces that operate outside of the therapy situation and outside of the realm of individual experiences and wishes.

In modern psychotherapy, the search is not for a cure of symptoms but for the understanding of personal destiny. Historically, within the framework of the psychoanalytic tradition, there has been a change in practice and in theory from the emphasis on symptoms and neuroses to the emphasis on personality and character disorders. A character disorder is the neurosis of destiny, the curse of a misunderstood and misspent life. This curse is removed through the magic ritual of secular psychotherapy, which puts the self at center stage and interprets destiny not within a cosmic frame of reference, as in religion or astrology, but within the narrowest core of personal experience. The most recent development (or fashion) in the psychotherapy subculture has been that of the narcissistic personality, a character disorder that is symbolic of both the suffering self and what is offered to it as a cure for its suffering. The psychotherapy subculture can be regarded as part of a wider self-actualization or counterneurotic social movement, a movement for the liberation of the individual self from its social shackles.

The Psychotherapy Subculture in Israel

Seeking psychotherapy is an admission of deficiency in areas central to the ego. It means "inadequacy on such central personal qualities as mental hygiene and general adjustment" (Nadler, 1986, p. 119). As such, it is a major threat to self-esteem because it conflicts with the cherished values of self-reliance and independence. For Israelis, admitting the need for psychological treatment is a confession of deviance from the conventional norm of toughness and independence (Lieblich, 1978 and 1983).

The ideology of modern psychotherapy has to be propagated, overcoming resistance, before it can be accepted and legitimized. The creation of a self-liberation movement in Israel became possible with the decline of traditional collectivism in word and deed. Lip service was being paid to collectivism in Israel long after its actual decline. The well-being of the nation, or at least the family unit, was generally accepted as a guiding principle for individual action as long as Zionism was struggling and gaining.

In the United States, we find a long tradition both secular and religious "mind cures," affected by positive thinking (Meyer, 1980). Such a tradition was completely absent in Israeli culture until the mid-1970s. The historical attitude toward psychotherapy in Israel was one of hostility:

> In fact, the aim of psycho-therapy which focuses on individual needs and self-realization conflicted with the national ideals that one must sacrifice, in the most intimate and personal sense, individual needs and aspirations. Above all, people were ex-

> pected to be tough, fearless, and ready to risk their lives for the defence and upbuilding of the country. There was a high degree of tolerance for eccentrics, provided, however, they accepted the goals of the group. (Palgi, 1963, p. 47)

Why the philosophy of psychotherapy was not accepted in pre-1973 Israel to the extent that it was in the United States is suggested by Moses and Kligler (1966). Israeli society, as of 1965, was still too collectivistic, and so the concepts of adjustment and self-fulfillment so popular in the United States were missing. "Literature focused on social goals and ideals rather than on the psychological dimension of the individual" (Moses and Kligler, 1966, p. 148). It took ten more years before the philosophy of self-actualization became the order of the day.

Psychotherapy in Israel was imported from Europe by immigrants who represented various European movements. A psychoanalytic institute was founded by Max Eitingon in Jerusalem in 1929, but for many years only a small group of followers were attracted to it. The Jungian psychotherapist Erich Neumann practiced in Tel-Aviv between 1935 and 1957. An Adler Institute was founded in Tel-Aviv in 1963. The Adlerians received a boost from several visits by Rudolf Dreikurs to Israel in the 1960s, and books by Dreikurs were translated into Hebrew, enjoying much popularity. Until the early 1970s, all of these activities represented something that was considered culturally marginal.

The first university-based training program in clinical psychology was started in 1965 at the Hebrew University in Jerusalem. It was aimed at training M.A. graduates in clinical practice according to a traditional model, which put diagnosis, rather than psychotherapy, at the center of training. The more expressive kinds of psychotherapy techniques (see Kaplan and Sadock, 1971; Mintz, 1971; Ruitenbeek, 1970; Yalom, 1985) aroused a strong resistance in Israel before 1973. Encounter groups (Schutz, 1971) first reached Israel in the mid-1960s but were used only within academic settings, as part of training programs in psychology and social work. Those who tried to introduce Esalen-type encounter groups had only a limited success, and Gestalt therapy was almost unknown (Bernet, 1971). The growth of psychotherapy in Israel has meant the appearance and acceptance of what Friedmann (1980) has called parapsychoanalytic psychotherapy, referring to such styles as Gestalt therapy, transactional analysis, and bioenergy. These are all unorthodox ways of practicing psychotherapy with undefined standards for the training of practitioners and undefined structures of therapeutic relationships.

Several developments indicate a revolutionary change in the status of psychotherapy in Israel since the 1960s and specifically since the 1973 War. The discourse of psychotherapy has gained legitimacy with the development of public psychological treatment facilities, of course. These services, offered in clinics and by the school system, have grown considerably in Israel since 1970. Their development has served as one basis for the growth of the psychotherapy subculture. Official reports of contacts with outpatient mental health clinics in the years 1966–79 show an increase of 288.9 percent, while the total population grew by only 37.5 percent. The rate of inpatient treatment remained stable during the same period (Rahav and Popper, 1980). The number of outpatient clinics in Israel almost doubled between 1965 and 1977, from thirty-seven to sixty-seven. The number of outpatient contacts grew from 144,000 in 1965 to 555,300 in 1977 (Popper and Rahav, 1980). What these data clearly show is a dramatic change in supply and demand for psychiatric services offered by psychiatrists, social workers, and psychologists. The change, from 60,000 per million (Jewish population) to 158,000 per million in the number of visits may indicate a growing need together with the growing availability of services and a growing legitimation of seeking help.

The profession of psychology in Israel achieved an unusual level of growth in the 1970s. The membership of the Israel Psychological Association was 170 in 1963, 289 in 1970, and 1750 in 1980. This put Israel on top of the list of the world's nations in psychologists per million inhabitants (437). As a point of comparison, the estimated rate of psychologists per million population in West Germany in 1983 was 286 (Brengelmann and Wittchen, 1986). This world record (Rosenzweig, 1982) reflects an impressive growth in the profession but gives us only a partial picture with regard to the growth in the number of psychotherapy practitioners. First, not all psychologists practice psychotherapy. Second, other professionals, and sometimes nonprofessionals, do. Estimating the number of psychotherapy providers in Israel is difficult, but it is estimated to include most psychologists together with hundreds of psychiatrists, social workers, counselors, and many individuals with no professional training.

A Psychology Law requiring the licensing of all psychological practitioners was passed in 1977. A register of psychologists was opened by the Health Ministry, and anybody using the title, of psychologist has to be registered and licensed. The Psychology Law has not stopped individuals from claiming that title or from offering psychotherapy while presenting themselves as counselors, sexologists, psychotherapists, or therapists. The general blooming of psychotherapy in Israel indeed meant that numerous individuals lacking any formal training have been successful in establishing psychotherapy practices. Some of them claim to be psychologists, while others present themselves as counselors, group leaders, or sexologists.

The most vivid evidence on the connection between the 1973 War and the blooming of psychotherapy in Israel is found in a book by Lieblich (1978). The author, a psychotherapist, reports on her experience in Gestalt therapy groups, in which war and loss are the major themes. She started running such groups in 1970, but it becomes clear that the 1973 War created an urgency and a need that were not there before. Despite the author's complete lack of any political analysis (she regards the recurring wars in the Middle East as similar to "living near a volcano" [p. 4], a natural phenomenon), she records faithfully the qualitative differences between this war and others. "The threat of defeat and individual loss has grown dramatically since the Yom Kippur War of 1973" (p. 4), and "for me, life has not been the same since the war. The confidence, the security, the sense of superiority, are gone" (p. 118). The response to the loss of confidence and superiority is an attempt to seek psychological awareness and to psychologize collective problems.

The characters in the Lieblich book are members of the elite who take part in therapy groups as part of their professional training or to deal with personal concerns. They express some concerns that are quite common to therapy clients everywhere: alienation, worthlessness, and meaninglessness. Beyond these "universal" complaints, however, they present some unique Israeli problems. There are really two psychological themes in the book. One is that of loss, mourning, and bereavement, which are mostly the business of women. The other is that of the role of the warrior and the psychology of the war hero, which are mostly the business of men. There is a strict division of labor between the sexes. Men are fighters and experience war firsthand. They are subject to danger, death, injury, and loss. Women experience war through men and experience directly only loss and bereavement. An Israeli woman is the mother, sister, wife or widow of a warrior. She has to support men, nurture them, indulge them, and then mourn them so that they will be able to carry out their manly duties as fighters.

Since the book is written from a psychological treatment perspective, contradictions in reality and ideology are neutralized as moral and ideological categories are translated into psychological ones. There are no moral or ideological conflicts or doubts; there are only reflections of the psychological aspects of individual personalities. Thus, when a woman is upset by the sight of a Palestinian refugee after the 1967 War, this is interpreted as a reflection of her identification with the refugee within her.

Immediately following the war, we see psychological treatment being offered as the answer to the problem of morale, and professionals offering solutions to the problems of bereavement and mourning. Why was professional intervention needed in this case? After all, there were 10,000 families in Israel who had lost sons in war before October 1973. The psychotherapeutic interpretation of reality, which views mourning as a natural and even growth-inducing process, had an obvious utility in dealing with the catastrophic loss of morale.

Following the decline in morale after the 1973 War, the Israel Defense Forces (IDF) started promoting the use of mental health professionals in all units. A new military classification was created, that of the mental health officer, known by its Hebrew initials as KBN. Today, the I.D.F. is the most saturated military organization in the world in terms of mental health professionals with mental health officers, usually social workers, in every battalion.

Mass media serve the function of legitimizing and setting up priorities for their audiences. In the case of psychotherapy in Israel, the mass media have performed this task effectively. The mass media have conferred legitimacy not only on mainstream professional forms of psychotherapy but also on practices promoted by nonprofessionals. The growing legitimacy of psychotherapy in Israel is demonstrated by the success of radio and television programs offering it to the masses, which have reached a remarkable level of popularity.

"Apple and Tree," a counseling program for parents and children was initiated in 1974, stopped in 1976, and renewed in May 1983. Of all the psychotherapy programs, it is the most down-to-earth because of its emphasis on practical problem-solving rather than self-actualization. "The Two of Us—Together and Apart" is a counseling program for couples that started in October 1978. It covers a wide range of topics, going far beyond marital problems and dealing with most kinds of psychological difficulties and since 1980 has been the most popular among nighttime radio shows. "Give Me Your Dream," started in May 1983, is the height of psychotherapy by radio. In this program listeners are invited to call in their dreams and are offered instant interpretation by recognized professionals in psychiatry and psychology. Listening to "Give Me Your Dream" means having people bare their souls on the airwaves and having psychotherapy professionals demonstrate the skills of modern psychological treatment. The manner displayed by the professionals in the radio studio is the proper therapeutic one. There is careful listening and reflection of the client's feelings. Interpretations are offered but not directions or suggestions. The Voice of Peace, an offshore radio station known for its pop music and liberal ideology, has started its own radio counseling program, hosted by a well-known Tel Aviv psychiatrist. Television viewers in Israel have been able to watch since 1985 "The Family Connection," which demonstates the principles of Adlerian psychotherapy with the help of actors, who perform case studies based on real problems sent in by viewers. The program has been immensely popular, especially among children and young people.

Est in Israel

Secular salvation movements are groups that propose and proclaim the advent of private salvation for all those willing to partake of it, through some new discovery of a psychological-philosophical principle. An example would be the sophrology, founded in 1960 by Alfonso Cayedo in Madrid. Sophrology claims to unify Eastern and Western approaches, to erase the prejudices of psychoanalysis and medicine, and to offer a revolution in psychology, medicine, and education (Boon et al., 1985). Secular salvation movements, such as est, present themselves as having global, if not cosmic, significance. Such groups put much effort into maintaining a group identity. Customers are treated as members, not just as clients, of a movement with more than just psychotherapeutic benefits.

The best illustration of the self-liberation movement and the creation of a psychotherapy subculture in Israel is the history of est in Israel. Est is the brainchild of John Paul Rosenberg, a.k.a. Werner Hans Erhard, a graduate of Dale Carnegie, Zen, Subud, Scientology, and a variety of secular psychotherapy schools. From all of these he distilled an essence, which has been sold to the public since 1971 (Bartley, 1978). Erhard demonstrates in his own existence the power of salvation through psychological, secular enlightenment (Fenwick, 1976). Est promises an experience of radical change: "There is only one thing powerful enough to transform the quality of your life in just four days—You."

The story of the coming of est to Israel involves Dan Carmon, born in 1942, who was never a part of the official est organization. Carmon, like Erhard, was a former salesman with one criminal conviction for drug possession (Etgar and Ella, 1980). During a stay in the United States in 1976, he took the est training and decided that such a venture would be profitable in Israel. Starting in 1978, he organized in Tel-Aviv what were known as "psychological marathons," in which thousands of Israelis took part. By all accounts, the Dan Carmon marathons were identical to the est training in format and philosophy. As opposed to the est organization, Carmon made two cardinal errors. First, he did not declare himself a nonprofit organization, as est did. Second, he did not care much for public relations.

In the spring of 1980, hostile reports about the Carmon marathons started appearing in the Israeli media. On March 21, 1980, a critical segment appeared on the Friday night news program of Israel television. The next move came from the Israeli Internal Revenue Service. Carmon was arrested for not reporting any of his substantial earnings. The marathons stopped. Then in 1982, Carmon was charged with practicing psychology without a license, under the terms of Article 2 of the Psychology Law, 1977. In 1984, Carmon, through plea bargaining, was sentenced to three months imprisonment (suspended) and a fine. By 1984, Dan Carmon was not the same man. His life had been miraculously transformed but not only through est. He was now a full-time Yeshiva student, sporting the long beard and the black skullcap of an Orthodox Jew.

Word of the unauthorized use of est technology by Dan Carmon reached est headquarters, and the result was the establishment of a branch in Israel. This branch was incorporated as a nonprofit organization in 1980, under the name "The Israel Center." Later on, the name was changed to "The Israel Center for Breakthrough." The first est training seminar was offered in Tel Aviv in December 1980. By 1984, the Israeli est center was offering a variety of workshops and activities. There was an activity scheduled for every day of the week. Most workshops, including the original est training and later the forum, were being conducted in English. According to est recruiters and to testimonials by graduates, language was no barrier. I myself recall hearing an Israeli est graduate in December 1980, who said that she could not understand a word of English, but the est training still changed her life. Other activities, especially those for youth, were in Hebrew. Among the workshops offered were "Making a Difference," "Experience of Integrity," a communication workshop for adults and another one for youth, "Self-Expression," and "Being Here Now." Other seminar titles included "Power of Being," "Empowerment Weekend," "About Money," and "The Body." The special est vocabulary in English, which usually sounds stilted to non-estees, has been rendered into Hebrew and sounds just as strange.

During an est guest seminar that took place in Haifa on May 29, 1984, the est trainer, Herb Tanzer, announced proudly that Israel held the world record in the rate of est participation. By 1987, the number of est graduates who have taken either the training or the forum, stood at 7500. To appreciate the success of est in Israel, it should be recalled that during the first six years of est activity in the United States, 175,000 trainees took the est training (Parloff, 1978). At the rate of est participation in Israel, given the differences between the population of the two countries (1 : 66), est participation in the United States should have reached 400,000 during the same period.

Est in Israel was a special success story in two kibbutzim where at least 50 percent of the members took the training and a significant number have become est volunteers. A list of est graduates in Israel reads like the Israeli *Who's Who*. It includes prominent figures in government service, the arts, the academic world, and the media. The editor and owner of one of Israel's leading newspapers, a man in his seventies, was among them. The participation of media people usually insures friendly coverage and a positive public image.

A significant minority of est graduates in Israel have become est volunteers, who commit themselves to working for est during their leisure hours. This commitment includes hosting est guest seminars at their homes and giving testimonials to potential clients. The est sales style is quite aggressive, and est volunteers adopt it and badger their friends and neighbors incessantly. The activities of est volunteers in Israel have enabled the organization to stop using salaried employees, except for one full-time director. Est volunteers answer the phones and stuff envelopes at est offices as well as sweep the floors and clean the restrooms during est training weekends. Since volunteers take care of every menial and nonmenial task necessary for the smooth and successful operation of the organization, the nonprofit "Israel Center for Breakthrough" was quite profitable for Werner Hans Erhard's worldwide organization.

The effects of private salvation through est could be best observed in these volunteers who have always been eager to tell their stories. An engineer who spoke at a meeting aimed at recruiting participants at the est Forum in late 1984 described his "conversion" mostly in "assertive" or selfish terms. After taking the est training, he made several major decisions about his life. The first was to stop working so hard. The second was to give less money to his only daughter, who lives with her mother. The third was to end a relationship with a woman who refused to have sex with him.

Z. G. was one of many est volunteers who do not fit the justified stereotype of the lonely, unsuccessful individual. Z. G. was married, the father of three, and a professor of engineering. He has studied and traveled abroad quite widely. Nevertheless, his life had been filled with frustrations before the remarkable transformation brought about by est.

Another est volunteer is Y., a widow for many years, who had been in psychotherapy with a well-known and controversial therapist to whom she was emotionally attached for several years. Then she became an est volunteer and was spending all her free time spreading the word. It should be mentioned that while being in psychoanalytic therapy did not have much of an impact on her life and she continued many self-destructive behaviors, since discovering est, she, like others who have found private salvation, has functioned very well.

No est trainer in Israel has ever been accused of practicing psychology without a license since the case involving Dan Carmon. The est organization has done an excellent job of promoting its image and has hired the services of journalists and attorneys of the first rank. When the Commission of Inquiry on Cults included est in its list of cults active in Israel, est went to the Supreme Court in Jerusalem and won an injunction against the publication of the Commission's report. It was represented in the proceedings by Ehud Olmert, who happened to be a Member of the Knesset (in Israel members of parliament can pursue such private business) and a major spokesman for the Likud party. As it turns out, Olmert did some private lobbying on behalf of est with M. K. Miriam Taasa-Glazer, chairperson of the Commission, without telling her that he was on a retainer by est (Yeffet, 1984).

Despite the effective est public relations campaign, which led to numerous positive media reports (e.g., Zadok, 1983; Yishai, 1981), it has been described as a cult in several newspaper articles. In one case, a man sued for divorce at the Tel-Aviv rabbinical court because his wife, according to the complaint, joined the "est cult" (Orenstein, 1983).

In order to improve its image and to be associated with social, not just individual, concerns, the Israel Center initiated in 1984 a large scale operation designed to encourage the use of safety belts. In Israel the law at the time mandated wearing a belt only on intercity highways. The 1984 operation had the commendable goal of persuading Israelis to wear safety belts while driving within city limits. The operation involved 4000 volunteers who met drivers at 200 gas stations during three days in November 1984 and offered them written "contracts" committing them to the use of seat belts. Drivers were invited to sign the "contracts." The operation, well-advertised in full-page newspaper advertisements, reportedly won 50,000 drivers over. The attempt to improve the image of the Israel Center failed. The fact that the Israel Center was really a branch of est, which was labeled a cult, was exposed with glee by the media. The operation was carried out under the auspices of President Haim Herzog and the Speaker of the Knesset, Shlomo Hillel. Following media reports about the connections between the safety belt campaign and a "mystical cult," the president issued a statement disclaiming any connection with the "est cult" (Gluska, 1984). Another discovery that hurt the est image was the disclosure that the Israel Center did not spend any of its own money on the campaign. As it turned out, the budget came from the government. The most substantial contribution on the part of the center were 4000 signed "contracts" that came from its graduates. Most of the volunteers were Boy Scouts.

Apparently, as a response to criticism that emphasized the narcissistic nature of est and its obliviousness to real problems in Israel, the est organization has started the Foundation for Mideast Communication. Michael Lame, who used to head the est effort in Israel, became the president and executive director of the foundation. The principles followed by the foundation include such statements as: "a non-positional, contextual approach opens up new possibilities for conflict resolution that are currently unavailable . . . a breakthrough in the Middle East is possible at any moment" (Foundation for Mideast Communication, 1986, p. 2). Foundation workshops are offered in the United States only, not in Israel, presumably because Americans may be more receptive to such an initiative. Even in the United States, only a few workshops have taken place with a limited number of participants. By late 1987, after 10,000 Israelis have partook of est weekends and workshops, the "Israel Center for Breakthrough" seemed to have exhausted its market segment. Another organization appeared on the scene, destined to inherit not only est's offices and phones but its clientele and ideological mantle.

I AM

A 1984 *Newsweek* report on cults around the world included a reference to a South African cult, based in Johannesburg and known as I AM. Its founder, Pat Grove, was also facing criminal charges but was planning to expand his activities overseas (Smolowe et al., 1984). Since then I AM is no longer prominent in South Africa, but the story of its rise and (relative) fall in Israel is instructive. In 1985, with the South African police on his heels, Pat Grove arrived in Israel. A couple of years later, I AM became known all over the country, its growth far surpassing that of est. By late 1987, I AM rented the large suite of offices that had been vacated by the shrinking est organization. Persons dialing the old est number were greeted to their great surprise by "I AM, good morning." Within four years of activity, 10,000 Israelis attended the I AM marathons. Stickers bearing the I AM logo could be seen everywhere in Israel. In 1989 Pat Grove encountered opposition from the psychiatric establishment when he wanted to offer special workshops for minors, sent by their parents.

A commission of inquiry was set up by the Health Ministry to investigate I AM following complaints about the workshops for minors, which were alleged to endanger their mental health. The commission was appointed in June 1989 and included three psychiatrists, a psychologist, and a social worker. After the commission submitted its report, the Health Ministry went to court in the fall of 1989 and obtained injunctions forbidding I AM from holding any workshops dealing with "psychology or psychiatry." The public uproar that followed did not help I AM, but it seemed that something else happened. Like est, it reached the magical number of 10,000, which is apparently the size of the potential market for the est-type groups in Israel. After the fall of 1989, Pat Grove left Israel for greener pastures elsewhere, and the operation has been run by his Israeli disciples. One of the committed promoters of I AM in Israel is Ronny Yarkony, born in 1956, who suffered from combat shock as a result of his participation in the 1982 Lebanon invasion. He has been suffering from numerous symptoms, such as claustrophobia and a fear of heights. A former paratrooper, he now spend his time organizing events for I AM graduates.

Psychotherapists as Culture Heroes

The process of growth, institutionalization, and legitimation of psychotherapy in Israel has been quick and intense. Within a few years, a psychotherapy subculture has grown comparable to those in New York, Buenos Aires, or Paris. The discourse of modern nonsymptomatic psychotherapy, which was totally nonexistent in Israel before the early 1970s, became a part of the culture by the late 1970s. "Self-awareness," "awareness," "experiencing," and "personal potential" were among the expressions that now have become familiar and prevalent. "Marathon" or "psychological marathon" has become a common term to signify intensive psychotherapy experiences conducted over weekends. Weekend workshops offering a variety of "human potential" psychotherapies are being offered and consumed by a growing clientele of the psychotherapy subculture.

> If I have identified this movement correctly, Tel-Aviv became locked on psychological treatment in the first months of '83. I may be the last one to notice it. During those months, more or

> less, started the trek of Tel-Avivers to know the lore of the soul, together with what grows out of a mass movement involving thousands. Friday night conversations, exchanging telephone numbers, rating the first league of recommended psychologists, rating those treating VIP's, rating those who specialize in freaks, rust removal, good and expensive ones, good and inexpensive. This avalanche of quasi-professional terminology has become part of the street language . . . client, treatment time, organic case, Oedipal stage, pre-Oedipal. If you are a pre- you are in bigger trouble. . . . We are talking about a session or two weekly, from 45 to 60 minutes. . . . Treatment takes place through long monologues . . . to really get out the pus, take into account three years. (Tzror, 1983, pp. 34–35)

That is how an unsophisticated Israeli journalist reported the final institutionalization of psychotherapy in Israel.

The experience of conversion through psychotherapy is described by a woman, who was age thirty-seven when she took part in a Carmon marathon in Tel Aviv in 1980: "I felt that somebody was yelling at me from the stage: 'You are responsible for your life. You alone will change it.' It is said that this kind of marathon does not change you. It is not a change, but a conversion. You follow the same route, but forward instead of backward, and you are aware of things happening to you" (quoted in Roman, 1984).

The success of transcendental meditation (TM) in Israel in the 1970s, when more than 40,000 Israelis learned to practice twice-daily mediation, should also be counted among the varieties of secular psychotherapy. For the majority of the Israeli meditators, what they learned was a relaxation technique, devoid of any religious meaning, and they learned it to deal with their personal distress in the form of subjective tension. The need for subjective relief, which is reflected in the highest rate per population of TM practitioners in the world, explains the openness to many forms of psychological treatment. The demand for psychotherapy, starting in the late 1970s, led to an environment in which most initiatives presented under the label of "psychological treatment" have had some success. Individuals with advanced, limited, or no formal training opened up "institutes" that have gained fame and fortune for their proprietors. By the late 1970s, one analyst observed that there was an enthusiasm in Israel for what he called more radical encounter group methods but also for "any new therapeutic approaches" (Berman, 1981, p. 171). Minor prophets of salvation have appeared on the scene, each with their own "institute" or group of followers and a word-of-mouth reputation growing in leaps and bounds. Irving Bronsky, described as a "charismatic psychiatrist," declares in a newspaper interview: "I am a teacher, I am a healer, I am a prophet . . . I have a lot of love in me, and a lot of intuition. A shocking intuition. I am amazed at myself to see how well I guess things" (Lan, 1991, p. 9).

One unique aspect of the psychotherapy subculture in Israel is the activities of a great number of practitioners who lack any formal training in the helping professions. In other countries the professional community of mental health professionals is quite jealous of its monopoly. In Israel, this community did not seem to worry about competition. In discussion with professionals, I have heard that the demand for psychotherapy was such, that it could not be met by legitimate professionals, so the nonprofessionals were providing relief, and the professionals did not feel threatened. Moreover, there have been many cases of recognized professionals collaborating with nonprofessionals in a variety of settings, such as weekend marathons.

The story of "humanistic" psychotherapy in Israel is illustrated by the odyssey of E. L., a prophet of self-liberation, with much honor in his hometown. E. L. came to Haifa in 1978, and started offering psychological treatment in individual and group settings. He is not a member of the Israel Psychological Association nor listed in the Ministry of Health directory of psychologists, a requirement for licensing, because of his lack of formal training. Nevertheless, he often refers to himself as a psychologist and is known as such by thousands. After a few months, E. L.'s activity as a psychotherapy entrepreneur was formalized in an "institute" defined as a "humanistic center for personal development." This institute, known as the Morag Center has offered a variety of workshops on such topics as "Human Relations and Interpersonal Communication," "Personal Development," "Personal Responsibility" ("we are the creators of our reality"), Gestalt workshops, and parents' groups. Most of the workshops have been offered by nonprofessionals.

The "Morag marathons" are described as "nonpsychotherapy," but this disclaimer in no way alters the perceptions and experiences of participants who recognize the goals and philosophy of secular psychotherapy in the "marathon" and does not change the meaning of "marathon" in spoken Hebrew, which denotes psychological treatment. Since 1978, the name "Morag" has become known to thousands around Haifa and its suburbs as synonymous with psychotherapy of the "humanistic" persuasion. Thousands have experienced it directly, and some of them have become committed clients who keep signing up for workshops and marathons and sometimes end up as group leaders in the same workshops and marathons.

E. L. has become a popular and sought-after speaker. His presentations before students at the University of Haifa have drawn standing-room-only crowds, and students line up long before the scheduled time in order to get seats. The topics include "Sexual and psychological maturity" and "Coffee and intimacy—how to live with others?" After a few short years, the Center has become not only a source of treatment and enlightenment but also a training facility. By 1982, it was offering a three-year course for group leaders, "designed for teachers, psychologists, social workers . . . and anybody who is in educational contact with others." This course has won recognition from the Education Ministry, which refunds the tutition of teachers taking part in it.

E. L. is an est graduate, and has collaborated with the Israeli est organization in est guest seminars in which new clients are recruited. He conducts est-style weekend experiences, which follow exactly the est format, except for their length (only one evening and oneday) and their price (much cheaper than est). The growing success of instant therapies such as est and unofficial marathons led to a media backlash in 1981, with professionals issuing warnings about the dangers of such practices (Kuperman, 1981). The backlash did not have much of an effect on the demand for this form of psychotherapy.

Dale Carnegie in Israel

The Dale Carnegie philosophy is a distillation of what secular psychotherapy is all about: "By talking to yourself every hour of the day, you can direct yourself to think thoughts of courage and happiness, thoughts of power and peace. By talking to yourself about the things you have to be grateful for, you can fill your mind with thoughts that soar and sing" (Carnegie, 1981, p. 12). This kind of positive thinking is at the root of all psychotherapy practices. The more sophisticated ones do not admit it, but Dale Carnegie did.

It was 1912 when Dale Carnegie offered to the public his first course in public speaking. In his 1936 book *How To Win Friends And Influence People,* he promised happiness and success in a few easy lessons. The Dale Carnegie brand of self-help is directed to teaching them that a firm handshake, a winning smile, and a memory for names are the key to success. In 1985, 118,000 people took the Dale Carnegie training in the United States (Bennett, 1986). The Dale Carnegie organization open a branch in Israel in 1972, during the days of euphoria and economic prosperity that preceded the 1973 War. It tried to reach business people at first, but after the war it extended its reach. Since then, about 20,000 Israelis have been enrolled in the organization.

One of the significant victories of the Dale Carnegie organization in Israel was noted in 1984. Shimon Peres, the labor party leader who in the 1981 election campaign enjoyed the services of an astrologer (see above), this time hired Mrs. Dalya Ayalon-Levy, the director of the Dale Carnegie center in Tel-Aviv. Mrs. Ayalon-Levy spent long hours with Mr. Peres weekly during the campaign. Mr. Peres gained friends, influenced people, and in the fall of 1984 became prime minister (Barzilai, 1984). Later on, of course, he was driven out of power, but this was not blamed on Dale Carnegie. Following missile attacks on Tel-Aviv in January 1991, the Dale Carnegie organization was one among several groups that offered workshops on how to deal with anxiety and improve functioning under stress. In this it joined other psychotherapy professionals (and nonprofessional practitioners) and showed again that its classification within the psychotherapy subculture was fully justified.

Co-Counseling (Reevaluation Counseling)

This psychotherapy movement, the combination of a self-help group with a hierarchical authority structure, which was started in the United States in the 1960s (Scheff, 1972), reached Israel in 1977 and developed significantly. It has involved since then perhaps thousands who have attended at least some sessions. Among the participants there is a considerable element of immigrants from English-speaking countries, and the group has been less successful in attracting native-born Israelis.

Unlike other psychotherapy movements, this one has a decidedly political, left-wing bent. In Israel this implies involvement with such issues as the rights of Palestinians, feminism, and the rights of homosexuals.

Minor and Major Prophets

The appearance, and the popular acceptance, of individuals calling themselves sexologists and offering advice on sexual problems is a unique Israeli phenomenon, and a unique Israeli addition to the realm of psychotherapy. Starting in the mid-1980s, sexologists have been writing newspaper columns, appearing on television, and giving lectures before a variety of groups. The term "sexologist" is not in normal use as a professional designation anywhere else in the world, and the individuals involved in this occupation in Israel are in most cases without any formal academic training.

Secular self-help books are the direct descendants of inspirational religion. Their message is quite similar: free will and positive thinking. Through self-help books, one enters a dialogue with an invisible psychotherapist whose voice is clearly heard. Though invisible, the writer-psychotherapist can induce acceptance, inspiration, and knowledge (see Rosen, 1987). Self-help books have been a part of the psychotherapy subculture first and foremost because the philosophy they embody is the secular, individualistic philosophy of psychotherapy, which puts responsibility for one's fate in one's mind (Campbell, 1974; Cordell, 1978; Dyer, 1976; Greenwald, 1973). Since the late 1970s, numerous self-help books have been published in Israel. Most of them were translations of self-help books published in the United States. The modern guru of pop psychology self-love, Leo Buscaglia, reached Israel in the 1980s through Hebrew translations of his best-selling books.

One form of psychotherapy that has appeared in Israel since the late 1970s is the self-help leaderless group. A survey of twenty-nine such groups in Jerusalem, showed that seventeen were started after 1978. The groups included Alcoholics Anonymous, Overeaters Anonymous, Bereaved Parents, Single Parents, and Al Anon (Bargal and Gidron, 1983).

Psychotherapy training programs, designed for psychiatrists, psychologists, and social workers, appeared in Israel in the late 1970s. The appearance in 1986 of *Conversations,* a periodical in Hebrew devoted to psychotherapy and written by professionals for professionals, marked the coming of age of the psychotherapy subculture in Israel. The Psychoanalytic Institute in Jerusalem, dormant for many years, gained a new vitality by the late 1970s with hundreds of professionals seeking admission into the analytical training program. Since the late 1970s, the psychoanalytic institute in Jerusalem has experienced a problem that is quite rare for most psychoanalytic institutes in the world: an increasing number of candidates who wish to join the ranks of the psychoanalytic guild. Hundreds have applied to become candidates and have been turned down, and their numbers have been growing steadily since the 1970s. Despite its remarkable growth and respectability, the psychotherapy "industry" in Israel, as of 1987, is still a far cry (or a far primal scream) from its equivalent in southern

California (cf. London, 1974). Still, what can be observed in the phenomenal growth of the psychotherapy subculture in Israel is the truth of the psychoanalytic statement that "when attachment to a common culture breaks down, the ego will attempt to fulfill its organizing functions by increased insight into internal processes" (Weinstein and Platt, 1969, p. 138).

5

Crisis and the Search for Salvation

I have grouped together four cultural developments, which I have called roads to salvation and which have all appeared during the same historical period in the same place. It seems obvious to suggest that these innovations are reactions to a serious historical crisis. The question, nevertheless, remains. Why have the reactions taken these forms and not other ones? After all, if it is a historical crisis, reactions should be in the political-ideological realm and not only through escapist personal salvation. The analysis of the rise and fall of belief systems has to be done within the framework or the sociology of knowledge. Ideas become acceptable or lose their acceptability within a certain social constellation following a particular zeitgeist. The idea has been expressed by Spengler (1919) among others and has become part of the received wisdom of historians of ideas. The most obvious and most plausible general explanation is that the appearance of new forms of faith and salvation indicates that the old ones are no longer satisfactory to the population involved. When there is a crisis in established institutions, individuals turn to alternative ones.

The deprivation hypothesis for the explanation of new religious movement is the most common in social science literature (Argyle and Beit-Hallahmi, 1975). In most general terms, it tells us that people deprived of satisfaction and happiness in this world look for them in fantasy. As objective conditions become more difficult and realistic coping does not lead to any change, humans turn to imaginary ways of coping. During times of stress and crisis, as during times of individual distress, there is a regression to "artistic," religious, or magical ways of thinking (Beit-Hallahmi, 1989). When realistic coping seems to be failing or futile, individuals may turn to magical or religious ways of coping. When all hope is lost, these ways of coping do seem worthwhile. In this particular case, a society that had enjoyed a high degree of cultural integration and uniformity has been undergoing a crisis of disintegration and anomie. This crisis has given rise to a variety of cultural innovations of an individualistic, escapist, and religious nature.

The first question we will have to answer is that of timing. Why did all of these movements appear on the scene at the same time? What is their historical context? While explanations for the appearance of salvation subcultures in modern society emphasize the themes of reactions to rationalism, industrialization, urbanization, and impersonality of social relations characterized by capitalist societies (cf. Löwy, 1978), the Israeli situation is unique and requires unique explanations. Israel is not a "normal" capitalist society. It is a garrison state without any real economic base, founded on a vision of national revival and on a practice of dispossessing the native population. The disenchantment in Israel leading to private salvation movements is first a disenchantment with the Zionist dream and with Israeli reality. Many Israelis seem to be without a coherent sense of their collective situation and see events unfolding around them as natural disasters, rather than man-made ones.

There were, of course, many political moves and political changes in response to the continuing crisis, and these touched much greater numbers of individuals than all the salvation movements we are covering here. Nevertheless, our focus here is on personal salvation only, not on political movements that attempt to affect the real causes of the crisis.

The Starting Point: 1973

We can distinguish two stages in the development of salvation movements in contemporary Israel. The stage of radical change, took place between 1973 and 1983, as these new movements first appeared and rapidly grew. Then after 1983, these movements entered a stage of stabilization, institutionalization, and even stagnation. One may speak of the initial stage of reactions to the shock, spasms, and convulsions between 1973 and 1983, which saw the greatest growth of the new salvation movements, followed by a period of stabilization and stagnation. Such cultural developments, indeed upheavals, have to be analyzed against the background of the crisis of Zionism and Israeli identity (cf. Beit-Hallahmi, 1991).

Israel before 1973 presented to the world a picture of relative cultural uniformity, great self-confidence and a hard-nosed attitude toward life. We might say that the high point in the history of Zionism was reached in 1967, but the war of attrition between Israel and Egypt, between September 1967 and August 1970, marred the feeling of triumph. The period between August 1970 and October 1973 can be seen as the point of triumph of Zionism, since there was almost no fighting anywhere along Israel's expanded borders, and economic prosperity reached unprecedented levels. Economic growth during the six years between 1967 and 1973 was the highest of any similar period in Israel's history. Between 1967 and 1973, per capita income went from $1131 to $2225, almost doubling itself, and the percentage of Israeli families owning an automobile went from 13.3 percent in 1967 to 22.1 percent in 1973 (Israel Statistical Abstracts, 1967–74). Optimism and self-confidence were characteristics of Israelis in the early 1960s, and reached their height after 1967 (Antonovsky and Arian, 1972). They were lowest after the 1973 War. Stone (1982) reports on how Israelis responded to the question: "How is your mood these days?" between 1967 and 1979. He shows that the two high points in national mood (based on monthly polls using representative samples) were in 1967, after the June War and in November 1977, after the historical visit to Israel by President Sadat of Egypt. The lowest level was reached between October 1973 and June 1974. Between August 1970 and October 1973, the mood reflected what Stone calls a period of "prosperity and development, confidence and optimism" (p. 121). The low point of Zionism, reached in 1973, was experienced not in terms of economic hardship but in terms of the loss of hope about the future.

Many years later, Israelis still speak of the 1973 War as the one event that pushed them over the edge of their ability to feel any security in the world around them. The illusion of Israeli invincibility and invulnerability was shattered in one decisive minute. What used to be taken for granted has now become ephemeral and shaky. Reality had to be tested again and its limits set anew. In social science literature, crisis is often defined as an event that has the "connotation of potential disruption of existing social structure" (Stallings, 1972, p. 314). In the case of Israeli since 1973, the threat is not of disruption but of termination, finality. In Israel since 1973, the term "Yom Kippur," which used to denote the holiest day in the Jewish calendar, has gained the connotation of a major disaster. The *intifada*, the Palestinian uprising which started in 1987, is now referred to as "another "Yom Kippur."

An Israeli psychoanalyst (Moses, 1983) describes the consequences of the 1967 war as "an inflation of the national ego, a narcissistic overevaluation, a tendency to believe in our omnipotence vis-à-vis our neighbors and enemies . . . an arrogant and superior attitude, a belief in an omnipotence that did not allow for the idea of a successful thrust by the enemy; therefore the threat did not exist." However, "after the Yom Kippur War came a deflation, a depression not only in response to the death of near and dear ones, but also because of the required change in self-image" (p. 125).

> The inflated balloon of Israeli grandiosity was painfully and saddeningly punctured. As in the Six-Day War, there was utter surprise, although quite a different one. . . . The depressive reaction that set it was only partially in reaction to the loss of life, the injuries, and the number of soldiers taken prisoner. It was more a response to the seemingly incredible fact that the Israeli Army could have been taken by surprise and overwhelmed, that the Barlev line, though impregnable, could have been broken, and that in this way the narcissistic grandiosity and omnipotence of the Israeli army, and therefore of the state, shared so widely by many of its citizens, was painfully shattered and suddenly deflated. Feelings of grandiosity and of omnipotence were replaced by those of vulnerability, helplessness, shame and humiliation. (p. 131)

We do not have to share the writer's psychoanalytic terminology to appreciate the dramatic changes he has described.

The events of 1973 and since in Israeli history have been nothing short of cataclysmic in their practical and psychological consequences.

> There are disasters that happen once and cover the world's light and darken everything, and later, the world turns slowly and comes out, and the pain moves away slightly, and loosens, and the light hesitatingly renewed, and we try to go on. And there are disasters that come once and then never leave. The world no longer turns, the light does not return, and the new morning cannot come out.

This is how Israel's greatest writer has described the effect of the 1973 War (Yizhar, 1975, p. 14). And indeed, for Israelis it has become the disaster that has not left them.

> The Yom Kippur War landed on the State of Israel like an all shattering earthquake. Even today, ten years later, there is no measure of the wounds it opened; and still nobody knows how many of the wounds, supposedly healed, still fester below the surface. One thing is universally accepted: the earthquake of the Yom Kippur War shook up this people, this state, so strongly, that even after the quake ended, even after a military victory was snatched from the throes of defeat, at a terrible price, the country has changed thoroughly, and Israel has not returned to what it formerly was. Possibly the bluntest change following the War is the loss of faith; unhesitating faith in the political and military leadership, that could not see the signs of the approaching quake; the automatic faith in the superiority of the Israel Defense Forces, that this time, only once since 1948, did not win a final, total victory; and above all the faith in the future, the vision that the State of Israel is the safe haven for the Jewish people, and the solution to the "Jewish problem". (Golan, 1983, p. 2)

That is how one Israel journalist saw the outcome of the events of October 1973.

Since the hour of 2:00 P.M. on October 6, 1973, Zionism has been facing its long hour of truth in an encounter with history that it wished very much to escape. Until that hour, Zionism was an amazing success story. Since then it has been coping with late twentieth-century history, in which its survival is very much in question.

> Until 1973 it seemed that Israel's survival was guaranteed. The first three days of battle in 1973 showed this assumption to be fragile. Accepting this reality was hard. . . . It was joined by the shock of the casualties and the reduced self-confidence of the leadership, and the nation descended into a collective depression. . . . The leadership, which saw itself charged with the fate of the people, found out that it committed a terrible mistake, that led the nation to the edge of the precipice. (Shapira, 1983, p. 17)

There was little need for finding a moral justification for Zionism while triumphant, and there was an urgent need for justifying and sustaining it when it was clearly on its way to defeat after 1973. Justifying the sacrifices became more of an issue with the apparent failure. The problem of the legitimation of Zionism and Zionists have been desperately casting about for sources of support and justification. The ideological problem, for most Israelis has been one of finding justification for the Zionist past and finding hope for the Zionist future, if one wants to go on with the Zionist enterprise, or finding an alternative source of meaning, if one does not choose that. "Where can we find the faith in the justice of our enterprise as individuals, as a society, as a nation, as children of that nation here?" writes a leading Israel poet in a letter to friends who lost their son in the war (Guri, 1974, p. 122). While the losses in the 1948–49 war amounted to almost 5700 dead (out of a population of 650,000), and the losses in the 1973 War to almost 2700 (out of a population of 3,000,000) the reaction in 1973 was much stronger. In 1948 the bereavement was muted by the recognition that the Zionist dream was being realized, that Zionism was seeing its hour of triumph, and that the sacrifice was worth it.

The trauma of the 1973 War and the doubts about Israel's future are expressed by Halkin (1977), who states that the war has given the country "a glimpse of its own mortality." The continuing Palestinian resistance after the war, expressed in terrorism, is also acknowledged by Halkin as raising doubts about Israel's future.

> [The 1973 War] shook Israel from its foundations to the very summit. A deep lack of confidence suddenly replaced the exaggerated arrogance, and was most noticeable among leaders and senior officers. Questions that had been perpetually pushed off at a tangent, resurfaced. Will we always live by our swords? Can we withstand more wars, when the gap is ever widening to the Arab benefit? . . . The war exposed the full hopelessness of Israeli leadership. (Schiff, 1974, p. 299)

Liebman and Don-Yehiya (1984) described the effects of the 1973 War in terms of "the decline of national morale, the sense of disintegration of Israel as a moral community" (p. 133).

Collective trauma is a "blow to the tissues of social life that damage the bonds attaching people together" (Erikson, 1979, p. 110). The effect of the collective trauma on individuals is in their feeling alone and lost in the world, having to cope with the calamity by themselves.

What has characterized Israeli subjective reactions to the crisis of Zionism has been the feeling of victimization. This experience shatters some primary operating assumptions that people use to construct the framework of their lives. These include a belief in personal invulnerability, and the perception that the world has order, meaning, and predictability (Janoff-Bulman, 1985). The threats to the survival of Israel are not just ideological. There are real and tangible dangers, given the continuing state of siege by Israel's implacable enemies. Continuing to fight in a permanent war requires faith in eventual victory, or at least survival. Such a shattering blow to optimism and self-confidence, as was dealt Israel by the 1973 War, can be mended by a strong faith, and the basis for such a faith did not seem to be available in reality. The 1967 War seemed to many Israelis a decisive victory that has changed the course of their history. It was to be the last war, since Israeli superiority could not be challenged. Israelis had, after 1967, everything they wanted. Their survival was not in doubt, their living standards were rising rapidly, and they could look forward to a future of security and prosperity. Their enemies may not have recognized their legitimacy, but there was nothing they could do about it. The future belonged to Israel. The air-raid sirens heard by everyone in Israel at 2:00 P.M. on Saturday, October 6, 1973, shattered this dream. In the wake of the war, the search for sources of faith started.

The worst thing about the 1973 catastrophe is that it left in its wake the feeling that it may happen more than once. That is the most threatening aspect of life in Israel after 1973. If it happened once, it may happen again, and it may be even worse than in 1973. What Israelis have realized after the 1973 War were two discouraging realities. First, the 1967 War was not the last war in the Middle East. Second, the 1973 War was not going to be the last one, either. Trauma affects both memory and future expectations, and that is what happened for Israel since 1973.

What sort of visions have Israelis had for their future? If after 1967 there were visions of total triumph and redemption, after 1973 the visions became apocalyptic with prophecies of total destruction. The 1973 War left many Israelis, perhaps because of their naive understanding of its causes, with a feeling of helplessness. They felt that this heavy blow dealt them had no justification or reason. It was again blind fate, and many felt that it was "Jewish destiny," acting against them and casting them again in the role of helpless victims. This created a marked readiness to identify with Jewishness and Jewish history. Some Israelis expressed the idea that they were not that different from their ancestors.

The years 1974–80 saw a real increase in the number of armed attacks by Palestinians against Israeli citizens. In 1974 alone, sixty-two civilians were killed in such attacks, the highest number ever. In the years 1974–80, 203 civilians were killed in such attacks. The October 1973 War was followed by an internal political crisis, by a change in government in 1977, by an increasing economic crisis, by the disastrous Lebanon invasion of 1982–85, and the *intifada*. "As if a man did flee from a lion, and a bear met him; or went into the house, and leaned his hand on the wall, and a serpent bit him" (Amos 5:19). The words of an Old Testament prophet seem to match the subjective feelings of many Israelis. Israel has been losing its self-confidence as one crisis led to another and every attempt at solution seemed to be making things worse. Gabriel Warburg, a professor at the University of Haifa, expressed his feelings in regard to Israel's situation thus: "For several years I have been living with a growing realization of a total failure; the failure of the State of Israel, of Zionism, of the path I have followed, and I have inspired others to follow. In such a state, despite my lack of illusions about being able to change the reality, the feeling of failure, when you do nothing to prevent it, is horrible" (1983, p. 66). The Israeli mood since 1973, more so since the Lebanon war of 1982–85, and even more so since the start of the Palestinian uprising in 1987, is one of fatigue and frustration.

What has happened in Israeli culture since 1973 has been a sea change, turning established ways upside down as the society was losing its bearing and its confidence in the face of mounting dangers to its survival. The end of identification with collective goals and meanings leads to the privatization of significance, which can be defined and experienced only within the self. The 1973 War was mentioned spontaneously by many of the saved as the starting point for their search. It has been mentioned as well by those interviewed in other studies (cf. Aviad, 1983).

Two examples of how the appearance of salvation movements followed by the 1973 earthquake are those of transcendental meditation (TM) and Scientology. TM was introduced to Israel in 1972 and drew only a few takers. The October 1973 War officially ended on October 23. In the weeks that followed, TM training centers opened all over the country, and in the months that followed there were thousands of satisfied customers. Scientology showed a different course of development. It was introduced to Israel in the early 1960s but only drew a handful of adherents. In 1970 there was an attempt by Yehoshafat Givon to recruit more, with no success. Despite some favorable publicity, which Givon engineered, the group remained small. In 1975 the Tel-Aviv Scientology Center was operating in offices that took a entire floor of an apartment building and later in 1977 moved to more spacious premises.

Stress and Its Consequences

The terminology of stress, originally coined in medical research (Selye, 1956) is a useful analogy in describing both social and individual processes. The stress model is a useful metaphor, moving from the body physic to the body politic. When stressors affect the social system, they bring about both social and individual reactions. A common term used in connection with the prevalence of stress is "social pathology." This is another useful metaphor, connecting the individual and the social. The language of social pathology represents a view of crime, deviance, and aggression as symptoms of "sickness" in a social system, possibly caused by social stress. Selye's stress theory has several important implications for the historical situation we are discussing here. According to the theory, stress reactions are additive. A reaction to any specific threat may be added to earlier reactions to earlier threats. Then, the damage caused by stress reactions accumulates over time. Finally, accumulated stress reaches a point of overwhelming the individual and causes severe pathology. It does not take much imagination to see how these claims may apply directly to the individual and collective experiences of Israelis over the last few decades.

After the individual has experienced, directly and indirectly, a succession of traumatic events, he may reach a point of being ready for new traumas without any feeling of being able to control events: "learned helplessness." The experience of traumatic stress, even if it does not lead to a feeling of helplessness, may lead to serious impairments. All possible sources of stress pale before the prospect of war, and the prospect of permanent war has been the lot of Israelis for the past four decades. The stress of life, as most Israelis experience it, includes feelings of a permanent threat, which is a threat to life, to familiar routines, and in general, to all aspects of life.

Any observer of Israel's history will conclude that the Israeli population has lived under conditions of extreme and prolonged stress (Breznitz, 1980, 1983). Freedman and coworkers (1975) and Kutash and Schlesinger (1980) in their overviews of the effects of prolonged and repeated stress, suggest that the following consequences can be expected: anxiety, tension, depression, psychosomatic illnesses, suicide ideation or attempts, marital problems and divorce, alcohol dependence, and violence. It is possible to show that these indications of prolonged stress have indeed appeared, as predicted, in Israeli society (Landau and Beit-Hallahmi, 1983). "The strength of groups, organizations, and even nations lies partly in people's sense of collective efficacy that they can solve their problems and improve their lives through concerted effort. Perceived collective efficacy will influence what people choose to do as a group, how much effort they put into it, and their staying power when group efforts fail to produce results" (Bandura, 1982, p. 143). If we adopt for the moment Bandura's concept of self-efficacy, it is clear that Israelis have lost their sense of collective efficacy over the past twenty years. Comparative surveys of Israelis and Americans found the former to perceive their environment as more threatening (Butcher and Gur, 1974; Butcher and Pancheri, 1976) and to be more fearful of physical harm (Goldberg, et al., 1975a and 1975b).

Disaster Syndrome

The concept of a "disaster syndrome" has appeared in the literature since the 1950s (Barton, 1970; Perry and Lindell, 1978; Wallace, 1956). The disaster syndrome, as described by Wallace (1956), grows out of the perception that "the entire visible community is in ruins . . . consciously or unconsciously interpreted as a destruction of the whole word." The individual "has been in effect, castrated, rendered impotent, separated from all sources of support, and left naked and alone, without a sense of his own identity, in a terrifying wilderness of ruins" (p. 127). It is plausible to assume that a large proportion of the Israeli population was suffering from a disaster syndrome after the 1973 War. The relevant comparisons seem to be a population hit by a tornado (cf. Fritz and Marks, 1954) or to the United States population immediately after the assassination of President John F. Kennedy in 1963 (cf. Sheatsley and Feldman, 1964).

For Israelis who lived through it, the 1973 War was an end of the world, and an end of an era. Psychologically, many were left as naked and as helpless as any victim of the disaster syndrome. Disasters have been found to lead to increases in mortality, psychosomatic diseases, mental health problems, physical symptoms, hospital admissions, and drug use (Raphael, 1986), but what is clear from experience in large and small disasters is that the vast majority of individuals do not suffer any serious problems, and only 10 percent of the victims develop significant symptoms (Kinston and Rosser, 1974). In a collective crisis situation, such as the aftermath of a natural disaster, the vast majority of individuals function realistically without any visible symptoms. A small minority react with stress-related symptoms, and an even smaller minority express a total psychological and/or physical collapse. Even in a severe crisis situation, most individuals do not panic, and the social reaction is not a total anomie. Many individuals react with realistic or fatalistic resignation.

What we have learned from research on disaster situations is that those who respond to stress by developing symptoms are individuals who have been the weakest and most vulnerable to begin with. We are using here the disaster concept as a metaphor, since only a small number of Israelis have been direct victims of combat experiences. Much larger numbers, possibly a majority, have experienced the loss of friends and relatives. Since 1948, almost 20,000 young Israelis have died in uniform, and about 100,000 have been injured. About 1 percent of the population are permanently handicapped because of war injuries. This means that the direct effects of war are known to most Israelis, but the wider effects of the 1973 catastrophe are recognized by all. Of course, a disaster without warning is likely to have more serious effects (Miletti et al., 1975; Erikson, 1976; Bolin, 1982), and such was the 1973 War. But "an anticipated disaster is a contradiction in terms. Without the element of surprise, defenses both material and psychological, may be erected. Much of the force of a disaster comes from the sudden manner in which it assaults unprepared societies, institutions, and psyches" (Barkun 1974, p. 57).

After the upheaval of 1973, changes in Israeli society have been both quantitative and qualitative. The accumulation of quantitative changes has led to a new level of stress and struggle. There is always a sense of impending doom, of a gathering storm. Following the initial trauma and the continuing crisis, many Israelis have lost their faith, which in this case means the loss of the will to fight on. The term *disaster* usually refers to describe a brief, climatic eruption that causes much damage and suffering within a short time. The aftermath of the disaster brings relief from suffering. Events in Israeli since October 1973 do not follow this pattern. There was first a disaster and a trauma, but then there was only mild relief. A period of continuing crisis was beginning.

Antonosky's theory of stress, based on the notion of coping resources, can be used to explain the increasing level of symptomatology in Israel. What was lost in the continuing crisis was the sense of coherence (see Antonovsky, 1980), the feeling that there is an underlying order in the world and events in it. The basic belief in a coherent world leads to a sense of control. Without coherence and control, coping becomes ineffective and pathology appears.

Thanatos and the Israeli Dream

I have dead people under the tables,
Lots of dead people under the tables,
and under the chairs, and beds, and dressers
The whole house filled with dead

> And I have in store dead for winter
> And a supply of dead for next year
> And in the long run I have some dead still living
> I am building on the dead, building with the dead,
> I eat the dead, breath the dead,
> Dead, dead, dead
> —Levin, 1975, pp. 82–83

Death in war has become an integral part of life in Israel. The consequences of this horrifying situation cannot be positive in any way imaginable. Encountering death firsthand through war or encountering death through the loss of relatives, friends, and acquaintances is quite common among young and not so young Israelis. "The public is tired of wars, tired of the endless bloodshed in which grandfathers who fought in the 1948 war find themselves walking behind the coffins of their soldier grandsons" (Marcus, 1985, p. 7).

Israelis have become regular contributors to the developing science of thanatology. The voluminous literature on death and dying, in addition to scores of symposia and conferences, following the 1973 War, including literature written by the bereaved (e.g., Zorea, 1975), reflects not only natural mourning but a wider preoccupation with the mortality of Israel itself (Klingman, 1980 and 1983; Florian and Har-Even, 1983; Florian and Kravetz, 1985; Rosenheim and Muchnik, 1985; Barinbaum, 1980; Florian et al., 1984; Smilansky, 1977).

The professional literature on mourning and the treatment of people during the mourning process in Israel grew by leaps and bounds after 1973. We can point to scores of articles written by members of the helping professions and published in professional and academic journals (e.g., Givon, 1974; Schindler, 1975; Golan, 1975; Kaffman and Elizur, 1979; Amir and Sharon, 1977; Palgi, 1973; Morawetz, 1982; Purisman and Maoz, 1977; Smilansky and Weisman, 1978).

Israel is not only a world leader in research on death awareness. As it turns out, this research has shown that Israeli children lead the world in their awareness of death. A tragic and chilling finding has proven that children in Israel are ahead of children in other countries in their correct and adult-like conceptualization of what death is. Smilansky (1980) found that Israeli children were the most advanced in the world in their mature conception of death. While children in other parts of the world realize the finality and irreversibility of death around the age of ten, in Israel such an awareness may be found in children of five (cf. Koocher, 1973). Moreover, Israeli kindergarten children know more about human death than about the death of animals. This is an amazing finding, contrary to everything that we know about children all over the world. One should expect children to know more about death in animals, something that can be readily observed in pets, and that is indeed what happens with children everywhere in the world, that is, everywhere except Israel. Another big difference between Israeli children and other children has been the paucity of erroneous explanations about death reported by Israeli children as compared with their peers abroad. So the finding is that Israeli children age four to six reach the level of death awareness typical of children age ten in other countries! This is a grim world record.

The professionalization of mourning and the increasing role of the helping professions with it reflect the severity of the crisis. Normal support systems were collapsing under the strain. Hundreds of workshops and courses were being offered between 1973 and 1977, all dealing with mourning, crisis, and stress. Scores of books and academic theses were written, and Israel became a world leader in research on loss, grief, coping, traumatic stress (see Jaffe and Rosenfeld, 1982; Levav et al., 1979; Milgram, 1986; Salomon et al., 1986).

An interesting piece of evidence, which supports the view of the 1973 as a "natural disaster" (from the point of view of many Israelis), is the high rate of psychiatric casualties in that war. The phenomenon of battle fatigue, "shell shock," or "psychiatric casualties," i.e., soldiers whose personality collapses in combat, was almost unknown in the Israel Defense Forces before 1973. When it became known in October 1973, it was in the form of massive numbers. The surprise of the war and the shock of the first days, with successful Egyptian and Syrian offensives, meant a world turned upside down, and soldiers fell apart under the strain (see Levav et al., 1979).

Estimates of psychiatric casualties during the 1973 War range as high as forty or fifty psychiatric casualties for every 100 physical ones (Shipler, 1983). Psychiatric casualties, almost unheard of before 1973, have been discussed openly since then, as the numbers of soldiers thus affected could not be ignored. New treatment techniques for psychiatric casualties and new successes with such techniques have been reported over the years (Gal, 1986; Soliman, 1979; Yalov, 1984).

One consequence of the 1973 War was the creation of a department of mental health within the Israel Defense Forces General Staff as a result of the high rate of psychiatric casualties (Dreman, 1981; Greenbaum et al., 1977). The growing use of behavioral sciences and mental health professionals in the Israel Defense Forces since 1973 reflects a decline in the morale of the military and the nation, since in Israel participation in the armed forces is universal. In 1948, 1956, and

1967, there were no "mental health officers" in the Israel Defense Forces, and their absence was not noticed.

Crisis and Collective Mourning

Using psychoanalytic parlance, the 1973 War was a severe narcissistic injury, but the blow was not just unconscious. It had to do with the very real question of Israel's future survival. The first casualty of the 1973 catastrophe was the collective sense of invulnerability and invincibility. Also damaged was the sense of coherence and meaning, since to many Israelis the events of October 1973 were simply incomprehensible, a volcanic eruption that hit them and was as unpredictable as any natural disaster. One can speak of a collective process of bereavement, with Israelis mourning over the loss of their dream, their confidence and pride.

Since 1973, Israel has been in the throes of a collective mourning process, which for some meant withdrawal and despair, and for others, attempts at revitalization. Mourning reactions include the images of a lost past and feelings of dejection and emptiness, loneliness, and panic (Parkes, 1973). The first stages of mourning consist of shock and denial. Then the new reality can no longer be denied. Anger and depression follow. Just like an individual in the early stages of shock, Israelis reacted by trying to wake up from a nightmare, only to discover that they are not asleep (Lindemann, 1965). What they had to mourn was the loss of their exaggerated feelings of invincibility and superiority, and they had to rebuild their perceptions of reality (Parkes, 1973).

We can accept sacrifices and hardships when we believe that they will be followed by a better future, or that they serve a higher or transcendent cause. We cannot accept them when we see them as senseless and we believe that the future will bring only more of the same. The great sacrifices by Israelis in the 1948 War were accepted with serenity and confidence because the war meant victory and achievement. The actual cost of Zionism has been mounting. Hope for the future has been declining. Can Zionism survive? Can it provide Israelis with a reasonable and liveable future? Those were the questions that led to the crisis of faith after 1973.

In historical cases of severe crisis, a variety of individual and collective responses. Table 5.1 presents response options along the poles of constructive-destructive and collective-private. The focus of this book is on private-constructive options, but we should briefly discuss other options as well.

Table 5.1. Reactions to Social Crisis

	CONSTRUCTIVE	DESTRUCTIVE
Collective	Revitalization movements	Emigration
Private	Private salvation	Suicide

The roads to private salvation described have been followed only by a minority of Israelis. The majority has coped with the crisis by carrying on despite anxieties and difficulties. A growing minority has left the country, and another growing minority has opted for self-destructive behaviors, mainly chemical dependencies and violence.

Self-Destructive Reactions to the Crisis

While Israel has experienced an epidemic of happiness found through self-constructive private salvation, this was paralleled by an epidemic of self-destruction. In this section we will look at some of the evidence. I am going to cover here measures of what is broadly known as "social pathology," i.e., aggregated deviant acts by individuals. There is a unique Israeli pattern of reactions to stress, reflected in stress related diseases and in self-destructive behaviors. I will present evidence indicating that all of these predicted increases in social pathology have appeared in Israel since 1973. Let us recall that Israel is a country with only 4.5 million inhabitants, and we have to see social pathology within this context. Problems are much smaller in absolute numbers, and in even relative rates, compared with most Western countries.

If stress leads to interpersonal aggression, then we should expect an increase in the rates of violence in Israel since 1973. And indeed, official statistics indicate a significant rise in the rate of homicide and attempted homicide (from 3.9 per 100,000 in 1974 to 5.7 per 100,000 in 1980) and robbery (from 6.5 per 100,000 in 1974 to 15.3 per 100,000 in 1980). There is also a significant rise in overall criminal activity (from 42 offenses per 1000 population in 1974 to 63 per 1000 in 1980) (Landau, 1984). It should be pointed out, however, that while overall rates of interpersonal violence in Israel are much lower than similar rates in the United States, they are higher than those of Western Europe.

While rates of violent crimes in Israel are still lower than those in the United States or Canada (and higher than those in Holland, Belgium, Norway, and Denmark), those rates have grown dramatically since 1973. Between 1973 and 1983, rates of attempted murder have gone up 230 percent and rate of other violent offenses (e.g., assault, rape, or armed robbery) have gone up by 50 percent (Landau and Beit-Hallahmi, 1983). What is significant about violence in Israel after 1973 is not its absolute rates, which may still be low in comparison to other countries, but its historical growth.

Between 1969 and 1985, the number of firearms permits issued by the Israeli Interior Ministry has grown from 38,000 to 188,000, and this happened after 70 percent of applicants have been rejected, i.e., the desire to obtain firearms was much greater, and about 600,000 have applied for permits. It is easy to suggest that many of those who have been refused hold firearms illegally. The increase in demand for firearms can be attributed to an increased fear of crime together with the fear of violent attacks by Palestinians (Landau and Beit-Hallahmi, 1983). By 1988, there were more than 200,000 firearm permits, and the number was growing at the rate of 1000 per month.

Chemical Dependencies

One common reaction to stress conditions is the appearance of addictive disorders (Miller, 1980). Tobacco use, alcoholism, and dependence on narcotics and tranquilizers all indicate that a population is seeking relief of stress and pain through the use of psychoactive drugs (Levison et al., 1983). The use of hallucinogens has never been prevalent in Israel, and even the use of cannabis (hashish or marijuana) has been less common than in the United States. Israel holds the world record in the consumption of minor tranquilizers, such as chlordiazepoxide (Librium) and diazepam (Valium). There is in Israel a subculture of heroin users, made up of members of the underclass of poverty and crime. The Shimron report on organized crime in Israel (1976) stated that the number of addicts to hard drugs was 4000. Still, the use of psychoactive drugs in Israel is much more limited in Israel than in the United States. Only in the use of tranquilizers and nicotine can Israelis be said to surpass Americans.

The consumption of nicotine and caffeine in Israel is significant and widespread. One can encounter many references to drug abuse on addiction in the Israeli media and in private discussions, but the references are exclusively to hashish or heroin. Alcohol or nicotine are not mentioned in this context. Most Israelis regard cigarette smoking as a normal and necessary activity, much like eating, and there are no signs that concerns about its health effects have had any impact in Israel. Moreover, there are indications that Israel is the only first-world country where cigarette smoking among the young is on the increase. A survey conducted by the Health Ministry in 1985 showed that 30 percent of Israelis between the ages of eighteen and twenty-one are addicted to cigarettes (Ben-Shaul, 1985).

There has been an extraordinary change in the use patterns of illegal hard drugs in Israel since 1973. While until 1975 the illegal drug market in Israel was exclusively dominated by hashish, a nonaddictive, or soft, drug, after 1976 the market has been transformed. According to official police records, heroin was first captured by Israeli police in 1976 and cocaine in 1977. On the basis of court files, it can be determined that by 1988, the market was dominated by heroin, and the number of consumers has grown significantly. In 1970, there was not a single case filed for the sale of illegal drugs; in 1974, there were six cases, and in 1975, 106. By 1987, the number was 1887. Data from the Israel General Security Services, the body charged with providing security clearances for top positions in intelligence units, showed that a majority of candidates for these positions, all of them individuals with outstanding military service records representing the Israeli elite, had used illegal drugs by 1988. In 1974, the first volunteer organization against drug abuse was formed, and in 1988, the Knesset passed a law creating a government authority for "the war on drugs." All the data quoted above have been supplied by this government body.

Rahav and colleagues (1985), who reviewed twelve surveys on drug use among Israeli high school students between 1971 and 1982, report on the increasing use of all drugs, from nicotine to opiates, over the years. In a survey of 1899 Israeli adolescents, done in 1982, it was found that drug use was more common among those coming from a higher socioeconomic background. This finding, contrary to most of the literature and common wisdom about deviance, shows that increasing drug use is a symptom not of poverty and low status but of growing up into the elite, which is being subjected to more and more stress.

Alcoholism turned out to be the most serious, and, historically, the most startling, problem. The whole cultural complex surrounding alcohol use and its effects, which is so much a part of Western culture (Critchlow, 1986) had been totally absent from Israeli culture. In the summer of 1975, I met with some experts on the study of alcoholism in the United States. I told them that in Israel they had a chance to study in vivo the development of alcohol abuse and alcoholism where none had existed before. I predicted that within ten years there would be a serious alcohol problem in Israel, and that is what has happened.

According to Health Ministry data, alcohol consumption in

Israel has doubled between 1969 and 1979. Data on annual changes in shopping habits are also instructive. In 1983, for example, liquor sales went up by 24 percent and wine sales by 22 percent (Cohen, 1983).

Whether we use the term "heavy drinker," "problem drinker," or "alcoholic," it is clear that the phenomenon of excessive alcohol use, which was virtually unknown in Israel until the late 1970s, has become a part of daily life. The prevalence of alcohol use and problem drinking has led one kibbutz to a decision to expel any member suffering from alcoholism who refuses treatment (Tenne, 1986).

The phenomenon of drunk driving, which used to be totally unknown in Israel, started appearing in police records in the late 1970s. In April 1983, the new situation was reflected for the first time in a legal regulation that defined drunkeness as having a concentration of 0.05 percent alcohol in the blood. By 1986, numerous traffic fatalities were attributable to drunk driving (Yudilovich, 1986). Blood alcohol levels were found to exceed the legal limit in 14 percent of the drivers and 13.4 percent of the pedestrians killed in road accidents from 1976 to 1980 (Siegel-Izkovich, 1984). In November 1986, the police were authorized to revoke a driver's license for thirty days, if a person was caught driving while intoxicated. This new regulation reflected the growing frequency of such cases.

By 1984 there was already an Alcoholism Division in the Welfare Ministry, which ran ten outpatient rehabilitation centers, and one inpatient treatment center. The head of the Alcoholism Division reported 12,000 alcoholics registered with it, and estimated that 2 percent of the population had a serious drinking problem (see Rudge, 1984). As of 1986, there were eleven outpatient clinics and one residential facility for the treatment of alcoholism in Israel. The residential treatment center, which was opened in December 1982, admitted 392 alcoholics since March 1986. The outpatient clinics had 457 new contacts between April 1985 and March 1986. The numbers may seem minuscule by foreign standards, but they indicate that alcoholism has become a part of life in Israel. Alcoholics Anonymous (AA) was started in Israel in 1975, imported by an immigrant from the United States. By 1985 there were branches in all major cities, and while the foreign flavor is still there, most members are Israeli-born (Rebibo, 1985). In 1986, a special program for the prevention of alcoholism became part of the official high school curriculum in Israel. By 1987, there was already a 24-hour emergency telephone service provided by the Association Against Alcoholism.

Drunkeness as a result of beer drinking led the Israel Defense Forces to ban sales of beer in military canteens in 1985. This was the end of a tradition started in 1948, when beer was sold freely in military units, but drunkenness was unknown (Oked, 1985). A survey of the adult Israeli population in March 1983 showed that 2 percent of the respondents could be defined as alcoholics by their own admission, 3 percent reported getting drunk at least once during the past month, 10 percent reported getting drunk more than once during the previous year, and 6 percent reported drinking more than twice a week. According to the Welfare and Labor Minister, Moshe Katsav, 6 percent of the Israeli population was addicted to alcohol as of 1984 (Fidel, 1984). By 1988, the problem of alcohol dependency and its attendant consequences and expenses seemed so serious that the Labor and Welfare Minister, Mr. Katzav, proposed levying a special tax of 1 percent on all alcoholic beverages. In explaining this proposal, Mr. Katzav mentioned that 4000 alcoholics were being treated by his ministry, creating a heavy financial burden (Tomer, 1988).

One clear measure of alcohol problems is death from alcohol overdoses, which usually occurs among alcoholics. In 1973, there were thirty-one such cases in Israel. In 1982, the number was seventy-five. There were two cases of death from drug overdoses in 1975, and forty-nine in 1982 (Namir, 1983). There were seventy-six cases of first hospitalization for alcoholism in 1966, and 144 such cases in 1975. The number of recurring hospitalizations was seventy-eight in 1966 and 262 in 1975 (Falik, 1977). The increase in new cases was 100 percent, while the population increase was only 20 percent.

Ideological Responses and Personal Salvation

Most of the responses to the 1973 shock were naturally political and almost as radical as the salvation movements. Public opinion polls show the sharpest jump ever in political discontent in Israel measured between 1973 and 1974 (Wolfsfeld, 1988). This wave of discontent peaked in 1977, when the ruling party lost an election for the first time in twenty-nine years. Before the 1970s, the term *right* was in itself quite stigmatized in Israel. The main issue of political divisions in Israel is the stance toward the Palestinian Arabs. While some on the left in Israel are ready to grant certain Palestinian rights (though in most cases not equality), those on the right solidly deny any such rights. The right wing nationalist position has been on the ascendant since 1973, as it has become clear that any left wing position means ceding some power and privileges to the Arabs. Most Israelis are simply not ready to countenance a real change in their privileged position vis-à-vis the native Palestinians.

The main change in Israeli political discourse regarding the right-left continuum has been that the term *right wing* has lost its negative connotations, and right wingers themselves use it, while formerly it was a term of opprobrium, used only by the left. At the same time, the term *left wing* has become a stigma, and it is used mostly as a way of designating those who are less than fervently nationalistic. To most Israelis, the term *leftist* has come to denote those who collaborate with the enemy, since leftists recognize Palestinian rights. (Right-wingers in Israel are not opposed to the welfare state. Some of them are declared socialists who at the same time are extreme nationalists.)

In 1949, the second largest party in the Knesset was Mapam (nineteen delegates), whose platform committed it to Marxism and whose rhetoric committed it to Stalinism. Mapam leaders referred to the U.S.S.R. as "the second homeland" and in 1953 mourned Stalin as "the father of nations, the rising sun." Recalling these facts makes it easier to appreciate the sea change in Israeli politics since then. The historical drift to the right started in 1967 and can best be illustrated through left-leaning intellectuals and writers, who since 1967, and especially since 1973, have espoused right-wing nationalism. Naomi Frenkel is a case in point. She is a best-selling Israeli novelist who was for many years a member of a Socialist-Zionist kibbutz. In 1983 she moved to Hebron in the occupied West Bank to join nationalist settlers there. Of the 1973 War she says, "The future will prove that this war became an historical trauma. During the war I experienced a psychological and spiritual revolution, which has created a barrier between me and others" (quoted in Omer, 1984, p. 22).

In 1962, a survey of political attitudes classified only 18.5 percent of Israelis as rightists, 32.1 percent were classified as clearly leftists, 16.1 percent were nonideological, and 23.4 percent were centrists (Antonovsky and Arian, 1972). The political change toward a conscious identification with right-wing ideology was reflected in the results of a survey of a representative sample of the Jewish adult urban population (n = 1088). The respondents were asked to rate the "ideal political party" for Israel on seven-point scale. When asked to rate it on the dimension of right/left, 55 percent of the respondents were three points to the right, and only 13 percent were three points to the left end; 32 percent were in the middle (Arian, 1983). A public opinion poll in 1985 showed that 45.4 percent of the respondents identified themselves as close to the right, while 28.4 percent said they were close to the left, and 24.0 percent could not define their position (Haaretz, 1985).

"The Six-Day War (1967) started a debate on the goals of Zionism, but the Yom Kippur War (1973) and the feeling that the whole Zionist enterprise is in danger shook up the consensus on which the political system was based. . . . The process of disintegration of the major political parties as coordinating agents in Israeli politics reached a climax following the 1973 War" (Galnoor, 1977, p. 23). That is how an Israeli political scientist described the major political change after 1973. The 1977 elections were a belated political reaction to the events of 1973. While in the 1973 elections the Labor Alignment still managed to get 39 percent of the votes, the continuing crisis led to its getting only 24.6 percent in 1977, in what has been called an "earthquake" in Israeli politics (Peretz, 1977). As Reich (1985) suggests, the 1984 general election results reflect a continuing shift to the right in the Israeli electorate as a whole "many of the forces set in motion by the Yom Kippur War and its aftermath seemed to coalesce to affect the situation in a tangible way when Israel's electorate went to the polls in May 1977" (Reich, 1985, p. 142). This was the real political earthquake which followed the earthquake of the 1973 War. It removed once and for all the historical leadership that had ran the state since 1948 and the Zionist movement before that time.

The most significant political change since 1973 has been a generational one. The move to the right in terms of political self-labeling and in terms of actual beliefs has been most noticeable among young Israelis. Israelis under the age of thirty have been leaning rather heavily to the right, while older ones have been more moderate. Such generational trends can be assessed in Israel by looking at votes in the military. All Israeli men between the ages of eighteen and twenty-one are in military service, and they vote in general elections during the service. The record of votes since 1977 shows a solid support for right-wing nationalist parties in such elections. Polls among high school students show an even stronger trend. In the 1981 and 1984 elections, both preelection and postelection polls showed that younger Israelis supported right-wing ideologies much more than older ones. The results of the 1984 general election showed right-wing parties gaining significantly among soldiers age eighteen to twenty-one.

Following the 1973 War there was a flurry of attempts at political revitalization with many new groups being started, usually without much success (Etzioni-Halevy, 1977). Various movements reached an embryonic stage soon after the war ended. In February 1974, several reserve officers, recently released after several months of active military service beginning October 6, 1973, started demonstrating against the government and the policies that led to the fiasco. This protest movement kept growing until the resignation of the government headed by Golda Meir. The year 1974 saw many spontaneous demonstrations and the formation of several political groupings. The most successful and best-known group started in the wake of the war was Gush Emunim, a nationalist group made up of mostly Orthodox (but not very Orthodox) individuals (Newman, 1985). Gush Emunim has become a Zionist revitalization movement, carrying out the Zionist vision of settling the land and taking it over from the natives. It has become the Zionist elite of the 1970s and the 1980s carrying the mantle of the left-wing settlers of the 1930s. Lehman-Wilzig (1981) has shown that the frequency of political protest in Israel in 1979 was five times greater than it was in 1960.

The reaction of Israelis to the crisis of their society after 1973 can be analyzed according to the model proposed by Hirschman (1970), which proposes three options for dealing with decline in organizations on the part of members or customers:

1. Exit, that is leaving the organization.
2. Voice, that is "any attempt at all to change, rather than escape from, an objectionable state of affairs . . . through various types of actions and protests" (p. 30).
3. Loyalty, that is, staying with the organization, despite its problems and possibly using Voice to improve it.

While it is clear that most Israelis have displayed Loyalty, a significant minority have chosen Exit, or has expressed Voice in a radical way. In addition to emigration, which has risen significantly after 1973 (see Sobel, 1986), some of the salvation movements can be classified as psychological, if not physical, Exit. Rejecting Jewish identity via the new religions or rejecting Zionism via extreme Judaization are clear Exit options. Rejecting any collective involvement via the psychotherapy subculture or the occult is also a form of Exit. In literary Hebrew, one may speak of a "migration to faraway districts of the soul." Indeed, those seeking salvation may accomplish a psychological migration, an internal move away from surrounding realities. They can go into an internal exile and ignore the crisis around them. All roads to private salvation represent attempts to turn away from collective distress, to ignore the political crisis, and to become apolitical.

Analogies to Israeli Private Salvation Movements

It is tempting to compare what has been taking place in Israel to events in other times and places. Salvation movements of all dimensions and fates come to mind. Nevertheless, we have to recognize the historical specificity of what we have observed in Israel, which is unlike any other similar phenomenon. Among the historical analogies that come to mind are the United States in the nineteenth century with a wealth of private and collective salvation movements, the rise of spiritualism, and the founding of so many new religions (e.g., Christian Science, Mormonism, Seventh-Day Adventists, and Theosophy). Czarist Russia during its last ten years with Rasputin and others, the United States in the 1960s, and contemporary South Africa have had another great awakening of salvation movements. Millenarian movements are likely to appear under conditions of social upheaval. "Following a disaster such as an epidemic, famine, revolution or war, people feel vulnerable, confused and full of anxiety, and they turn to millenial beliefs in order to account for the otherwise meaningless events. The disaster is given meaning as a prelude to the messianic period so that the deepest despair gives way to the greatest hope" (Sharot, 1980, p. 401).

The frenzy of the last years of the Weimar Republic in Germany included not only militant political movements of the left and the right but also new religious movements, experimentation in psychology, the development of psychotherapy, and an incredible boom in the occult business (30,000 astrologers in Berlin in 1929). McFarland (1967) describes popular religious movements in Japan as responses to "endemic social crisis" in Japanese society since the nineteenth century. Since the cataclysmic events of 1945, new religions have boomed, and it has been estimated that 20 percent of the Japanese have taken part in their activities. The Sabbatian movement in the seventeenth century is another example that comes to mind readily. This messianic upheaval was unprecedented in Jewish history and engulfed the whole Jewish world of the time (Löwy, 1984; Scholem, 1973; Sharot, 1980).

A naive, intuitive explanation offered by many Israelis for the appearance of salvation movements in Israel is U.S. influence. The notion that every American fad is adopted by Israelis five years later is expressed quite often in Israel. When we examine this claim we discover, not too surprisingly, that importation of trends in American culture is rather selective. Quite a few fads and fashions prevalent in the United States have not reached Israeli shores, such as feminism, ecology, the antinuclear movement, smoking marijuana, the struggle for students' rights, the antismoking campaign, and antiwar sentiments. While it is clear the the content of some salvation movements (new religions, psychotherapy, and the occult) is imported, there is no wholesale adoption of foreign culture. On the contrary, the combination of roads to private salvation presented here is unique to Israel and uniquely Israeli, reflecting the Israeli cultural context and Israeli history.

Some of the phenomena observed in Israel in recent years bring to mind cultural developments in the United States in the 1960s. In the two cases, we can observe a society in crisis, but the reactions to the crisis in Israel, despite the surface similarities to the United States, are more radical. In the United States the salvation movements that flourished in the 1960s were in place long before. Religious salvation traditions, a psychotherapy subculture, and political protest did not appear *ex nihilo* in 1966. They existed for decades before and experienced a resurgence. The United States has had "a long history of nominally deviant religious subgroups that created life styles antithetical to the cultural and social traits of most citizens, e.g., the Seventh-Day Adventists, the Amish, the 19th-century communards" (Damrell, 1978, p. 181). In the United States there is a long history of religious and secular psychotherapies, starting in the early nineteenth century (Fuller, 1982). Unlike the continuous and rich history of deviant religions and salvation movements in the United States, Israel's history is totally lacking in such. In Israel there were no salvation movements or subcultures. It is the unprecedented crisis, much more serious than the 1960s crisis in the United States, that has brought about the astounding development of private salvation movements in Israel after 1973.

Any comparisons of the salvation movements in Israel since 1973 with similar phenomena in the United States in the 1960s would be definitely out of place. Anyone who remembers the glorious sixties will be sadly disappointed if he or she comes to Israel to look for the lost spirit. There have been no radical student movements and no tear gas on Israeli campuses. In Israel students demonstrate only when their parking privileges are in jeopardy, and young Israelis, compared with their elders, are notoriously right wing. There is little dope being smoked on campuses, and few attempts at communal living. Not only is there no discussion of possible revolution, but there is little hope for a better future. The atmosphere of experimentation, freedom, and a coming revolution of the young is totally missing from the Israeli scene.

Unlike American society in the 1960s, where the main problem for youth, according to Keniston (1967), was "the achievement of individual identity" (p. 250), the cultural uniformity of Israeli society and the permanent state of war solved this problem for Israeli youth. They were expected to grow up and then accept the roles of loyal citizens and soldiers, and they did—that is, up to a certain point. It is important to remember that the majority of Israelis still follow the norms. The difference between 1964 and 1984 in Israeli is in the existence of a significant minority that refuses to go on with the prescribed roles and norms and are ready to opt for hitherto inconceivable identity possibilities.

Some of the phenomena described here in the Israeli context have become prominent in an American context, where they are known as "New Age" ideas. But the differences are greater than the similarities. While the content of beliefs regarding psychological salvation, the occult, or new religions, is, of course, identical, and Scientology in Tel-Aviv, in terms of beliefs, is the same as Scientology in Los Angeles, viewing the phenomena described here as the result of wholesale importation is patently wrong. The importation of such ideas to Israel is very selective. Some basic building blocks of New Age consciousness, such as "psychic research" and spiritualism, are totally missing in Israel (cf. Rossman, 1979). Can all the phenomena we are dealing with be compared with the manifestations of the American "Me Decade" of the 1970s? There are certain similarities, no doubt, and what is common is an ideology of individualism that becomes pronounced for many individuals in both societies. However, the differences are more striking than the similarities. An ideology of individualism is not a startling cultural innovation in the United States. It may be such in Israel, and the development of a movement for self-liberation in Israel is indeed a significant cultural change. When we examine the specific components of cultural changes in Israel and in the United States in the 1970s, the major difference is in the tendency, evident in Israel but not the United States, for reliance on religion and the occult as ways of understanding and transforming the self.

The situation of whites in apartheid South Africa has seemed like a fairly close analogy to that of the Israelis (Beit-Hallahmi, 1987 and 1991). Both groups have been under serious threat and have been concerned about their physical survival, as they should be. Both were overwhelmed by the huge numbers of the third-world natives surrounding them. In the 1970s and 1980s, tension in both Israel and South Africa was mounting, as both nations were becoming more isolated, under growing threat. The exclusion of South Africa from the United Nations General Assembly in 1974 was followed by the General Assembly resolution on Zionism in 1975. Increasing internal and external pressures on Israel in the 1970s was followed by the rise of resistance to apartheid in South Africa in the 1980s.

If I am indeed correct in pointing to the connection between Israel's uncertain future and growing despair among its citizens and the phenomena of private salvation in recent years, we should expect similar developments in South Africa. This is indeed the case. South African whites also have miracle stories to tell about visits to fortune tellers who knew almost everything in their private lives just by looking at them (Crapanzano, 1985). They too tell stories of sudden conversions that changed lives completely. The charismatic movement is spreading in South African churches, as whites speak in tongues and experience the spirit of the Lord. White South Africans have been finding private salvation in psychotherapy, old religions, and new ones (see Hochschild, 1980; Crapanzano, 1985). Many South African whites were in the 1980s engaged in "religious renewal" seeking "to escape through a transcendental religious language . . . through Oriental mysticism and pointillist world games . . . and still others, . . . through projects of departure" (Crapanzano, 1985, p. 30). Others go to astrologers and other fortune tellers. Still others join more charismatic, "enthusiastic," churches.

Among those who "take refuge in otherworldliness" is Zachary, a young white South African who grew up in Rhodesia. He "has studied Hinduism and other Oriental mysticisms. He has been an adept of an Indian guru and once thought seriously of joining a Zen monastery in England. He has been involved in several spiritualist groups . . . and has more recently been attending the services of a neognostic society whose members come from the wealthiest strata of Johannesburg's spiritually enlightened" (Crapanzano, 1985, p. 174). But old religions are experiencing a renewal as well.

> Charismatic Christianity is . . . spreading among South African whites. The Renewal is particularly important in the Anglican Church, in the Catholic Church, and in such Pentecostal Churches as the Baptists and the Assemblies of God. . . . Among Jews . . . the Lubavitch movement . . . is spreading. Members of this movement, like many members of the Christian Renewal, remove themselves from active political engagement and concern. . . . Members of the renewal . . . tell stories of extraordinary conversions, miraculous healings, and "groups overcome mightily by the spirit of the Lord." . . . Trances, praying in tongues, visions, and extraordinary auditory phenomena are understood as the inflowing of the Spirit of the Lord." (Crapanzano, 1985, pp. 210–11)

The atmosphere among South African farmers, as described by Crapanzano (1985), is charged with anxiety and uncertainty, which creates a readiness to accept stories of doom and anger, about the

Illuminati, Anti-Christ, and satanic churches and, on the other hand, stories of miracles and transformations.

South African roads to private and collective salvation are unique to South Africa, of course, just as the Israeli equivalents reflect a unique Israeli context. What is similar is the general historical situation, and people's attempts to escape from despair to private and instant salvation. All comparisons provide us with important insights, but any cultural upheaval has to be understood in its own context. This book is committed to historical uniqueness. Salvation movements in Israel share much with similar movements in dissimilar times and places, but the whole complex of phenomena is unique and will never be repeated. There is nothing unique about the contents of salvation movements in Israel since 1973. The same beliefs and the same practices are found all over the world. What is unique in the Israeli case is the short and amazing history of these movements.

6

Forming and Preserving the New Self

The most poignant demonstration of the Israeli yearning for security in the face of annihilation threats is the group known as Immortality, which is the Israeli branch of a United States group known as the Eternal Flame Foundation. The Eternal Flame is a U.S. "New Thought" group "dedicated to building a deathless world." It was founded in Scotsdale, Arizona, in the late 1960s by Charles Paul Brown (born 1935), a former Presbyterian minister and nightclub singer. Brown had a vision of Jesus Christ together with the revelation of physical immortality in the spring of 1960. He was joined in leading the group by BernaDeane Brown (born 1937) and James R. Strole (born 1949). The group's doctrine is connected to Christian theology and claims:

> Death is actually a fabrication or lie imposed on our minds and bodies by a ruling death consciousness in order to control the species of man and keep him in eternal bondage . . . there will never be lasting peace on earth until the LAST ENEMY OF MAN, WHICH IS DEATH is abolished . . . most religions believe that physical immortality will eventually take place in the bodies of mankind upon the earth. However, it is always projected into some future dispensation due to misconceptions and religious dogmas. We feel the time IS NOW for an immortal species of mankind to be birthed upon the planet.

Immortality was started in 1988 by an Israeli couple, Raya and Shmuel Ben-Dror, who met the leaders of the Eternal Flame in Britain. It was love at first sight, and the Ben-Drors decide to bring the message to their homeland. Within a few months, they gathered around them scores of followers, some of them personal friends, relatives, and business associates. The Ben-Drors do not represent the oppressed and downtrodden by any means. Raya Ben-Dror is the heiress to a significant fortune. Her husband is a successful businessman in his own right. Many of the people in the immortality faith are well-to-do. It isn't clear if all the members in the group, which meets at least twice a week, really believe in physical immortality, but they are all attracted to the incredible optimism that such a faith reflects. The group's meetings are devoted to mutual criticism, testimonials ("how life has changed since I became physically immortal"), and mutual support.

What can we say about this incredible phenomenon of individuals who proclaim their own literal, physical, immortality? A fascinating and puzzling question for both "naive" observers and social scientists is how people change their attitudes, beliefs, and identities so radically and so dramatically, with serious costs and consequences for themselves and others. We are in need of explanations for the new group membership, for the changed identity, and for the high level of ego involvement.

Psychological explanations of the process have focused on two factors:

1. A "deviant" process of persuasion, often referred to by the popular term *brainwashing*.
2. A deviant personality structure of the recruits, who are judged to be psychologically disturbed.

Brainwashing, or Thought Control

Brainwashing is most often used in the mass media (Nordheimer, 1974), but it really has little conceptual meaning in psychology. Such terminology is never used when a person joins an old religion, only when he joins a new one. Joining a small, deviant group arouses opposition and calls for an explanation. From the observer's point of view, it just doesn't make sense. When a young Israeli joins ISCKON, the identity change involved is so dramatic that many observers will react with horror and prejudice. Those using the term *brainwashing* usually mean a system of persuasion based on deception, group pressure, and coercion (Scanlon, 1966; Ungerleider and Wellisch, 1979). The whole brainwashing approach is predicated on the notion that deviant groups have been amazingly successful in their recruiting efforts. A look at the history of these groups shows that noting could be further from the truth.

New religious groups have not been any more successful than other new social movements and have been much less successful than most secular movements. Actually, new religions have been quite unsuccessful in both recruiting and keeping members, which explains their limited impact and their limited rate of survival. Most popular explanations of the rise of new religions, and even some of the questions raised in academic articles, are merely expressions of prejudices about minorities and other cultures. Magical prowess in recruiting new members is often attributed to new religions, while in reality they remain small and usually fail in their attempts to recruit new members. If we want to examine seriously the recruitment practices of new religions, what we discover are normal attempts by true believers to persuade others to follow them, which mostly fail miserably, and possibly a special readiness or openness among those who are ready to accept the new message. In addition, we tend to forget that there are differences in the involvement and commitment among group members. Some are passionately and totally committed, while others are merely curious.

> The typical adherent of these new religious . . . movements established a peripheral, transitory relationship to one of these groups and then drops out. . . . It is possible to distinguish two forms of participation. In one form, persons . . . commit a large proportion of their time, feelings, and identification. Such memberships become a major source of meaning, values, and norms for individuals involved. . . . Such "committed members" provide the core of central cadre for these movements. . . . Other persons, however, may have a more peripheral or transitory form of affiliation. (Bird and Reimer, 1982, p. 4)

All forms of individual salvation we are discussing are rather precarious. Personality transformation under dramatic conditions is notoriously unstable (Levine, 1984). The individual is always in danger of reverting to his or her old self because of internal (psychological) or external reasons. Whether this will happen or not depends on both personality and social circumstances. Salvation obtained through the occult or through psychotherapy is notoriously short-lived and unstable. Religious identity change will also be susceptible to reversals. In Israel, it is easy to predict that Judaization will be the more permanent form of religious identity change, because of the considerable societal support it enjoys, and this indeed is the case. New religions in Israel, often subject to external opposition, are mostly unstable groups with unstable members that need extraordinary luck and leadership to survive and prosper.

Conversion and Commitment

Continuity in behavior, though it is the rule rather than the exception, does not require explanation; discontinuity does. Ninety-nine percent of religious believers carry the exact same religious labels as their parents before then. Less than 1 percent have changed labels, and this tiny minority gets our well-deserved theoretical attention. A modern definition of conversion refers to it as a "radical reorganization of identity, meaning, life" (Travisano, 1970, p. 594). Conversion has been the classical topic in the psychology of religion and has been studied earlier and more extensively than many of its students today realize (Leuba, 1912; Pratt, 1920; Starbuck, 1903; Thouless, 1923). As Allport (1950, p. 37) attested, "No subject within the psychology of religion has been more extensively studied than conversion."

There are three theoretical approaches to the phenomenon of dramatic transformation in religious identity:

1. Cognitive quest (Heirich, 1977).
2. Positive solution to conflict (Allison, 1968).
3. Pathological solution to an unconscious conflict (Salzman, 1953).

The psychodynamic view of conversion, starting with Freud's *tour de force* on religious experience (1928), delineates an unconscious conflict, which finds a defensive solution through a sudden reorganization of impulses and attachments. The specific content of religious beliefs and commitments is secondary to the real process, a mere epiphenomenon (Allison, 1968 and 1969; Christiansen, 1963; Kliegerman, 1957; Salzman, 1953).

Conversion has been regarded as the model of an adolescent identity crisis and its resolution. Since the nineteenth century, when psychologists such as G. Stanley Hall, William James, and Edwin D. Starbuck have turned their attention to this matter (Hall, 1904; James,

1902/1961; Starbuck, 1899), religious conversion was rightly considered an adolescent phenomenon or even an essential part of adolescence (Argyle and Beit-Hallahmi, 1975). Modern society is characterized by a prolonged adolescence, and many of the conversion cases we are discussing fit into the time frame of this period, which may extend into middle age (Wittenberg, 1968; Beit-Hallahmi, 1977). Returnees to Judaism in Israel and some of the members in new religions do not fit the image and the reality of the typical convert in other countries, who is an adolescent (Argyle and Beit-Hallahmi, 1975). In Israel many of the converts and the seekers are older, sometimes middle-aged.

It is important to recall that not all members of new religious or returnees to Judaism have experienced private salvation, as described here, and not all have the same degree of involvement in their new identity. Some, despite outward appearances, are not fully committed. While only a relative minority has experienced salvation, a larger minority has experimented with various salvation modes and has adopted part of their ideology. Not all of these who have joined religious groups or who have experienced intensive psychotherapy have also gone through the private salvation experience, but all those who have had private salvation thrust upon them have followed one of the roads we have dealt with.

Systematic psychological studies on "converted" individuals indicate that these individuals experienced a personal crisis prior to achieving private salvation and that their relations with their parents were more problematic, compared with controls. Ullman (1982) in a comparative study of converts and individuals with a stable religious identity showed that converts' perceptions of their parents was more negative and that the incidence of father absence was higher in their life histories. Converts described their childhood and adolescence as unhappy and recalled more traumatic childhood events. Personal stress was reported as characterizing the two-year period preceding the conversion. These findings were regarded as supporting closely the psychodynamic view of conversion.

Beit-Hallahmi and Nevo (1987) compared returnees to Judaism with their secular counterparts. Fifty-nine men, who had all been born and raised in Israel in secular Jewish families but had switched to Orthodox Judaism and kept practicing it for at least a year, were the experimental group. They were administered a structured interview, based on the one used by Rabin and Beit-Hallahmi (1982), aimed at assessing life experiences on several dimensions. Items dealing with religion and the search for meaning were especially added. Following the interview, each individual filled out a biographical inventory, developed by Nevo (1983). Forty of the respondents filled out, in addition, a Hebrew version of the *F* scale (Adorno et al., 1950), and a self-concept questionnaire.

The control group was selected as follows. Each biographical inventory filled out by a member of the experimental group was used to find him a close match. The variables used for matching were: age, marital status, occupation, rank in the military (military service in Israel is compulsory for Jews), number of siblings, the parents' places of birth and occupation, and socioeconomic level. On the basis of these variables, a secular match was found, and the same instruments were administered to him. We used only men born in Israel in order to avoid other confounding variables. From the interview, the biographical inventory, and the questionnaires, thirty measures were extracted and used in comparing the two groups. The measures used to compare the two groups can be divided into four content areas: (1) ideology and religion, (2) family relations, (3) social contacts, and (4) self-perception.

Not too surprisingly, there are significant differences on all measures in the first area. The "born again" are higher on the *F* scale (measuring authoritarianism), higher on attachment to religion, report a major identity change among their life events, and report more religious experiences. In the area of family relations, the only significant difference is in the lower identification with the parents on the part of the "born again." In the area of social contacts, they report fewer relationships with women, but they are more ready to ask other people for help when faced with personal problems. The "born again" are also lower on two different measures of self-esteem and lower in their level of aspirations.

Interpretations of changes in religious identity as the result of a search for meaning have to account for the fact that while alienation and meaninglessness may be experienced by many, only a few choose a religious answer to their quest. Who are those that make up this relative minority? The picture that emerges from this study is one of a certain weakness, meekness, or vulnerability in those who choose the religious option. Dittes (1969, p. 636) stated that "religion functions to meet the needs of those who feel frustrated, threatened, inadequate, or deprived." Our findings indicate that a move in the direction of religion, for a formerly secular individual, is associated with subjectively felt deficiencies, which are dealt with through authoritarianism and religion.

While authoritarianism and comitment to religion are the end result of religious identity change, certain characteristics of "born again" individuals may explain why they have sought this solution to their personal quest. They seem to move away from their parents, while being still more dependent. They are less active physically and sexually, have fewer ambitions, and lower self-esteem. The religious framework of belief in an ordered world, together with the warmth of religious institutions and religious "recruiters" in a secular, stressful society, provide the right setting for meeting their needs. Those who share the same stress without opting for a religious solution seem to be more active and more self-confident. Our results in this particular case are in accord with earlier research and theorizing, in that they show family relations to be an important antecedent for identity change. "Born again" Jews in Israel are broadcasting a message of alienation and rebellion to their secular parents, just like the born again adolescents described by William James (1902) and G. Stanley Hall (1904) almost a century ago.

Because most secular Israeli parents are nominally Jewish, the message of a child's conversion is one of denouncing parental hypocricy and shallowness. On a collective, generational level, finding new identities is a total ideological rebellion. The new religious identities constitute in many cases rejection of the Zionist faith of the parents and of the parents' everyday materialistic lifestyle.

For young people, and sometimes for older ones, joining a deviant group and choosing a new identity is an act of rebellion against their parents and parental authority "the inner struggle with the problem of hatred toward the father or toward father symbols—that is, towards authority—results in overwhelming anxiety and can result in the conversion experience" (Salzman, 1953, p. 186). In terms of individual and family dynamics, every identity change is a rebellion against one's parents, who usually created a former identity, and against one's past. When a young Israeli who grew up in the average secular family turns Orthodox or joins a new religion, he is declaring a revolt against his parents. He may rebel also through finding a new better parent in a secular psychotherapist.

Vulnerability, Hunger, and Love as Factors

A necessary factor in holding onto beliefs that are deviant or clearly disconfirmed is social support. It is hard for one individual to hold onto deviant or disconfirmed beliefs. It is much easier for a group (Festinger et al., 1956). There is no doubt that during the recruitment process and through group membership, recruits enjoy a great deal of love and concern, something they may have not experienced before. The literature tends to underestimate the impact of friendship. People often follow their close friends on their salvation trek. Recruitment is often by personal friends and not by unknown recruiters. While researchers have used the concepts of persuasion, attitude change, and group membership to describe recruitment to salvation perspectives, they have missed one essential component in the process, that of personal attachments that create new committed relationships. We should consider the possibility that the most efficient model we can use to understand the intensity and suddenness of the private salvation experience may be that of an intense emotional attachment, which may be just as sudden and dramatic.

Falling in love, in Western culture, means an intense, often seemingly sudden, attachment to an object, which becomes highly valued. This commitment to another is accompanied by a rise in self-esteem and general well-being. If we listen to a person newly in love, he or she sounds amazingly like a person newly converted. In many cases of private salvation, we find an attachment to a charismatic authority. In secular psychotherapy, the charismatic authority figure is the therapist. In religious conversion, it is a teacher or a fellow convert. Attachment to that other individual is crucial for the process. To use the psychoanalytic terminology, what happens to the ego in the process of private salvation is a revitalization through a new internalized love object, which is totally positive. Two metaphors seem most relevant to the experience of those saved: hunger and love. It was the felt emptiness inside that sent them on their way toward salvation. It was redemptive love that formed the center of the salvation experience. The new love object has conquered all previous deficiencies and deprivations, at least for a while.

What I would like to propose here is that the emphasis on recruitment techniques by deviant groups, especially new religions, neglects the most important element in the process, which is the recruit and his or her needs. The emphasis on recruitment views the new member as passive, subject to more or less sophisticated recruited techniques, which determine his or her future course of behavior. Most explanations of recruitment regard recruits as passive recipients rather than active seekers. I would like to propose that the recruit is not passive. He or she may be an active seeker who plays an important role in the process. He or she may be a vulnerable and needy individual who translates an inner hunger for meaning and belonging into active seekership, or at least an openness to new messages. This openness to new ideas is the sine qua non of joining new deviant groups that offer a radically different worldview.

We should regard those who have found private salvation as active seekers who share a self-definition of stress and distress with an active search for personal change. Their initial openness to salvation messages is the crucial factor in their recruitment to a new worldview. The change is not just one of adopting a new cognitive paradigm. It may involve every aspect of one's life. The seekers yearn for meaning, for answers to the questions that keep them awake all night.

The phenomenon of the conscious seeker was brought home to me most dramatically while visiting a ISCKON center. It was a Saturday afternoon, and a few curiosity seekers came to the center and were received graciously by the ISCKON members. Two of them asked me for a ride, and a conversation ensued. To my great surprise, I discovered that W. was not just a curious onlooker. He was a young man of twenty-two on a search. Deliberately and consciously, he was spending his time travelling around Israel and meeting with various groups or reading their literature while staying at home. It was clear to him that at the end of this journey he would commit himself to the group found to be most convincing and satisfying. What was unique about W. was his methodical approach and his awareness. Others go through the same search but are unsystematic and confused. A former member of the Divine Light Mission said in an interview: "The root is that you go to the group in a real search. I was looking for something that would fill the void."

This openness to unconventional ideas is related to personality factors but must also reflect social realities. When confidence in accepted ways is lost, there is a readiness to listen to new ways of approaching reality, even if we used to consider these new ways crazy only a short time before. The seekers do not care about our diagnosis of philosophical differences between religion and the occult, on the one hand, and secular psychotherapy, on the other. Their distress is great, and they will try anything that promises even mild relief, not to mention salvation. For them, the main consideration is their own burning internal need for meaning and solace. So they'll try anything in their desperation, without any concern for consistency.

Openness to new ideas means a heightened responsiveness or suggestibility, as opposed to resistance and critical reception of beliefs offered by others. Suggestibility assumes a "tendency to respond uncritically to suggestions" (Turner and Killian, 1957, p. 84). Some individuals are so susceptible to the new message that no great amount of persuasion and no great effort at recruiting them are necessary. They carry with them a strong inner need for attachment, meaning, and faith, and whoever arrives with a new message will have their allegiance. Under these conditions, recruitment becomes likely even without much effort or a special technology being used by the recruiting group. Given the initial openness (growing out of despair and confusion) changing attitudes and the acquisition of new beliefs come naturally. Private salvation is achieved through dialogue and exchange with an individual saver, leading to an autobiographical reassessment and then to epiphany, the actual moment of salvation, following the dialogue stage. This is what was reported by Uri Zohar, Israel's leading convert (see Chapter 2).

Private salvation is based on a recruitment to a deviant world-view. Members of new religions adopt ideas that seem to us bizarre and unproven. This cognitive focus on the part of researchers may be exaggerated or misguided and reflects our own biases. Most members of new religions and religious converts in general, are not intellectuals. They do not share with academics our overly developed habit of critical thinking. Indeed, they may approach the world and other people uncritically, searching not for the truth or probable truths but for other kinds of solace and comfort. Persuasion, in such cases, may be rather easy. Knowledge of beliefs, in the case of some members, may be quite superficial. Researchers may be more knowledgeable than members about elaborate belief systems, and there are cases where presumed members do not really understand what they are supposed to believe. Still, the group may have a strong hold on them because they are attached to another person rather than a conviction in some abstract faith. The attachment may not even be to a charismatic leader but to a close friend, who introduced them to the group and now stands by them.

This gap between the experience of group members and our interpretation may be another example of how social scientists overvalue ideas while ignoring simple human connections (see Rochford, 1982; Snow et al., 1982). What amazes us about many of the seekers, especially those who have adopted a full faith in a new religion, astrology, or macrobiotics, is their gullibility and readiness to accept the absurd. What we tend to forget while looking at these individuals is how much most members of modern societies, with the exception of professional intellectuals, are lacking in critical thinking and are used to depending on the opinions of others, accepted unthinkingly.

The Seekers

The customers for various modes of salvation are the population of seekers, individuals in crisis, who are open (or vulnerable) to accepting new self-definitions or, at least, new ways of looking at the self. The seekers are those who hunger after meaning, support, and love.

They are more vulnerable and insecure than their next-door neighbors, and they are ready to experiment and experience new and unknown roads to happiness. What seekers are after is oftentimes an escape from their past and their present (Balch and Taylor, 1976).

We can list their social background characteristics, which explain why they have become the seekers and the saved. Beyond the social background, what all these individuals share is at the psychological level an openness, or vulnerability, to new ways of defining themselves and their potential happiness. This psychological factor can explain the change possibly better than theories that claim a special power to the message offered the seekers, or the special power of the medium conveying the messages. The seekers are motivated by a desire to escape from an unwanted self, a quest for community, and the pursuit of meaning (cf. Neal, 1970). The exact social location where they end up may be attributed to chance and circumstance, but it is the quest that makes them the candidates for membership.

Thus, the appearance of the new modes of salvation is a reflection of the crisis of Israeli identity. What can be seen in some of these modes of salvation is the explicit formation of a new identity; a return to Jewish identity in the case of the "returnees"; a non-Jewish, non-Israeli identity in the case of ISCKON and other new religions; a distancing from collective identity in the case of involvement in psychotherapy. What has developed in Israel is a population of individuals, mainly under the age of thirty, who are active seekers or passive recipients of the new messages. The crisis and the decline of existing institutions and cultural support systems create an openness to cultural innovations on the part of some or many individuals. An openness to the religious frame of reference is the sine qua non of joining the new religions. This openness is found among a significant minority of secular Jews in Israel, and it is leading them to either Orthodox Judaism (Aviad, 1983) or to the new religions.

Students of new religions in North America (Stark and Bainbridge, 1984; Robbins et al., 1978) have stated that the rise of new religious movements is tied to the decline of old religious traditions and structures and is occurring at their expense. In Israel it seems that the appearance of new religions has paralleled the movement of return to the old religion of Judaism. What society has experienced has been a rise in the acceptibility of religious options, both old and new.

What James (1902) suggested is that a profound personal crisis is always the prelude to the dramatic personality change observed in those who have found their salvation in one way or another. And we hear about this profound crisis in the testimonies of those who have been saved, through psychoanalysis, Judaism, Emin, or est. This crisis of self-confidence, the restlessness that leads to the search for an answer is the sine qua non for the transformation of the self through salvation. A general social-psychological explanation for the openness of certain individuals to new modes of experiencing the self and the world has to do with their immediate social relations. Individuals who are in the midst of transitional periods or transitional social situations are more open (or vulnerable, according to some views) to new self-definitions and new groups. Examples of such individuals include adolescents and people without family attachments.

Many studies show that those likely to adhere to new religious groups and to seek salvation in secular forms are overwhelmingly unattached, and that women outnumber men among them (Argyle and Beit-Hallahmi, 1975; Harrison, 1979; Schofield, 1964). Those who do not feel a sense of belonging to any immediate primary social group are the most likely to feel detached from wider ideologies and to be open to new ideas. The boundaries of legitimacy, as defined by society at large, do not hold the same authority for those who become seekers. The seekers are, of course, a minority, and only a minority of Israelis demonstrate openness to the new roads to salvation. The majority is adjusted, desensitized, cynical, or just too desperate and dispirited to seek new alternatives. The seekers may be those who are more sensitive to contradiction, ambiguity, and lack of structure. They need external supports and an orderly world around them. The privatization of collective crisis and distress is but one reaction, limited to a minority of the population, but this reaction can be quite effective when the individual finds comfort in private salvation.

The seekers represent on an individual level the deepening cultural crisis. A society under siege and under a real threat to its survival cannot allow its members to waver in their loyalties. Israeli society, for its survival, demands from its members an absolute loyalty to the idea of the State. In other countries such loyalty is not called for, because national survival is not in question. In Israel survival cannot be taken for granted, and the legitimacy of the State has to be asserted precisely because it is called into question by both external and internal forces. The difference betwen "normal" Western alienation and what is experienced by Israeli seekers is that in Israel the spectre of collective annihilation is added to individual feelings of emptiness. Ideological challenges from the outside and inside attack the legitimacy of Zionism because it cannot be reconciled with secular, democratic ideals of equality. From other quarters there is the less serious challenge of traditional Judaism, which does not accept Zionism because of its secular nationalist ideals.

Psychopathology as an Explanation

Beyond the recognition of social and historical factors that led to the appearance of salvation movements, there are questions about the salvation careers of individuals. Psychological readiness, or vulnerability, or individual psychopathology may be called upon to explain why particular individuals, and not others in similar social situations, have chosen, or have grown into, private salvation experiences.

There is a parallel, noted by James (1902), between the psychological state of despair preceding the experience of conversion or salvation and the elation and happiness following it. One might suggest that the intensity of any salvation experience is going to be matched by the despair that preceded it. It is those disturbed individuals, often quite seriously disturbed, who are more likely to experience such sudden transformations, which in themselves are evidence of severe pathology. The enthusiastic believers who tell us about their private salvation may be covering up a deep depression. Pruyser (1968) is among those who suggest that sudden religious conversion is an indication of severe psychological crises and, at the same time, provides a way of warding off a total breakdown.

The minority of individuals who report experiencing private salvation may be regarded as being more vulnerable and more disturbed in terms of psychopathology. At the same time, we should view them also as extremely sensitive, in a way similar to that of those considered disturbed or even deranged. This is the sensitivity of those who do not follow social conventions and who speak out to tell us what we all sense but dare not say. The seekers may function like the proverbial canary in a coal mine. They feel the earth tremor long before the majority of the population and know early on that the foundations are really shaking. The vocabulary of psychopathology does not lack terms to describe those more likely to find their salvation in religion or secular miracles: dependent and inadequate personalities, borderline personalities, hysterical tendencies leading to dissociative states, or outright psychosis. All these labels seem to be appropriate. Recent reports clearly indicate that those saved by religion show much higher rates of serious psychiatric illness (Witztum et al., 1990). This does not explain the historical phenomenon but indicates that personal vulnerability is indeed a factor in seeking personal salvation.

When traditional support systems decline in the face of growing strains, new devices will be relied upon. Individuals will seek psychotherapy as a secular option or will turn to new and old religions. We can safely predict, in view of research findings that those likely to tell us dramatic salvation stories are also likely to be socially isolated. A change in religious affiliation has been found to be related to personal deficiencies (Wallace, 1975). These deficiencies could be in social rewards (occupation, income, and education) or in coping with a crisis situation. Vulnerability can be defined by a psychological label, such as *neuroticism* or *anxiety,* and it can be defined as stemming from low social status, economic deprivation, and other factors leading to insecurity. Loneliness is, of course, a major factor in personal vulnerability.

> A remarkably similar set of social circumstances characterizes people who develop tuberculosis and schizophrenia, become alcoholic, are victims of multiple accidents, or commit suicide. Common to all these people is a marginal status in society. They are individuals who for a variety of reasons . . . have been deprived of meaningful social contacts. (Cassel, 1976, p. 110)

The active seekers may indeed be the marginal, vulnerable members of society. The vulnerability of certain individuals that leads to dramatic conversions of identity and mood can be covered by the psychological terms of low self-esteem and depression and by a limited network of social support. When social support is so weak, those friends that one is forced to rely on become crucial, and they may be followed on the rosy road to salvation (see Witztum et al., 1990).

The psychopathology view, in its bluntest form, claims that those experiencing miraculous transformations are members of the small percentage of individuals who are psychotic, or nearly so, and the transformations save them from active psychosis (and sometimes do not). Those with more sensitive egos are more likely to respond to a collective crisis, often by seeking new identities and support groups. All forms of private salvation are self-constructive. They allow the self an escape from external pressures and internal deprivations.

Individuals who have few personal ties to others and a weak sense of identification with family and friends are more likely to develop salvation careers. Social isolation means that individuals are detached from structures that would channel them into conventional activities. Isolated individuals are likely to experience more distress and discontent, which will be channeled into "deviant" activities. In a situation of crisis and social disintegration, individuals with weaker personalities and borderline functioning will be more sensitive and will react with symptoms, psychological breakdowns, or by finding new solutions. Individuals with low self-esteem will join small groups holding deviant political or religious beliefs, which are likely to raise the self-esteem of members.

In many cases, the effect of joining a group is clearly therapeutic. Severely disturbed individuals are held together by group support and group practices. From these observations and the research literature, we can conclude that disturbed individuals are attracted to groups that offer private salvation. There is a whole range of pathology involved, from neurotic to actively psychotic. Joining a group often provides structure and support and often improves individual functioning significantly.

I had a chance to observe a debate between a woman member of ISCKON and a returnee to Judaism at an ISCKON center in Israel. The returnee was quite aggressive. She was gentle and mild. As the debate went on, he became more vicious in his attacks. She refused to respond directly but at some point started chanting "Hare Krishna." She seemed on the verge of collapse, but withdrawing into the chant was her way of gaining strength. It was her way of keeping herself together, an external device taking the place of missing internal structures. Chanting and praying while under stress provide such externalized supports, when the inner self falters.

There is little doubt that private salvation, especially with group support, helps the individual rebuild his or her ego and function better. It is also possible that the same process of rehabilitation operates for group leaders themselves and other individuals who serve in leadership roles in salvation moments. Occult "advisers" are often severely disturbed, and through their service to others, they gain recovery from psychosis. The miracle workers, all the minor prophets of salvation, through miraculous psychotherapy or a miracle cure or conversion, are the modern Shamans "whose autistic defenses against . . . threats and anxieties obtained 'solutions' of which his society stood in dire need" (La Barre, 1972, p. 138). Many of the modern shamans, the prophets of salvation, are themselves tragic figures, lonely, disturbed, and unhappy, who find some satisfaction in life through their salvationist role.

Ideologies of Salvation

When there are alternative ways of viewing the self and the world in the same society, representatives of these alternatives are going to compete rather aggressively. This competition is very much in evidence in Israel. There are several roads to self-transformation, which individuals may choose. They stand in contrast to life choices that do not involve a dramatic self-transformation and to life choices that involve self-destruction, such as drug addiction. When an individual experiences personal distress, which is not directly related to a physical ailment or limitation, there are (at least) five ways of defining the sources of distress and, accordingly, five ways of its alleviation:

1. Organic: Source of distress is to be found in invisible organic disequilibrium. Change will be affected by a change in diet, exercise, or special healing.
2. Psychological: Source of distress is to be found in invisible psychological disequilibrium. Change will occur through psychotherapy.
3. Religious: Source of distress is in the individual's alienation from invisible cosmic powers, which control the universe. Change will come through creating a psychological tie with those powers.
4. Occult: Source of distress may be in a variety of visible and invisible forces (e.g., the planets or witchcraft). Change will come through knowledge and manipulation of forces.
5. Political: Source of distress is in the social divisions of power existing around the individual. Change will come through changing these divisions.

Ideological options for interpreting reality and subjective experiences, especially subjective distress, are always available. Ideological changes determine which of these options will become more acceptable or fashionable. At the individual level, a person in distress interacts with these five perspectives. At the collective level, the five perspectives may compete, experience growth, and decline in popularity over time. One of the questions we are dealing with here is the growing acceptability of certain perspectives in Israel since 1973.

The nature of the salvation experience within a group context is such that membership in this group is going to neutralize any other commitment. It is quite clear that choosing any of the roads to salvation covered here means giving up the option of active and direct political involvement. Those committed to the liberation of the self are too busy with that to liberate others or to change society. Betrand Russell (1957) had the last word on it: "The natural impulse of the vigorous person of decent character is to attempt to do good, but if he is deprived of all political power and of all opportunity to influence events, he will be deflected from his natural course and will decide that the important thing is to be good" (p. 33). This description is especially apt to portray the situation of many Israelis in the 1970s and 1980s. Faced with the deepening crisis of their society and with their inability to do anything about it, more and more Israelis have decided to take care of themselves first and foremost. In the face of an external crisis, individuals have the choice of attempting to transform their selves or the world around them. Psychotherapy as a response to crisis aims at transforming the self, religion aims at transforming both, and a political reaction aims at changing the real world (Foss and Larkin, 1978). This march of the saved and near-saved is an Israeli Children's Crusade in which the energy expended and the individual sacrifices do not lead to any change in the reality that brought about the march in the first place.

There are cases where individuals can pinpoint a moment of conversion to a political ideology, the exact time at which a new commitment or a new enlightenment were achieved. However, these are not accompanied by elation, but rather its opposite. The revolutionary's commitment is serious, even grim. The experience of personal salvation is associated with a retreat from involvement in political activities. Not only is salvation in this case private, but its social context is one of an intimate community. Political activity is public and often impersonal. I do not claim that the individuals involved in new religious have been involved in political activities and then withdrew from them. I suggest that the available political options in Israel have decreased in number over the years since 1973 and that the individuals today involved in new religious belong to the same social stratum that used to constitute the left-of-center political parties in Israel.

Some may suggest that these salvation groups are actually revolutionary, in the sense of a will for a complete transformation of society. Are they, indeed, revolutionary? They are, in the sense of having a vision of what a radically different society would look like. Such visions are expressed in the teachings of Orthodox Judaism and of some new religious. They are less explicit in psychotherapy (but they can be found, e.g., Bugental, 1972), and only rarely are they found in the lore of occultism. Nevertheless, while a radical vision is there, the means to bring it about are conceived of in totally nonpolitical terms. What many of the saved have in common is the certainty that a revolution is coming, a consciousness revolution that will convert the world to their point of view and bring about a total world liberation. Both secular and religious believers have this certainty, which they are happy to proclaim to the rest of the world.

Predictions about the coming "new consciousness," like predictions about the coming of messiahs, have been heard often enough in recorded history and have been proved wrong just as often. It is is sufficient to mention the wave of New Age predictions that were heard in the United States in the 1960s and 1970s. The Aquarian Age (Roszak, 1976) still has not come, and much more work is needed to bring about even lesser changes in the real world.

All four roads to salvation discussed here are roads to self-enhancement and ego support. Returning to the old religion, joining a new religion, graduating from est, or visiting a fortune teller all lead, in the vast majority of cases, to a better feeling about oneself and to a better functioning in the real world. Our egos cannot function well for long without outside supports and structures, and the roads to salvation lead to new ego supports. Thus, any of these roads, though we may regard them as escapist and illusory, is better than other ways of coping with stress, such as drug addiction, which is clearly self-destructive. Roads to salvation are roads to the reconstruction of the self through a radical transformation.

There are clear philosophical differences among the different paths to self-salvation. Religion and mysticism, of all kinds, emphasize the existence of forces external to the person, which have to be dealt with and considered. Secular psychotherapy, on the other hand, emphasizes the forces inside the personality, and the lonely self in its struggle for autonomy and growth. What all these ideologies have in common is the avoidance of looking critically at social arrangements around the lonely self (cf. Beit-Hallahmi, 1974). A crisis may lead to a complete surrender, and religious movements may express resignation and hopelessness (Vidal, 1983). Thus, the content of a movement, as Vidal suggests, may be the expression of a complete despair, a complete acceptance of a death verdict.

The relationship between the return to Orthodox Judaism and the new religions is paradoxical. The return to Judaism movement has reinforced the potential for new religions because it has put the religious issue on the agenda. Defining problems in religious terms is what the old and the new religions share. This perspective of problem-definition (and solution) is crucial for joining both old and new religious groups (cf. Lofland and Stark, 1967). If religious problem-definitions and solutions are generally on the agenda for more and more individuals, there is a greater openness to religious answers, and even deviant ones are likely to get a hearing by some individuals at least. Thus, the Judaization movement has helped to create greater basic readiness for joining even deviant new religions.

If we are asked to define the major cultural change that explains the rise of private salvation in Israel, then we would say that it is the greater readiness to define personal problems in religious or psychological-individualistic terms (cf. Lofland and Stark, 1965). While Israelis used to pride themselves on being hard-nosed and practical, and thus suspicious of salvation through religious or psychological means, some of them have lost enough of their hard-nose attitude to start experimenting with the new roads to salvation. Once a basic openness to these alternative views exists, the next step toward conversion is possible. Private salvation discourse has been part of the United States culture for a long time (James 1902/1961). In Israel it represents a startling cultural innovation, and its acceptance is a consequence of some cultural changes. For the private salvation discourse to be accepted as legitimate, notions of individualism, romanticism, and psychologism have to prevalent. Given the the cultural pressures in Israeli society, the resulting changes include a greater readiness to turn to psychotherapy, a return to Orthodox Judaism, and the appearance of new religions as a significant social presence. The greater readiness to define problems in psychological terms, and the greater readiness to adopt religious ideas, then interact with a variety of social forces, including strong opposition to certain worldviews. That is why the greatest number of individuals have had some contact with the occult, the second largest group has engaged in psychotherapy, the third largest has turned to Judaism, and the smallest number have turned to new religions.

Israeli salvation movements can be divided according to the themes of revitalization and protest. Some of their manifestations are attempts to respond to crisis by revitalizing collective or individual faiths. Zionist Judaization is a clear movement of revitalization and renewal seeking to offer Zionism a new lease on life. Non-Zionist Judaization is a protest movement, as are the new religions that reject collective and individual Jewish identity. Psychotherapy and the occult revitalize the dispirited individual, but in their extreme escapist forms, they also constitute manifestations of protest. The growing ideology of individualism in Israel is clearly reflected in the changing themes of Israeli novels. While Hebrew novels until the 1960s were grounded in the reassuring worldviews of Zionism and Jewish identity, later on they started focusing on the trials and tribulations of deviant, struggling individuals, doubting the validity of Zionist visions (see the novels by Amos Oz).

Selfishness as Ideology in Israel

A television interview with a young philosophy instructor at Tel Aviv University created an uproar in Israel in early 1975. There was a wave of newspaper articles and heated debates. The man who created this uproar was Moshe Kroy, Ph.D., born in 1947, who became Ayn Rand's prophet to the Israelis. Later on, he presented his thinking in a book (1975) on rational existence and objective happiness, which became a best-seller. The book was described as the author's adieu to the State of Israel, whose regime embodied the opposite of everything advocated by him. The exposition relied mostly on Rand's books (Rand, 1964 and 1967), which were recommended as further reading. Kroy advocated unfettered capitalism and rational selfishness with individuals acting as free commercial agents. It is interesting to note that the book was dedicated to "My friend Mordecai Kedar, who knew dangers and suffering without betraying his consciousness." Kedar was a legendary criminal in the early 1950s, who got away with murder, and then was recruited by Israeli Intelligence for an overseas assignment. While being groomed for his mission, he killed his superior agent, and was brought back to Israel to stand trial under the strictest secrecy. His trial in 1957 became public knowledge only about thirty years later. He spent seventeen years in prison, was released in 1974, and become a hero to some because he seemed to be totally unaffected by his long time in prison. Then he joined the Israeli group of objectivists around Dr. Kroy. Choosing a hardened murderer as a hero could not be a better symbol of the post-1973 anomie that has led to the appearance of selfishness as a philosophical position.

Despite Kroy's claims that there are a few places in the world where as much openness to objectivist philosophy existed, he indeed said adieu to Israel and moved to Australia in 1976. The ranks of his followers, no doubt feeling orphaned and abandoned, thinned considerably. He discovered that the eternal soul does indeed exist and so became religious. He first joined Scientology and then became a follower of an obscure Indian guru. He now regards the writings of Ayn Rand as containing a gnostic message.

In late 1987 he returned to Israel, and in a series of media appearances announced his latest discoveries. He believes that the world is ruled by the forces of Evil, but the final battle between the Sons of Good and the Sons of Evil is at hand. Then God and goodness will rule. In February 1988 he was invited to speak before a group of seekers in Haifa. He never arrived, and a few days later his body was found in Tel-Aviv. He committed suicide.

We can point to an individualist movement in Israeli society, a movement for the liberation of the self, which parallels social and political developments since 1973. All private salvation is a rebellion against collective responsibility, a cry against collective oppression. There is a disappointment with the collectivity, which leads to more investment in personal happiness. What can be described as selfishness on a personal level is paralleled by the success of right-wing ideology in politics, which can be regarded as selfishness on a collective level. All private salvations are selfish vis-à-vis the need for collective solutions to the crisis. The liberation of the self is possible through humanistic-rational psychotherapy, which emphasizes individual responsibility and self-determination, or through the magic of the occult, which emphasizes external forces controlling human destiny.

Ideas about the external control of the self are, of course, much more prevalent, and much older than ideas of human self-determination. All religions promote the idea of an invisible world inhabited by various creatures, gods, angels, and devils, which control much of what happens to us. Actually, the occult ideology is halfway between self-control and total helplessness, as we have some capacity of affecting those external forces or at least knowing more about them. Religious and occult beliefs share the quality of offering certainty and completeness by placing the self within a cosmic order. The willingness to accept a totalistic belief system, which provides the answer to all of life's questions, should surely be regarded as an expression of the need to "escape from freedom" (Fromm, 1941). Giving up one's autonomy in return for absolute ideological security is a powerful motive. Some of the transformations described so far may fit the escape from freedom model. The individual joins an intensive group situation, offering collective identity, charismatic leadership, and a form of messianic hope. "The search for the strong, supportive, and protective figure who conveys absolute sureness fits into the magical thinking and messianic wishes of hundreds of thousands of people" (Liff, 1975, p. 116).

Romanticism as Ideology in Israel

A worldview that serves as a basis and a common framework for some of the new cultural developments we are looking at is that of romanticism, meaning a general preference for the emotional over the rational, for the old over the new, and for intuition over critical thinking. Romanticism always expressed the victory of spirit over matter, and the triumph of will over reality. It praises the internal world of experience, dreams, and daydreams. The buzzwords of romanticism are miracle, secret, mystery, and darkness, and they all exist internally, in one's psychological private world. Romanticism expresses a disappointment with reason and a turning away from it. It proclaims a readiness to try nonreason in the face of the failure of rationalism. A romanticist worldview creates an openness to religion, old and new, to the occult, and to some forms of psychotherapy. The prevalence of a romanticist worldview is historically tied to the rise of the right wing in politics. In Israel this parallel is perfect. The success of right-wing political approaches is tied to the rising tide of cultural romanticism, expressed in the various roads to salvation. Romanticist thinking can be compared to artistic thinking, reflecting a "regression in the service of the ego" (Kris, 1951), which may go beyond services to the ego.

All human beings share this readiness to regress from reality in favor of imaginary solutions. In certain historical situations, this potential regression expresses itself in a social movement, such as the Ghost Dance, and "crisis cults" in general (La Barre, 1971 and 1972). In the dreamlike thinking of the prophet and the artist, all things are possible, and artistic solutions become preferable to changing reality the hard way. Part of the romanticist worldview is the notion of expanding the powers of individual ego through the use of intuition and arcane knowledge. The antidote to materialism was the development of innate but atrophied powers of intuition in order to perceive hidden supernatural worlds. Such ideas have been explicitly promoted by Rudolf Steiner, the founder of anthroposophy, G. I. Gurdjieff, and other modern prophets.

The rise of Israeli romanticism, together with the rise of an authentic Israeli right-wing ideology, may be seen as comprising the appearance of an authoritarian culture in Israel (Adorno et al., 1950). Indeed, most elements of authoritarian ideology, as described by Adorno and coworkers, seem to exist in Israel and provide an ideal background for new modes of salvation. Authoritarianism includes a contempt for rationality and "hyprocritical" morality, and hidden and not so hidden wishes for power. Religions (of any variety) and the occult are clearly promoted by an authoritarian worldview. An openness to mystical ideas is one of the hallmarks of the authoritarian ideology. There seems to be one coherent framework for describing an ideology that combines openness to religious and occult beliefs with right-wing political thinking and that is the idea of authoritarianism. And indeed, if we examine the political ideology that seems to dominate Israeli political discourse since 1973, a diagnosis of authoritarianism seems appropriate. This can be ascertained not only in terms of the trend toward a right-wing majority but in terms of the basic worldview expressed in everyday political discussions.

There is a class of new cultural heroes in Israel who represent the arts of divination and healing together with modern psychotherapy. They all work by means of charisma, which is felt and held by their convinced clients, who are ready to offer testimonials and payments. Many of the occult entrepreneurs, the successful purveyors of psychological and miraculous healing, and the active recruiters into religious movements fit Weber's description of the charismatic actors:

> All *extraordinary* needs, i.e., those which *transcend* the sphere of everyday economic routines, have always been satisfied in an entirely heterogeneous manner: on a *charismatic* basis. It means the following: that the "natural" leaders in moments of distress—whether psychic, physical, economic, ethical, religious, or political—were neither appointed officeholders nor "professionals" in the present-day sense, but rather the bearers of specific gifts of body and mind that were considered "supernatural." (Weber, 1968, pp. 1111–12)

And in Israel of recent years we see these extraordinary needs being created and then being met by a mass of new "natural" leaders who offer their followers miracles and private salvation.

Epilogue

We have now reached a view of private salvation as a reaction to deprivation and oppression, an oppression that is not always visible to the naked eye but is subjectively experienced by the seekers who have found salvation and by those who are still looking for it. Their suffering and anguish is no less serious than those of natives in faraway places who join Cargo Cults. They may appear to be young, strong, and capable, but inside themselves they know only debilitating weakness. More or less deviant solutions, from the point of view of the majority in society, can, and should, be viewed as a rebellion against the majority, a rebellion and a cry uttered by a minority that feels itself to be oppressed and misunderstood within the majority culture. We, together with the majority, can see members of the minority as deficient, morally or psychologically, but we can also be impressed with the crisis that led to this rebellion. If salvation testimonials reflect only cyclical changes in manic-depressive individuals and results from a deteriorating psychological adjustment, why did an epedemic of such manic-depression start in Israel in 1973 and not earlier or later?

The crisis since 1973 is one of identity, belonging, and loyalty. Israelis respond to it by becoming more chauvinistic and moving to the right, by leaving the country altogether, or by joining one of the new salvation movements. New ideologies, which became acceptable after 1973, are individualism, on the one hand, and romanticism, on the other. The former is more of a threat to the state, while the latter can be integrated with right-wing ideology and traditional religion.

Possible reactions to the appearance of new roads to personal salvation on the part of the "establishment" may be ignoring, suppressing, or keeping under control. In Israel, different roads to salvation are treated differently, according to the threat they pose to the survival of the state. Thus, the return to Judaism is supported in a major way, psychotherapy and the occult are somewhat supported, and only new religions are the target for condemnation and suppression. New religions are a clear threat to Jewish identity and represent a historical continuation of Jewish conversions to other religions. During the modern history of the Jews, secularization has become the norm, but converting to other religions is still looked upon as a serious deviation. In joining ISCKON, a young Israeli is indeed converting to another religion, and such an act will shock even most secular Jews. The establishment reaction is in some direct proportion to the degree of perceived threat. The new religions are the most extreme form of rebellion among Israeli youth. Compared with the return to Orthodox Judaism, which is a "conformist" rebellion, or the narcissistic psychotherapy movement, which does not challenge Zionism in any way, the new religions are a palpable threat and a palpable alternative to Zionist loyalties. The state has to react to this challenge because it cannot afford to have open competition over ideological hegemony.

The growth of new religions in Israel can be regarded as a sort of political protest because it parallels, in terms of time periods and the social background of the individuals involved, movements that are more clearly political. If during the same period, members of the same social group, given to the same pressures and drives, invest much energy in joining new groups and developing new identities, we might suspect that similar basic processes are involved and that circumstances and individual differences may account for different individual commitments. And indeed, in Israel we find these parallels as well as indications of stress and crisis during the same time period. Private salvation is a sanctuary from harsh realities, an escape from the collectivity and its crisis.

The phenomena under discussion in Israel may be compared to Cargo Cults (Barber, 1941; Worsley, 1959; Worsley, 1969) and the Ghost Dance (La Barre, 1972; Mooney, 1965; Wallace, 1956), religions of crisis in other times and places. The new religions represent desperate efforts to cope with a terrible reality, which cannot be humanly changed without a miracle or an apocalypse. Like Cargo Cults in Melanesia, the new salvation movements in Israel are a rebellion against the seeming rationality and the real irrationality and inhumanity of an oppressive social system. These movements within Israeli culture are innovative and revolutionary. Salvation movements in Israeli society can be regarded as an active and passive rebellion against Zionism. The price of Zionism is getting too steep, and so the reactions range from leaving the field altogether, by emigration, or by changing the psychological field through individual salvation.

As we have seen, reactions to the crisis take four essential forms:

(1) an attempt to continue with normal coping, with general passivity toward the causes for the crisis itself, which is the majority response; (2) changing the situation by either leaving the field (emigration) or by political initiatives; (3) a destruction or injury to the self in the face of stress; or (4) a positive transformation of the self, which is the topic of this book. The experience of private salvation, as reported by our many informants, is a clear form of escape, from collective troubles to individual solutions and resolutions. Private salvation is also a cry of suffering and protest, the cry of the oppressed creature as describe by Marx.

The individual personality is always in need of external support structures, and weaker personalities are in need of stronger supports. When society is in crisis, weaker personalities are the first to sense a deterioration of support structures. Individuals may either crumble or find new, less traditional sources of succor. Thus, we may see the search for and discovery of private salvation as a way for disturbed individuals to avoid collapse and find reintegration for their suffering and dying souls. The individuals involved are indeed more sensitive and vulnerable, a minority that reacts with more panic to the collapse of an orderly world around them. From the seekers' point of view and in their direct experience, their search is for meaning, human community, and love. From the observers' point of view, it is an attempt at compensation for alienation and personal deprivations. For the seekers who have found their private salvations, the voice of faith is used to silence the inner and outer voices of doubt and despair.

The real issue in the crisis and the real question for every Israeli is not secularization, modernization, or alienation. The real issue is unique to Israel and similar to that facing apartheid South Africa: the survival of the whole state and a whole culture in a future filled with growing threats and difficulties. The mortality of the State of Israel is at stake. Israelis have always lived under a threat of annihilation, but since 1973, they have lived in its shadow, and that shadow has moved closer.

Is it possible that all of these salvation movements could have appeared in Israel anyway, even without the 1973 catastrophe, just because of the process of growing modernization and alienation? This seems unlikely. Israel was never a third-world country undergrowing modernization. It was quite modern, by all standards, before 1973. While the rise in living standards and leisure time can bring about more openness to psychotherapy, the phenomena observed are too dramatic and too sudden to be explained as part of some Westernization process. If explanations that suggest the effects of modernization or the upheaval that follows economic prosperity are correct, then we should have expected the appearance of private salvation movements in Israel during the period of 1970–73, which Stone (1982) indeed characterized as a time of "prosperity and confidence." Nothing of the kind was in evidence, however. The prosperous and confident Israelis of 1970–73 had no need for private salvation and remained completely indifferent to religious, magical, and psychotherapeutic messages.

The Israeli crisis of faith since 1973 is a crisis of meaning, and meaning is tied to the future. "What lends meaning to history? The promise of the future. If there is no promise, there is no meaningful history. Significance is contingent on vision and anticipation, on living the future in the present tense" (Heschel, 1967, p. 127). The future for Israelis since 1973 is one without promise and with an anticipation of more suffering to come. Living such a future in the present tense is a bitter fate, to be refused and resisted but not to be avoided.

The dominant mood in Israel after 1973 has been one of exhaustion: fatigue coming from the experience of past warfare and the prospect of future warfare and crises. The catastrophe of the 1973 War was the beginning of a continuing crisis, as Israel's fortunes seemed to be going from bad to worse. In November 1974, Yassir Arafat, the leader of the Palestine Liberation Organization (PLO), was invited to speak at the United Nations. A year later the United Nations General Assembly passed a resolution denouncing Zionism as a form of racism. These two events signaled a low point in the history of political Zionism. The struggle of Zionism in the world arena for almost 100 years focused on obtaining legitimacy for itself and political rights for Jews in Palestine, while denying the same legitimacy and the same rights to the Arab natives of Palestine.

This struggle has been eminently successful and culminated in the Partition Resolution of 1947, passed by the United Nations General Assembly, and the creation of the State of Israel in 1948, which eliminated the entity known as Palestine from the maps and the world's consciousness (see Beit-Hallahmi, 1991). After the 1967 War, the Palestinians began to reappear in the world arena, and with the help of the now extant third-world ideology gained a measure of legitimacy within a few years. The recognition given by the world community and by the United Nations to the Palestinians was a shock and a threat to Israel's future. By 1975, the number of countries recognizing the PLO was higher than the number of countries recognizing Israel, and Yassir Arafat was being received as a head of state all over the world. Israelis were feeling isolated, as they really were, and threatened, as the very legitimacy of their state was called into question. It was clear that in the political arena, as well as in the military one, Israelis were headed for harder times.

For many Israelis then, the years since 1973 consist of a series of traumas and failures for their society, with its future more and more in doubt. The Lebanon War of 1982–85 has been considered by most Israelis as an unmitigated disaster, similar in kind to the 1973 catastrophe. Mr. Begin himself, after the Lebanon invasion of 1982, said that this new war would erase the trauma of the 1973 War. As is well known, Mr. Begin went into seclusion in 1983 and has been spending his time in bed ever since as a result of the failure of that attempt to erase a trauma. What all Israelis are aware of, sometimes only in the back of their minds, is their historical predicament, the ticking clock which reminds them that things are not getting better and their enemies are not getting weaker. The experience of Iraqi missile attacks during the 1991 Gulf War has only reinforced these feelings. Israel's continuing precarious situation in West Asia will insure a steady demand for private salvation.

Gnawing doubts and nagging questions about the Zionist dream and the Israeli future created the openness to new answers and new ideologies of the religious, occult, or secular-individualistic variety. The doubts and questions have been there all along, but the trauma of the 1973 War gave them energy and vitality. The questioning voices within became louder until they drowned the old certainties in their deafening noise. Private salvation might be seen as a form of individual protest resulting from the lack of any channels for effective political action or expression. The search for the meaning of one's personal destiny, if though psychotherapy or through astrology, reflects an alienation for collective goals and meanings. It is an escape from the national to the human. Astrology is a human answer, not a national one.

Against the background of the 1973 catastrophe and the crisis following it, the confidence of the religious minority vis-à-vis the majority has grown. The non-Zionist segment of the Orthodox camp sees this crisis as justifying its stand, which views Zionism as a passing episode in Jewish history. Judaism, coherent and eternal, stands triumphant over the shambles of the unsuccessful Zionist experiment, and Orthodoxy gains new vitality. The Zionist-religious segment, on the other hand, shows secular Zionists that it alone still has the energy and the faith to continue the struggle, which means the continued war against the natives of the Middle East. It alone can go on justifying the dispossession of the Palestinians, can go on doing it, and can offer hope for a better, sometimes messianic, future. Every encounter between any individual secular Israeli and an Orthodox one takes place in the shadow of this gap in confidence. The secular majority and secular individuals can offer only feeble negations to Orthodox confidence, but they cannot offer an alternative vision.

When individual salvation is tied to the explicit rejection of Zionism, be it in the form of Orthodox non-Zionist Judaism or in the form of a new religion, the societal reaction is uniformly negative. The rebellion against Zionism cannot be allowed to take an active form. It can be more easily tolerated. When young people are involved in identity change, they are rebelling against their parents, who have handed them certain identities which are now rejected. When many young people choose to reject their handed-down identities, we may be observing a rebellion that is no longer an individual but rather a collective phenomenon. The involvement of thousands of young Israelis in the deliberate choice of new identities is a rebellion against the social order. As we have seen, some of the salvation movements, particularly some new religions, are a threat to the dominant ideology and identity in Israeli society, and they have been treated accordingly. New religions in Israel are clearly a religious innovation, and as such, it causes much opposition. It is also a heresy in terms of Israeli society.

The phenomenon of new religions in Israel plays a special role, and deserves a special discussion in our analysis. Since the 1950s, the boundaries of religious experimentation in Israel have greatly expanded in practice. The question is whether a real religious pluralism has been created. The answer is clearly negative, because in Israel Orthodox Judaism still holds a monopoly, and not even lip service is paid to an ideal of pluralism. This means that joining a new religion in Israel remains the most deviant form of private salvation. If we draw a scale of deviance for the roads to salvation described in this book, the occult is the least deviant, followed by psychotherapy and a return to Judaism. Adopting a new religion means, in most cases, going beyond the pale. It is a form of exit (Hirschman, 1970) similar to emigration from Israel. It is the most threatening and most challenging to both religious and secular institutions.

To what extent can these recent developments be regarded as a breakdown of the narrow confines of the Israeli identity, which should augur a new era of pluralism and openness? To some extent, this is true, as Israelis, or at least a minority of them, are feeling free to shop around in the new market place for identities. In terms of ideological commitments, it is clear that all the choices we are dealing with here represent alienation from Zionism, as it has been known in Israel since 1948. The appearance of this new pluralism is clearly a reflection and a consequence of the decline of the old consensus. The old framework of identity and self-actualization is broken and withering, which creates the new openness to experimentation and private salvation. This alienation from Zionism makes possible the acceptance of alternative belief systems. Given, on the one hand, the overwhelming cultural uniformity of Jews in Israel and, on the other hand, the sensitivity to any threats to that uniformity, it is easy to predict the level of tolerance for anything outside the boundaries of that uniformity. Israeli society has been marked, since its inception, with an atmosphere of intolerance for anything outside the boundaries of religious legitimacy, which includes old religions, new religions, and even Reform Jews.

There is definitely more openness now to a variety of deviant religions and secular salvation options for individuals, as we have seen, but open challenges to the dominant Jewish identity of the culture are still opposed and suppressed. The move toward pluralism is only relative, and Israel cannot be compared (or confused) in this respect with the United States or Western Europe.

The threat posed by alternative belief systems is clear. Society cannot tolerate the living evidence of individuals and groups within it who seem to be marching happily to the beat of a different drummer. A societal response is necessary in the case of Israel, a society under constant threat, and which has enjoyed a high degree of cultural uniformity in the past. If Jews are indeed a normal people, like the French or the Danes, why cannot Jews belong to different religions, like the French or Danes? The identity between religion and national identity has not been breached by Zionism or by the State of Israel. Thus, Zionism has not created a "normal" secular national identity for Jews or for Israelis.

Can the appearance of new religions in Israel be viewed as a breaking down of the monopoly of Judaism in Israeli culture? Not at all. It is important to recall that new religions is Israel represent a minority, which is far from a real threat to Judaism. The number of individuals who have returned to orthodox Judaism since 1973 is greater than the number of those who have joined new religions, and some of the new religions adepts have returned to Judaism. What the appearance of new religions in Israel represents is a crisis of Israeli secular identity. To the extent that this identity is still tied to Judaism and dependent on it, this is a threat to Judaism as well. But it is important to remember that new religions have not gained any degree of legitimacy in Israel which would challenge the monopoly of Judaism. Some of the new religions, and they represent a small minority, reflect a real break in cultural uniformity. ISCKON, the Divine Light Mission, Ananda Marga and other small groups are made up of individuals who have given up their Israeli-Jewish identity and have become members of a new non-Jewish minority in Israel. This is an unusual development that seemed to be inconceivable only a few years ago. It is possible that the openness to both old religion, in the form of the return to Judaism, and to new religions, among more and more Israelis, will create a greater openness to Christianity as a religious option. Indications for that trend may be seen in the growth of such groups as Messianic Jews and Jehovah's Witnesses.

There is a connection between the phenomenon of the return to Judaism and that of new religions. The sanctioned process of individual and collective Judaization puts the religious solution to private distress on the agenda. It proclaims the superiority of religious answers and thus unintentionally creates an openness to non-Jewish religious solutions. The attraction of religious options, both old and new, to nonobservant Israelis is based on "group identification, as opposed to individualism, sharing in place of competition, and asceticism or spiritualism instead of materialism" (Levine, 1979, p. 601). These are the elements that both the return to Judaism and most new religions in Israel share. Both old and new religions agree that the cure for private distress is in adopting a religious way of life. The disagreement is only over the precise kind of way, but this basic agreement gives minority religions a lease on life among Israeli seekers of private salvation.

Can we now speak of a counterculture of salvation in Israel or only of a subculture? (Yinger, 1960). While it is clear that there are subcultures of salvation, most of them are quite conformist. "On the ideological level, a counterculture is a set of beliefs and values which radically reject the dominant culture of a society and prescribes a sectarian alternative. On the behavioral level, a counterculture is a group of people who, because they accept such beliefs and values, behave in such radically nonconformist ways that they tend to drop out of the society" (Westhues, 1972, p. 10). From this definition it is clear that only the subculture of new religions in Israel is a counterculture as well.

The salvation movements we have described in this book are not going to take over Israeli culture. They will remain the domain of minorities, but they have become a permanent part of the cultural landscape. Despite the various salvation subcultures that have grown in Israel, the situation cannot be compared with what exists in the United States where similar and larger subcultures have been around longer. If an Israeli today wants to start the self-discovery trip taken by Rubin (1976) or Rossman (1979) in the 1960s and 1970s, the choices are more limited and the range of experiences narrower.

Since private salvation, as intense as it may be, does not transform society in a significant way, all the energy fuelling individual salvation movements has not touched the real causes of despair, and it is still there and growing. A kibbutz member writes in 1986:

> In the second generation to our redemption, there is already a crying void of nonsense and illusion. No wonder that many of our sons and daughters seek refuge in worlds of dreams: drunkenness, drugs, cults and the Jewish cults of the "returnees." . . . Despite the State and our political independence, our army and our sovereignty, our sun stands still, our time has stopped. . . . There is no God, no human beings, no law, and no vision.

Israelis see themselves as being in a desperate situation with no way out. They want to keep the world as they know it and like it, the only world they can survive in. The Zionist vision promised to end the incredibly tragic history of the Jewish people. As time goes on, it becomes transparent that Zionism has done nothing of the kind, and the State of Israel becomes just another chapter in the calamitous history of the Jews. With interminable fighting and interminable "strategic" dead ends, such as the 1973 War and the Lebanon War, Israelis have become more cynical and more desperate about their fate. And who could blame them? If all they have to look forward to is more fighting and more hollow victories, their behavior becomes more understandable. They feel themselves to be trapped, completely helpless in the face of a menacing world, regardless of what they do.

The point of departure for any serious thinking about the future must be pessimism. This is the question. So far, Zionism has been a success, but it may be short-lived because of the rising forces of opposition to it. Discussing the lengthy celebrations of Israel's fortieth anniversary in 1988, a Knesset member states: "Only in a place where there is no confidence in a tomorrow, people stick to any yesterday with a desperate passion. . . . When it is uncertain whether we will celebrate seventy, or sixty, or, to be safe, fifty, . . . we have to use any opportunity to celebrate, and any excuse for a party" (Sarid, 1987, p. 9). And in a public opinion poll in 1987, 18 percent of Israelis were found to believe that there is a real possibility that the Arabs would destroy Israel within twenty years (Salpeter, 1987).

Collective self-doubt is translated into individual insecurity and feelings of subjective worthlessness. Hopelessness and helplessness characterize both society and its members at this stage. The growing acceptability of magical thinking in a group reflects collective anxiety and loss of confidence. The rise of the occult into cultural prominence in Israel since 1973 is the most serious symptom of the historical crisis it faces, for such ideas gain in popularity when a society has lived through "a loss of confidence in established symbols and cognitive models of reality. . . . Occult practices are appealing . . . because they are seemingly dramatic opposites of empirical practices of science" (Tiryakian, 1972, pp. 510, 494).

When one trauma is followed by another, and nothing seems to go right for a person, the result is often the magical idea of a curse. Why are all these things happening to me? Why am I helpless to change reality? When instrumental coping fails, magic seems like the only recourse (Malinowski, 1925). A collective feeling of helplessness in the face of a "curse" may lead to a collective acceptance of fatalism, religion, and the occult. Generalizations across historical situations are most plausible at the psychological level, the level of individual dynamics. What contemporary Israelis have in common with Cargo Cultists and Ghost Dancers is the wish and the need to escape from an impossible reality, through the mechanism of salvation. But Cargo Cultists and Ghost Dancers offered not only private salvation, and their members did not just tell private salvation stories as contemporary Israelis do. Israelis are neither Cargo Cultists nor Ghost Dancers, but some of them, committed to miraculous answers to their crisis, do offer others both private and public salvation. The salvation movements in Israel are not Ghost Dance movements nor are they Cargo Cults. Still all these movements have something basic in common, which can be enumerated only in the calculus of human despair and deliverance.

References

Abramovitz, A. Assad votes Likud. *Maariv,* May 4, 1984a, (in Hebrew).

Abramovitz, D. Judaization? No such cult. *Koteret Rashit,* June 5, 1984b. (in Hebrew).

Adams, P. R., and Adams, G. R. Mount Saint Helen's Ashfall: Evidence for a disaster stress reaction. *American Psychologist,* 1984, *39,* 252–260.

Adiran, Y. Contractor claims: My partner spent company money on astrology. *Yediot Aharonot,* November 20, 1984 (in Hebrew).

Adorno, T. W. The Stars Down to Earth: The Los Angeles Times Astrology Column. *Telos* 19:13–90, 1974.

Adorno, T. W., Frenkel-Brunswick, E., Levinson, D. J., and Sanford, R. N. *The Authoritarian Personality.* New York: Harper and Row, 1950.

Albee, G. W. The Protestant ethic, sex and psychotherapy. *American Psychologist,* 32:150–61, 1977.

Allen, S. *Beloved Son: A Story of the Jesus Cults.* Indianapolis: Bobbs-Merrill, 1982.

Allison, J. Adaptive regression and intense religious experience. *Journal for the Scientific Study of Religion,* 5:452–63, 1967.

———. Religious conversion: Regression and progression in an adolescent experience. *Journal for the Scientific Study of Religion,* 8:23–28, 1969.

Allport, G. W. *The Individual and His Religion.* New York: Macmillan, 1950.

Allport, G. W., and Vernon, P. E. *Studies in Expressive Movement.* New York: Macmillan, 1933.

Amdur, M. Campaigning against cults. *Newsview,* February 2, 1982.

American Psychiatric Association. *Diagnostic and Statistical Manual,* 3rd ed. Washington, D.C.: American Psychiatric Association, 1980.

Amir, Y., and Sharon, I. Factors in war widows' adaptation. *Megamot,* 25:119–30, 1979 (in Hebrew).

Antonovsky, A. *Health, Stress and Coping,* San Francisco: Jossey Bass, 1980.

Antonovsky, A., and Arian, A. *Hopes and Fears of Israelis.* Jerusalem: Jerusalem Academic Press, 1972.

Aphek, E., and Tobin, Y. Cartomancy as a discourse and social semiotic system. *Kodikas/Code,* 3:315–24, 1981.

Appelbaum, S. A. *Out In Inner Space: A Psychoanalyst Explores The New Therapies.* Garden City, N.Y.: Doubleday, 1979.

Arad, N. Employees are anxious, management tries to help them relax. *Yediot Aharonot*, February 12, 1991 (in Hebrew).

Archer, D., and Gartner, R. Violent acts and violent times: A comparative approach to postwar homicide rates. *American Sociological Review*, 41:937–63, 1976.

———. Homicide in 110 nations: The development of the comparative crimes data file. *International Annals of Criminology*, 16:109–39, 1977.

———. Peacetime casualties: The effects of war on the violent behavior of non-combatants. In I. L. Kutash, S. B. Kutash, and L. B. Schlesinger (eds.): *Violence: Perspectives on Murder and Aggression*. San Francisco: Jossey Bass, 1978.

Argyle, M., and Beit-Hallahmi, B. *The Social Psychology of Religion*. London: Routledge and Kegan Paul, 1975.

Arian, A. *The Elections in Israel—1977*. Jerusalem: Academic Press, 1980.

———. *The Elections in Israel—1981*. Tel Aviv: Ramot, 1983.

———. *Politics in Israel: The Second Generation*. Chatham, N.J.: Chatham House Publishers, 1985.

Armin, R. *The Poem of the Church of Emin Coils*. London: Cobwebs Press, 1978.

———. *The Journey: The Archives of the Emin Foundation*, vol. 1. London: The Regal Print Company, 1979.

———. *Cobwebs and Tears*. London: The Regal Print Company, 1982.

Artziely, M. The Judaization offensive. *Haaretz*, November 30, 1984 (in Hebrew).

Atlas, Y. The Maharishi to the aid of the stock market. *Yediot Aharonot*, February 1, 1984 (in Hebrew).

Aviad, J. *Return to Judaism: Religious Renewal in Israel*. Chicago: University of Chicago Press, 1983.

Avidan, D. Fascism in literature, first discussion. *Yediot Aharonot*, June 6, 1986 (in Hebrew).

Avidan-Barir, B. The lion. *Haolam Hazeh*, August 3, 1977 (in Hebrew).

———. Electricity in your palms. *Laisha*, December 12, 1983 (in Hebrew).

Avissar, A. An astrological adviser to Prime Minister should be appointed. *Maariv*, May 5, 1988 (in Hebrew).

Avneri, A. Uri Zohar against the Guru Maharaj Ji and Hare Krishna. *Yediot Aharonot*, March 12, 1982 (in Hebrew).

———. Graphologist: Sensitive and honest. *Yediot Aharonot*, February 26, 1984 (in Hebrew).

Avron, S. Sandwiches, as if there is no tomorrow. *Hadashot*, March 1, 1985 (in Hebrew).

Azolay, O. Addiction. *Yediot Aharonot*, November 7, 1980 (in Hebrew).

Balch, R. W., and Taylor, D. Salvation in a UFO. *Psychology Today*, October 1976.

Bandura, A. Self-efficacy mechnism in human agency. *American Psychologist*, 17:122–47, 1982.

Barber, B. Acculturation and messianic movements. *American Sociological Review*, 6:663–69, 1941.

Bargal, D., and Gidron, B. *Self-Help/Mutual Help Groups In Jerusalem. Explora-*

tory Study. Jerusalem: The Baerwald School of Social Work, The Hebrew University, March 1983.

Barinbaum, L. Death of young sons and husbands. In R. A. Kalish (ed.): *Death and Dying*. New York: Baywood, 1980.

Bar-Kadma, E. Finkel settles the score. *Yediot Aharonot*, March 9, 1983 (in Hebrew).

Barkun, M. *Disaster and the Millenium*. New Haven, Conn.: Yale University Press, 1974.

Barnea, N. On the way from the polls. *Koteret Rashit*, July 25, 1984 (in Hebrew).

Bar-On, Y. Two are better. *Bamahane*, May 1986a (in Hebrew).

———. Dudu Topaz—writing and counting. *Bamahane*, July 16, 1986b (in Hebrew).

Bart, P. The myth of a value free psychotherapy. In W. Bell and J. A. Mau (eds.): *Sociology and the Future*. New York: Basic Books, 1972.

Bartley, W. W., III. *Werner Erhard: The Transformation of A Man, The Founding of est*. New York: Clarkson N. Potter, 1978.

Barton, A. H. *Communities in Disaster*. Garden City, N.Y.: Anchor Books, 1970.

Bartzky, N. The private side: Dvora Omer. *Maariv*, November 7, 1986 (in Hebrew).

Barzilai, A. Elections 84, elections 85. *Haaretz*, February 17, 1984 (in Hebrew).

Becker, B. "A little self-respect goes a long way". Excerpted from B. Becker, *Decisions: Getting What You Want*. New York: Grosset and Dunlap, 1978. *New York Post*, August 1, 1978.

Be'er, Y. Emin painting exhibition stopped. *Kol Ha'ir*, January 21, 1983 (in Hebrew).

———. The State of Israel vs. the cults. *Kol Ha'ir*, December 10, 1982 (in Hebrew).

Beit Hallahmi, B. Religion and nationalism in the Arab-Israel conflict. *Il Politico*, 38:232–43, 1973.

———. Salvation and its vicissitudes: Clinical psychology and political values. *American Psychologist*, 29:124–29, 1974.

———. On the "religious" functions of the helping professions. *Archive für Religionpsychologie*, 12:48–52, 1976.

———. Humanistic psychology: Progressive or reactionary? *Self and Society*, 12:97–103, 1977a.

———. Identity integration, self-image crisis and "Superego Victory" in postadolescent university students. *Adolescence*, 12:57–69, 1977b.

———. *The Israeli Connection*. New York: Pantheon, 1987.

———. *Prolegomena to the Psychological Study of Religion*. Lewisburg, Pa.: Bucknell University Press, 1989.

———. *Original Sins: Reflections on Zionism and Israel*. London: Pluto Press, 1991.

———. *Dictionary of Modern Religious Movements, Sects, and Cults*. New York: Richards Rosen, 1992.

———. Naming traditions and identity problems in Israel. Unpublished manuscript. University of Haifa, 1987.

Beit-Hallahmi, B., and Nevo, B. "Born-again" Jews in Israel: The dynamics of an identity change. *International Journal of Psychology,* 22:75–81, 1987.
Ben-Ari, D. A wedding at dawn. *Laisha,* May 26, 1986 (in Hebrew).
Ben-Dov, Y. Bar-Ilan will surrender. *Haaretz,* March 2, 1984 (in Hebrew).
Ben-Meir, J., and Kedem, P. Index of religiosity of the Jewish population of Israel. *Megamot,* 24(3):353–62, 1979 (in Hebrew).
Ben-Ner, Y. Don't do it. *Maariv,* March 12, 1982 (in Hebrew).
Bennett, A. Who made Iacocca not quite so shy? It was Dale Carnegie. *The Wall Street Journal,* June 16, 1986.
Bennett, J. G. *Gurdjieff: Making of a New World.* New York: Harper and Row, 1973.
Ben-Shakhar, G., Ben-Hillel, M., Bilu, Y., Ben-Abba, E., and Flug, A. Can graphology predict occupational success? Two empirical studies and some methodological ruminations. *Journal of Applied Psychology,* 71:645–53, 1986.
Ben-Shaul, D. Smoking more. *The Jerusalem Post,* April 12, 1985.
Ben-Zakkai, T. Look for the woman. *Maariv,* November 27, 1981 (in Hebrew).
———. Bourgeois on the Heights. *Maariv,* January 15, 1982 (in Hebrew).
———. Who is afraid of 1984? *Maariv,* June 17, 1983 (in Hebrew).
Berger, P. L. Towards a sociological understanding of psychoanalysis. *Social Research,* 32:26–41, 1965.
Berman, E. Dilemmas of psychotherapy in Israel. *American Journal of Psychoanalysis,* 41:169–72, 1981.
Bernet, M. M. Is Israel ready for encounter? Is encounter ready for Israel? *AACI Bulletin,* April 1971.
Binyamini, M. An astrological forecast for election day. *Haolam Hazeh,* July 18, 1984 (in Hebrew).
Bird, F., and Reimer, B. Participation rates in new religious and para-religious movements. *Journal for the Scientific Study of Religion,* 21:1–14, 1982.
Bitzur, Y. Reform's "War of deception." *Maariv,* October 31, 1986 (in Hebrew).
Bloch, N. The future lies in numbers. *Yediot Aharonot,* March 5, 1982 (in Hebrew).
Boettcher, R. *Gifts of Deceit.* New York: Holt, Rinehart and Winston, 1980.
Bolin, R. *Long-Term Family Recovery from Disaster.* Boulder, Colo.: Institute of Behavioral Science, University of Colorado, 1982.
Boon, H., Davrou, Y., and Macquet, J. C. *La Sophrologie.* Paris: Retz, 1985.
Boshes, H. No chance to destruction. *Haaretz,* October 16, 1984 (in Hebrew).
Boshier, R. Conservatism and superstitious behavior. In G. D. Wilson (ed.): *The Psychology of Conservatism.* London: Academic Press, 1972.
Brengelmann, J. C., and Wittchen, H. U. Professional psychology and private health service: Developing trends in the Federal Republic of Germany. *American Psychologist,* 41:306–8, 1986.
Breznitz, S. Stress in Israel. In H. Selye (ed.): *Selye's Guide to Stress Research,* pp. 71–89. New York: Van Nostrand Reinhold, 1980.
——— (ed.). *Stress in Israel.* New York: Van Nostrand Reinhold, 1983.
Broughton, J. M. The genetic psychology of James Mark Baldwin. *American Psychologist,* 36:396–407, 1981.

Burg, A. Followers of the Messiah. *Davar,* May 22, 1984 (in Hebrew).

Burridge, K. *New Heaven, New Earth.* New York: Schocken, 1969.

Burton-Bradley, B. G. The psychiatry of cargo cult. *The Medical Journal of Australia,* 2:388–92, 1973.

Butcher, J. N., & Gur, R. A Hebrew translation of the MMPI. *Journal of Cross-Cultural Psychology,* 5:220–27, 1974.

Butcher, J. N., & Pancheri, P. *A Handbook of Cross National MMPI Research.* Minneapolis: University of Minnesota Press, 1976.

Cahnman, W. J. Religion and nationalism. *American Journal of Sociology,* 49:524–29, 1944.

Campbell, D. *If You Don't Know Where You're Going You'll Probably End Up Somewhere Else.* Niles, Ill.: Argus Communications, 1974.

Caplan, N., and Nelson, S. D. On being useful: The nature and consequences of psychological research on social problems. *American Psychologist,* 28:199–211, 1973.

Carnegie, D. In Thought-Fuel. *Comments,* January 1981 (official publication of Dale Carnegie and Associates, Inc.).

Cashmore, E. *Rastaman.* London: Allen and Unwin, 1981.

Caspi, A. Are graphologists fooling us all? *Koteret Rashit,* June 13, 1984 (in Hebrew).

Cassel, J. The relation of the urban environment to health: Implications for prevention. *Mount Sinai Journal of Medicine,* 40:539–50, 1973.

Cavaglion, G. The societal reaction to "cults" in Israel. Unpublished M.A. Thesis, Institute of Criminology, The Hebrew University. Jerusalem, 1990.

Central Bureau of Statistics, *Statistical Abstracts of Israel,* Jerusalem, 1966–83.

Central Bureau of Statistics, *Victimization Survey, 1981,* Special Series No. 729. Jerusalem, 1983.

Christiansen, C. W. Religious conversion. *Archives of General Psychiatry,* 9:207–16, 1963.

Cohen, E., and Grunau, H. *Minorities in Israel.* The Hebrew University, The Institute for Asian and African Studies, 1972 (in Hebrew).

Cordell, D. *Take 10 to Grow.* Niles, Ill.: Argus Communications, 1978.

Cox, H. *Turning East.* New York: Simon and Schuster, 1977.

Crapanzano, V. *Waiting: The Whites of South Africa.* New York: Random House, 1985.

Critchlow, B. The powers of John Barleycorn: Beliefs about the effects of alcohol on social behavior. *American Psychologist,* 41:751–64, 1986.

Cromer, G. Repentent delinquents. A religious approach to rehabilitation, *The Jewish Journal of Sociology,* 23:113–22, 1981.

———. Sad tales and happy tales: The politicization of delinquent life-histories. *Political Communication and Persuasion,* 55:179–90, 1988.

Darell, J. *Search for Identity: Youth, Religion and Culture.* London: Sage, 1978.

Dankner, A. Last winter it all looked different. *Haaretz,* June 29, 1981 (in Hebrew).

Dar, Y. More than 20 conversions to Christianity in Naharia. *The Jerusalem Post,* January 6, 1984.

Davar, June 29, 1983. Membership in the cult—or in the kibbutz (in Hebrew).
Davis, K. The application of science to personal relations: A critique of the family clinic idea. *American Sociological Review,* 1:236–47, 1936.
Deshen, S. Israeli Judaism: Introduction to the major patterns. *International Journal of Middle East Studies,* 8:141–69, 1978.
"Dial Dr. Toni for therapy". *Time,* May 26, 1980, p. 95.
Dittes, J. Psychology of Religion. In G. Lindzey and E. Aronson (eds.): *The Handbook of Social Psychology,* vol. 5 (2nd ed.). Reading, Mass: Addison-Wesley, 1969.
Dohrwend, B. C. Sociocultural and social-psychological factors in the genesis of mental disorders. *Journal of Health and Social Behavior.* 16:365–92, 1975.
Dreman, S. B. The Yom Kippur War: The soldier on the front and his family. *American Journal of Family Therapy,* 9:56–64, 1981.
Durkheim, E. *Suicide.* Glencoe, Ill.: The Fress Press, 1951.
Dyer, W. *Your Erroneous Zones.* New York: Avon Books, 1976.
Eden, M. After services, the orthodox went to demonstrate against a Messianic community. *Yediot Aharonot,* December 9, 1984 (in Hebrew).
Ehrenreich, B., and Ehrenreich, J. The Professional-Managerial Class. *Radical America,* 11(2):7–31, 1977.
Ehrlich, E. Well conected. *Haaretz,* December 23, 1988 (in Hebrew).
Eister, A. W. Culture crises and new religious movements: A paradigmatic statement of a theory of cults. In I. I. Zaretsky and M. P. Leone (eds.): *Religious Movements in Contemporary America.* Princeton, N.J.: Princeton University Press, 1974.
Eival, D. Before becoming a butterfly. *Davar,* August 24, 1984 (in Hebrew).
Eli, R. Ceauşescu and Elana: An autopsy. *Maariv,* January 26, 1990a (in Hebrew).
———. A nation's sign. *Maariv Magazine,* October 19, 1990b (in Hebrew).
Eliom, D. The macabre is the refuge of the kind in heart. *Hotam,* April 6, 1984 (in Hebrew).
Elkayam, S. Driving the mouse crazy. *Haolam Hazeh,* July 1, 1981 (in Hebrew).
Ella, S. Witch hunt. *Yediot Aharonot,* October 2, 1981 (in Hebrew).
Ellenberger, H. F. *The Discovery of the Unconscious: The History and Evolution of Dynamic Psychiatry.* New York: Basic Books, 1971.
Emin Society Israel. Leaflet for art exhibit, Jerusalem, December, 1982.
Erikson, K. T. *Everything in its Path: Destruction of Community in The Buffalo Creek Flood.* New York: Simon and Schuster, 1976.
———. *In the Wake of the Flood.* London: Allen and Unwin, 1979.
Etgar, L. A ticket to heaven. *Yediot Aharonot,* December 2, 1983 (in Hebrew).
———. "The stars don't like Reagan." *Yediot Aharonot,* October 30, 1984 (in Hebrew).
Etgar, L., and Ella, S. A bitter marathon. *Yediot Aharonot,* May 9, 1980 (in Hebrew).
Ettinger, S. He played it big. *Shahaf,* April 20, 1984 (in Hebrew).
Etzioni, A. Human beings are not very easy to change after all. *Saturday Review,* June 3, 1972.

Etzioni-Halevy, E. *Political Culture in Israel.* New York: Praeger, 1977.
Fairbairn, W. R. D. *Psycho-Analytic Studies of the Personality.* London: Tavistock, 1952.
Falik, A. The problem of alcoholism. *Briut Hatzibur,* 19:465–66, 1977 (in Hebrew).
Fenwick, S. *Getting It: The Psychology of Est.* New York: Penguin Books, 1976.
Festinger, L., Riecken, H. W., and Schachter, S. *When Prophecy Fails.* Minneapolis: University of Minnesota Press, 1956.
Fidel, Y. Six in hundred addicted to alcohol. *Hadashot,* September, 17, 1984 (in Hebrew).
Fine, F. *Psychoanalytic Psychology.* New York: Jason Aronson, 1975.
Finkel, N. J. From cathartics to catharsis: Psychology's emergence from medicine. *Connecticut Medicine,* 40:269–71, 1976.
Fisher, R. Hundreds of young people in Haifa fall prey to mysterious cults from the East. *Kol Haifa,* November 30, 1979 (in Hebrew).
Florian, V. War widows: Intervention in the first period of mourning. *Advances in Thanatology,* 5:1–8, 1982.
———. Children's concept of death: An empirical study of a cognitive and environmental approach. *Death Education,* 9:133–41, 1985.
Florian, V., and Har-Even, D. Fear of personal death: The effects of sex and religious belief. *Omega: Journal of Death and Dying,* 14:83–91, 1983.
Florian, V., and Kravetz, S. Fear of personal death: Attribution, structure and relation to religious belief. *Journal of Personality and Social Psychology,* 44:600–607, 1983.
Florian, V., and Kravetz, S. Children's concepts of death: A cross-cultural comparison among Muslims, Druze, Christians and Jews in Israel. *Journal of Cross-Cultural Psychology,* 16:174–89, 1985.
Florian, V., Kravetz, S., and Frankel, J. Aspects of fear of personal death, levels of awareness and religious commitment. *Journal of Research in Personality,* 18:289–304, 1984.
Florian, V., and Shurka, E. Psycho-social aspects of loss. *Saad,* January 1974, pp. 5–8 (in Hebrew).
Foa, U. G., and Donnerwerth, G. W. Love poverty in modern culture and sensitivity training. *Sociological Inquiry,* 41:149–59, 1971.
Foss, D. A., and Larkin, R. W. Worshipping the absurd: The negation of social causality among the followers of Guru Maharah Ji. *Sociological Analysis,* 39:157–64, 1978.
Foulkes, S. H. My philosophy of psychotherapy. *Journal of Contemporary Psychotherapy,* 6:109–14, 1974.
Foundation For Mideast Communication Newsletter, vol. 1, no. 2, Spring 1986.
Frank, J. D. *Persuasion and Healing* (rev. ed.). New York: Schocken, 1974.
Freed, J. *Moonwebs.* Toronto: Dorset, 1980.
Freedman, A. M., Kaplan, H. I., and Sadock, B. J. *Comprehensive Textbook of Psychiatry.* Baltimore: Williams and Wilkins, 1975.
Frenkel, S. Cults are the target. *Haolam Hazeh,* September 20, 1983 (in Hebrew).

Freud, S. A religious experience. In *The Standard Edition of the Complete Psychological Works of Sigmund Freud,* vol. 21, London: The Hogarth Press, 1961 (1928).

Friedmann, D. Les groupes "parapsychanalytiques": leurs animateurs et participants. Paris: CNRS (CORDES) Document de recherche, 1980.

Friedmann, G. *The End of the Jewish People?* Garden City, N.Y.: Doubleday, 1967.

Fritz, C. E., and Marks, E. S. The NORC studies of human behavior in disaster. *Journal of Social Issues,* 10:26–41, 1954.

Fromm, E. *Escape From Freedom.* New York: Avon, 1964 (1941).

Fuller, R. C. *Mesmerism and the American Cure of Souls.* Philadelphia: University of Pennsylvania Press, 1982.

Galili, L. The inhabitants of the no man's land of faith. *Haaretz,* March 16, 1984a (in Hebrew).

———. Being logical is only half of science. *Haaretz,* April 20, 1984b (in Hebrew).

Galili, Y. "Messianic merchandise" on the streets of Haifa. *Kol Haifa,* February 12, 1982 (in Hebrew).

Galnoor, Y. Changes in the Israeli political system since the 1973 War. *Medina, Mimshal, Veyahassim Beinleumiim,* 1977, no. 11 (in Hebrew).

Galzan, O. Getting married at 49 (and a half). *Haolam Hazeh,* April 25, 1984 (in Hebrew).

Gardner, M. *Fads and Falacies In the Name of Science.* New York: Dover Publications, 1957.

Gartner, A., and Riessman, F. *The Self-Help Revolution.* New York: Human Sciences Press, 1984.

Gat, B. Who are you, Vicky Shiran. *Yediot Aharonot,* September 16, 1983 (in Hebrew).

Gault, A. *The Founders of Psychical Research.* London: Routledge and Kegan Paul, 1968.

Geffen, Y. Ticket to heaven (first class). *Maariv,* October 21, 1982 (in Hebrew).

———. The 5744 fad. *Maariv,* November 6, 1981 (in Hebrew).

Genossar, S. How are soldiers returned to Judaism. *Davar,* February 5, 1986 (in Hebrew).

Givon, D. Crisis intervention with bereaved families. *Saad,* 17:3–11, 1974.

Glock, C., and Stark, R. *Religion and Society in Tension.* Chicago: Rand McNally, 1965.

Gluska, A. No connection with est (letter). *Haaretz,* December 11, 1984 (in Hebrew).

Goell, Y. Everything we were promised about Emanuel has been delivered. *The Jerusalem Post,* January 20, 1984.

Golan, A. The Hermon fortress: The wound. *Yediot Aharonot,* September 16, 1983 (in Hebrew).

Golan, N. Wife to widow to woman. *Social Work,* 20:369–73, 1975.

Golan, S. Show me your palm and I'll tell you. *Davar,* February 15, 1991 (in Hebrew).

Golden, F. It's in the stars, Mr. President. *Discover,* January 1985.

Goldberg, J., Yinon, Y., and Cohen, A. A cross-cultural comparison between the Israeli and American fear survey inventory. *Journal of Social Psychology,* 97:131–32, 1975a.

———. A factor analysis of the Israeli fear survey inventory. *Psychological Reports,* 36:175–79, 1975b.

Gonen, J. Y. *A Psychohistory of Zionism.* New York: Mason/Charter, 1975.

Green, H. *Fit for America.* New York: Pantheon Books, 1986.

Greenbaum, C. W., Rogovsky, I., and Shalit, B. The military psychologist during wartime: A model based on action research and crisis intervention. *The Journal of Applied Behavioral Science,* 13:7–21, 1977.

Greenwald, J. *Be the Person You Were Meant to Be.* New York: Dell Publishing Co., 1973.

Guberman, J. Cults in Israel. *The Advisor,* August/September 1982.

Gumbel, E. Psychoanalysis in Israel. *Israel Annals of Psychiatry And Related Disciplines,* 5:89–98, 1965.

Guri, H. Letter. *Shdemot,* no. 53, Winter 1974 (in Hebrew).

Gutwirth, J. Religieux et laïcs en Israël: Forces opposées ou complémentaires? *Archives de Sciences Sociales des Religions,* 49:61–66, 1980.

Haaretz, Ways to stop youth from joining guru cult discussed. October 28, 1981 (in Hebrew).

Haaretz, 45 percent of public: Our views are closer to the right. May 14, 1985 (in Hebrew).

Hacohen, E. The young are more "lenient." *Al Hamishmar,* October 24, 1984 (in Hebrew).

Hadashot, Original Celebration. March 21, 1984 (in Hebrew).

Hale, N. G., Jr. *Freud and the Americans.* New York: Oxford University Press, 1971.

Halevy, D. The crystal ball, black ointment, and the king of the devils. *Monitin,* June 1980 (in Hebrew).

Halkin, H. *Letters To An American Jewish Friend: A Zionist's Polemic.* Philadelphia: Jewish Publication Society of America, 1977.

Hall, G. S. Adolescence: Its psychology and its relations to physiology, anthropology, sociology, sex, crime, relgion, and education. New York: Appleton, 1904.

Halleck, S. L. *The Politics of Therapy.* New York: Science House, 1971.

Halloran, J. Emin, Armin, Amen. *Private Eye,* March 28, 1980a.

———. Salvation Armin. *Private Eye,* April 11, 1980b.

———. Emin Chorus. *Private Eye,* May 9, 1980c.

———. Leo tarred. *Private Eye,* May 23, 1980d.

Halmos, P. *The Faith of the Counsellors.* New York: Schocken, 1970a.

———. *The Personal Service Society.* London: Constable, 1970b.

Hammer, Z. Letter to Miriam Glazer Ta'asa. February 5, 1982.

Handwerker, H. In the name of the Jewish people and Jesus its Messiah. *Haaretz,* December 3, 1980 (in Hebrew).

Haolam Hazeh, Religious rehabilitation for prisoners. April 9, 1986 (in Hebrew).

Haolam Hazeh, Hava Yaari on everybody else. June 11, 1986 (in Hebrew).

Harrison, J. F. C. *The Second Coming: Popular Millenarianism 1780–1850.* New Brunswick, N.J.: Rutgers University Press, 1979.

Hashavua Bakibbutz Haartzi, September 27, 1973 (in Hebrew).

Heirich, M. Change of heart: A test of some widely held theories about religious conversion. *American Journal of Sociology,* 83:653–80, 1977.

Herman, S. N. *Isralis and Jews: The Continuity of an Identity.* New York: Random House, 1970.

Hertzberg, A. *The Zionist Idea.* New York: Atheneum, 1971.

Heschel, A. J. *Israel: An Echo of Eternity.* New York: Farrar, Straus, and Giroux, 1967.

Hine, V. H. Bridge burners: Commitment and participation in a religious movement. *Sociological Analysis,* 31:61–66, 1970.

Hirschman, A. O. *Exit, Voice and Loyalty.* Cambridge: Harvard University Press, 1970.

Hochschild, A. In the final days. *Mother Jones,* November 1980.

Hochstadt, M. Women are waiting for the fortune teller. *Maariv,* September 28, 1981 (in Hebrew).

Hoffer, E. *The True Believer.* New York: Harper and Row, 1951.

Hoffman, V. Idyllic idea for the 'Year of Destruction'. *The Jerusalem Post,* October 30, 1982.

Holland, J. G. Behaviorism: Part of the problem or part of the solution? *Journal of Applied Behavior Analysis,* 11:163–74, 1978.

Hurvitz, M. Arson in a Tiberias hotel following missionary activities. *Haaretz,* December 26, 1983 (in Hebrew).

Hurvitz, N. Psychotherapy as a means of social control. *Journal of Consulting and Clinical Psychology,* 40:232–39, 1973.

———. Manifest and latent functions in psychotherapy. *Journal of Consulting and Clinical Psychology,* 42:301–2, 1974.

Insensee, W. Havens for troubled minds. *USA Today,* January 24, 1984.

Israel Ministry of Religious Affairs. *Report on the Activities of the Ministry.* Jerusalem, 1975.

Israel National Police, Special Service Branch. The "Guru Maharishi" Cult. *Intelligence Report,* May 3, 1974.

Israel Pocket Library: *Religious Life and Communities.* Jerusalem: Keter Books, 1974.

Jaffe, Y., and Rosenfeld, H. Field dependence, handling of hostility, and sexual identification in post-traumatic Yom Kippur War veterans. In C. D. Spielberger, I. G. Sarason, and N. A. Milgram (eds.): *Stress and Anxiety,* vol. 8. Washington, D.C.: Hemisphere, 1982.

James, W. *Radical Empiricism and a Pluralistic Universe.* London: Longmans, Green and Company, 1900, 1943.

———. *The Varieties of Religious Experience.* New York: New American Library, 1902, 1961.

Janoff-Bulman, R. The aftermath of victimization: Rebuilding shattered assumptions. In C. R. Figley (ed.): *Trauma and Its Wake: The Study and Treatment of Post-Traumatic Stress Disorder.* New York: Bruner/Mazel, 1985.

Jenkins, C. D. Epidemiological studies of the psychosomatic aspects of coronary heart disease. *Advances in Psychosomatic Medicine,* 9:1–19, 1977.

The Jerusalem Post, Aloni: Jehovah's Witnesses now being forced to serve in army. December 30, 1975.

The Jerusalem Post, 'Messiah' Center tightens its grip. February 10, 1979.

The Jerusalem Post, Church arson was an "antimissionary action." January 8, 1984.

Joshi, V. *The Awakened One.* New York: Harper and Row, 1982.

Judah, J. S. *The History and the Philosophy of the Metaphysical Movements in America.* Philadelphia: Westminster Press, 1967.

Kaffman, M. "Emin" and the kibbutz—peaceful coexistence? *Hashavua Hakibbutz Haartzi,* June 17, 1983 (in Hebrew).

———. The attraction of the cults. *Skira Hodshit* (Israel Defence Forces Monthly), December 1983 (in Hebrew).

Kaffman, M., and Elizur, E. Children's bereavement reactions following death of the father. *International Journal of Family Therapy,* 1:203–29, 1979.

Kaplan, H. I., and Sadock, B. J. *Comprehensive Group Psychotherapy.* Baltimore: Williams and Wilkins, 1971.

Karasu, T. S. Toward unification of psychotherapies: A complementary model. *American Journal of Psychotherapy,* 33:555–63, 1979.

Kardiner, A. The social distress syndrome of our times. *Journal of the American Academy of Psychoanalysis,* 6:89–101, 1978.

Keinan, G., Barak, A., and Ramati, T. Reliability and validity of graphological assessment in the selection process of military officers. *Perceptual and Motor Skills,* 58:811–21, 1984.

Keniston, K. *The Uncommitted.* New York: Dell, 1967.

Kessler, G. Give us a break, Mr. Aridor. *Maariv,* November 13, 1984 (in Hebrew).

Kessler, R. C., and Cleary, P. D. Social class and psychological distress. *American Sociological Review,* 45:463–78, 1980.

———. A disaggregation of the relationship between socio-economic status and psychological distress. *American Sociological Review,* 47:752–64, 1982.

Kfiri, A. Missionaries in Haifa distributing "corrected" Passover Hagaddah. *Kol Haifa,* April 12, 1984 (in Hebrew).

Kiev, A. Subud and mental illness. *American Journal of Psychotherapy,* 18:66–70, 1964.

———. Primitive religious rites and behavior: Clinical considerations. *International Psychiatry Clinics,* 5:119–31, 1969.

Kinston, W., and Rosser, R. Disaster: Effects on mental and physical states. *Journal of Psychosomatic Research,* 18:437–56, 1974.

Kisslev, R. Truth from Ramat-Hasharon. *Haaretz,* November 9, 1983 (in Hebrew).

———. The kingdom of Or Sameah. *Haaretz,* March 23, 1984 (in Hebrew).

Klerman, G. L. The efficacy of psychotherapy as the basis for public policy. *American Psychologist,* 38:929–34, 1983.

Kliegerman, C. A. Psychoanalytic study of the *Confessions* of St. Augustine. *Journal of the American Psychoanalytic Association,* 5:469–80, 1957.
Klingman, A. Death education through literature: A preventive approach. *Death Education,* 4:271–79, 1980.
———. Simulation and simulation games as a strategy for death education. *Death Education,* 7:339–52, 1983.
Kohn, M. Teaching tolerance. *The Jerusalem Post,* July 8, 1984.
Kolbo. Emin cult penetrates suburb? December 5, 1982 (in Hebrew).
Koocher, G. P. Childhood, death, and cognitive development. *Developmental Psychology,* 9:369–75, 1973.
Kramer, M. The returnees. *Jerusalem Post Magazine,* May 18, 1972.
Kroy, M. *Rational Existence: The Conditions For Objective Happiness.* Tel-Aviv: Metziut, 1975 (in Hebrew).
Ksafim. The prophecy that came true. May 14, 1984 (in Hebrew).
Kulka, R. A., Veroff, J., and Douvan, E. Social class and the use of professional help for personal problems: 1957 and 1976. *Journal of Health and Social Behavior,* 20:2–17, 1979.
Kuperman, A. Caution: Marathons! *Haaretz,* February 24, 1981 (in Hebrew).
Kutash, I. L., and Schlesinger, L. B. (eds.). *Handbook on Stress and Anxiety.* San Francisco: Jossey Bass, 1980.
La Barre, W. *The Ghost Dance.* New York: Dell, 1972.
Lan, S. "I am a teacher, I am a healer, I am a prophet." *Haaretz Magazine,* January 4, 1991 (in Hebrew).
Landau, S. F., and Beit-Hallahmi, B. Aggression in Israel: A psychohistorical survey. In A. P. Goldstein and M. H. Segall (eds.): *Aggression in Global Perspective.* New York: Pergamon Press, 1983.
Lanternari, V. *The Religions of the Oppressed.* London: MacGibbon and Kee, 1963.
Lazarus, A. A. Notes on behavior therapy, the problem of relapse and some tentative solutions. *Psychotherapy: Theory, Research and Practice,* 8:192–94, 1971.
Lazerwitz, B., and Harrison, M. American Jewish denominations: A social and religious profile. *American Sociological Review,* 44:656–66, 1979.
Lehman-Wilzig, S. Public protest and systematic stability in Israel 1960–1979. In S. Lehman-Wilzig and B. Susser (eds.): *Comparative Jewish Politics: Public Life in Israel and the Diaspora.* Ramat-Gan: Bar-Ilan University Press, 1981.
Leibovitz, S. The other cheek. *Koteret Rashit,* May 30, 1984 (in Hebrew).
Leuba, J. H. *A Psychological Study of Religion.* New York: Macmillan, 1912.
Lev, Y. To be alone, together. *Maariv,* May 6, 1984 (in Hebrew).
Levanon, N. Under the sign of Dolly. *La'isha,* May 19, 1986 (in Hebrew).
Levav, I., Greenfeld, H., and Baruch, E. Psychiatric combat reactions during the Yom Kippur War. *American Journal of Psychiatry,* 136:637–41, 1979.
Levi, L., and Anderson, L. *Psychosocial Stress—Population, Environment and Quality of Life.* New York: Spectrum, 1975.
Levin, H. *Schitz.* Tel Aviv, 1975 (mimemo) (in Hebrew).
Levin, T. M., and Zegans, L. S. Adolescent identity crisis and religious con-

version: Implications for psychotherapy. *British Journal of Medical Psychology,* 47:73–82, 1974.

Levine, S. V. Role of psychiatry in the phenomenon of cults. *Canadian Journal of Psychiatry,* 24:593–603, 1979.

———. *Radical Departures.* New York: Harcourt Brace Jovanovich, 1984.

Levinstein, E. 166 possibilities for a romantic relationship. *Haaretz,* April 21, 1986 (in Hebrew).

———. The cranes are flying again. *Haaretz,* February 24, 1988 (in Hebrew).

Levison, P. K., Gerstein, D. R., and Maloff, D. R. (eds.). *Commonalties in Substance Abuse and Habitual Behaviors.* Lexington, Mass.: Lexington Books, 1983.

Levy, A. The 5 electrical centres in the human body. *Teva Ubriut,* October 1981 (in Hebrew).

Lieblich, A. *Tin Soldiers on Jerusalem Beach.* New York: Pantheon Books, 1978.

———. Between strength and toughness. In S. Breznitz (ed.): *Stress in Israel.* New York: Van Nostrand Reinhold, 1983.

Liebman, C. S. Religious and political integration in Israel. *Jewish Journal of Sociology,* 17:19–26, 1975.

———. The meaning of Jewish identity. In C. S. Liebman and E. Don-Yehiya (eds.): *Religion and Politics in Israel.* Bloomington: University of Indiana Press, 1984.

Liebman, C. S., and Don-Yehiya, E. Separation of religion and state in Israel: A program or a slogan? In C. S. Liebman and E. Don-Yehiya (eds.): *Religion and Politics in Israel.* Bloomington: University of Indiana Press, 1984.

Liff, Z. A. The charismatic leader. In Z. A. Liff (ed.): *The Leader in the Group.* New York: Jason Aronson, 1975.

Lifton, R. J. *Though Reform and the Pyschology of Totalism.* New York: Norton, 1961.

Lincoln, C. E. *The Black Muslims in America.* Boston: Beacon Press, 1961.

Lindemann, E. Symptomatology and management of acture grief. In H. J. Parad (ed.): *Crisis Intervention.* New York: Family Service Association, 1965.

Lindop, G. Divination. In J. R. Hinnells (ed.): *The Penguin Dictionary of Religions.* Harmondsworth: Penguin Books, 1984.

Lior, G. Come dance with us at the cemetry. *Yediot Aharonot,* April 22, 1981 (in Hebrew).

———. Who are you, Yonah Avrushmi. *Yediot Aharonot,* January 27, 1984a (in Hebrew).

———. The police against "the missionaries." *Yediot Aharonot,* August 14, 1984b (in Hebrew).

Lipson, J. G. Jews for Jesus: An illustration of syncretism. *Anthropological Quarterly,* 53:101–10, 1980.

Lofland, J. *The Doomsday Cult.* New York: Irvington, 1981.

Lofland, J., and Stark, R. Becoming a world saver. *Review of the Religious Research,* 1965.

London, P. From the long couch for the sick to the push button for the bored. *Psychology Today,* June 1974.

Löwy, M. Idéologie révolutionnaire et messianisme mystique chez le jeune Lukacs (1910–1919). *Archives de Sciences Sociales des Religions,* 45:51–63, 1978.

———. Pour une sociologie de la mystique juive. *Archives de Sciences Sociales des Religions,* 57:5–13, 1984.

Lynn, D. B. Personal philosophies in psychotherapy. *Journal of Individual Psychology,* 17:49–55, 1961.

McFarland, H. N. *The Rush Hour of the Gods.* New York: Macmillan, 1967.

McNeill, J. T. *History of the Cure of Souls.* New York: Harper and Row, 1951.

Maimon, S. Rutti Navom: A new Jewess. *Yediot Aharonot,* June 13, 1986 (in Hebrew).

Mandler, N. Texts and notebooks. *Haaretz,* April 21, 1987 (in Hebrew).

Mansur, A. The underground of converted Jews in Israel. *Haaretz,* October 26, 1984 (in Hebrew).

Marcus, Y. Wars aren't made in heaven. *Haaretz,* September 24, 1985 (in Hebrew).

Margalit, H. The end of the world is coming. *Al Hamishmar,* October 6, 1981 (in Hebrew).

Marmorstein, E. *Heaven at Bay.* London: Oxford University Press, 1969.

Marx, K. *Early Writings.* New York: McGraw-Hill, 1964.

Mazori, D. Star wars. *Maariv,* October 2, 1981 (in Hebrew).

———. Curing by tickling. *Maariv,* December 17, 1982 (in Hebrew).

Mauskopf, S. H., and McVaugh, M. R. *The Elusive Science: Origins of Experimental Psychical Research.* Baltimore: Johns Hopkins University Press, 1981.

Meislisch, S. *The Return to Judaism.* Tel Aviv: Masada, 1984 (in Hebrew).

Meller, D. I lost a son. *Maariv,* October 18, 1985 (in Hebrew).

Meltzoff, J., and Kornreich, M. *Research in Psychotherapy.* New York: Atherton, 1970.

Meroz, T. Beware of the Guru. *Haaretz,* May 3, 1974 (in Hebrew).

Meyer, D. *The Positive Thinkers: Religion as Pop Psychology from Mary Baker Eddy to Oral Roberts.* New York: Pantheon, 1980.

Michael, B. "Change the State's Birth Date." *Hadashot,* October 31, 1984 (in Hebrew).

Mileti, D. S., Drabek, T. E., and Haas, J. E. *Human Systems in Extreme Environments: A Sociological Perspective.* Boulder, Colo.: Institute of Behavioral Science, University of Colorado, 1975.

Milgram, N. A. (ed.). *Stress and Coping in Time of War: Generalizations from the Israeli Experience.* New York: Bruner/Mazel, 1986.

Miller, W. R. (ed.). *The Addictive Behaviors.* New York: Pergamon, 1980.

Mintz, E. E. *Marathon Groups: Reality and Symbol.* New York: Appleton-Century-Crofts, 1971.

Mooney, J. *The Ghost Dance Religion and the Sioux Outbreak of 1890.* Chicago: University of Chicago Press, 1965.

Morawetz, A. The impact on adolescents of the death in war of an older sibling. *Stress and Anxiety,* 8:267–74, 1982.
Mor, E. Investment according to the stars led to disaster. *Yediot Aharonot,* June 26, 1982 (in Hebrew).
Moses, R. Emotional responses to stress in Israel: A psychoanalytic perspective. In S. Breznitz (ed.): *Stress in Israel.* New York: Van Nostrand Reinhold, 1983.
Moses, R., and Kligler, D. S. A comparative analysis of the institutionalization of mental health values: The United States and Israel. *Israel Annals of Psychiatry and Related Disciplines,* 4:148–61, 1966.
Nadler, A. Self-esteem and the seeking and receiving of help: Theoretical and empirical perspectives. *Progress in Experimental Personality Research,* 14:115–63, 1986.
Neal, A. G. Conflict and the functional equivalence of social movements. *Sociological Focus,* 3(3):3–12, 1970.
Needleman, J. *The New Religions.* Garden City, N.Y.: Doubleday, 1970.
Needleman, J., and Baker, G. (eds.). *Understanding the New Religions.* New York: Seabury Press, 1978.
Nelson, B. Mental healers and their philosophies. *Psychoanalytic Review,* 25:275–80, 1961.
Nevo, B. The validity of graphology in Israel. *Nihul,* no. 52, October 1986 (in Hebrew).
Newman, D. (ed.). *The Political Impact of Gush Emunim.* London: Croom Helm, 1985.
Nordheimer, J. Experts feel Miss Hearst may have undergone brainwashing. *New York Times,* May 28, 1974, p. 30.
Nuriel, A. The Orthodoxization of religious Zionism. *Nakuda,* December 9, 1986 (in Hebrew).
O'Dea, T. F. Sects and cults. In D. L. Sils (ed.): *International Encyclopedia of the Social Sciences,* vol. 14. New York: Macmillan, 1968.
Omer, D. The devil's urine. *Haolam Hazeh,* April 4, 1984 (in Hebrew).
Oren, D. The secret in numbers. *Haaretz,* March 4, 1983 (in Hebrew).
———. The logic of a Kahanist. *Haaretz,* December 21, 1984 (in Hebrew).
———. Coming home. *Haaretz,* November 29, 1985 (in Hebrew).
Orenstein, A. Is membership in the est cult a cause for divorce? *Maariv,* December 22, 1983 (in Hebrew).
Orwell, G. *Nineteen Eighty-Four.* London: Secker and Warburg, 1949.
Ozerman, E. Ambassadors from another world. *Haaretz,* January 9, 1976 (in Hebrew).
Palgi, P. Immigrants, psychiatrists, and culture. *Israel Annals of Psychiatry and Related Disciplines,* 1:43–58, 1963.
Parkes, C. M. *Bereavement.* New York: International University Press, 1973.
Parloff, M. B. Shopping for the right therapy. *Saturday Review,* February 1976, pp. 14–20.
———. How Werner got it. *Psychology Today,* November 1978.
Parsons, T. *The Social System.* Glencoe, Ill.: The Free Press, 1951.

Peretz, D. The earthquake—Israel's ninth Knesset elections. *Middle East Journal,* 31:251–66, 1977.

Peretz, I. The Messianic cult will not proselytize in Rehovot. *Hadashot,* December 16, 1984 (in Hebrew).

Peri, Y. The skullcap and the ingratiation. *Davar,* August 9, 1985 (in Hebrew).

Perry, R. W., and Lindell, M. K. The psychological consequences of natural disaster: A review of research on American communities. *Mass Emergencies,* 3:105–15, 1978.

Peterson, D. R. Is psychology a profession? *American Psychologist,* 3:572–81, 1976.

Pfeffer, L. The legitimation of marginal religions in the United States. In L. I. I. Zaretsky & M. P. Leone (eds.): *Religious Movements in Contemporary America.* Princeton, N.J.: Princeton University Press, 1974.

Poewe, K. On the metonymic structure of religious experiences: The example of charismatic Christianity. *Cultural Dynamics,* 20:361–80, 1989.

Popper, M., and Rahav, M. Trends in psychiatric hospitalization in Israel during the past two decades. Paper presented at the Second Annual Meeting of the Israel Epidemiological Society, Beer-Sheba, 1984.

Pratt, J. B. *The Religious Consciousness.* New York: MacMillan, 1920.

Prister, R. The battle over the "Castel." *Haaretz,* May 31, 1985 (in Hebrew).

Pruyser, P. W. *A Dynamic Psychology of Religion.* New York: Harper and Row, 1968.

Purisman, R., and Maoz, B. Adjustment and war bereavement—some considerations. *British Journal of Medical Psychology,* 50:1–9, 1977.

Rabi, A. Interior Minister: Pardon to all returnees. *Hadashot,* May 29, 1985 (in Hebrew).

Rabin, A. I., and Beit-Hallahmi, B. *Twenty Years Later: Kibbutz Children Grown Up.* New York: Springer, 1982.

Rafaeli, A., and Klimeski, R. J. Predicting sales success through handwriting analysis: An evaluation of the effects of training and handwriting sample content. *Journal of Applied Psychology,* 68:212–17, 1983.

Rahav, M., and Popper, M. Trends in the delivery of psychiatric services in Israel in the years 1965–79. Paper presented at the 1980 Pinhas Sapir Conference on Development, Tel Aviv, December 1980.

Raimy, V. C. *Training in Clinical Psychology.* New York: Prentice Hall, 1950.

Rapaport, S. Police investigating parents' complaints about their children being drawn to a "pagan ritual". *Maariv,* March 26, 1974 (in Hebrew).

Rand, A. *The Virtue of Selfishness.* New York: Signet, 1964.

———. *Capitalism: The Unknown Ideal.* New York: Signet, 1975.

Raphael, B. *When Disaster Strikes.* New York: Basic Books, 1986.

Raviv, Y. *The Open Door: Electronic Communication With the Dead.* Tel Aviv: Reshafim, 1981 (in Hebrew).

Rebibo, J. A drink too many. *The Jerusalem Post,* August 17, 1985.

Reich, B. *Israel: Land of Tradition and Conflict.* Boulder, Colo.: Westview Press, 1985.

Reuveni, Y. Yehudit Ravitz: A slight panic. *Yediot Aharonot,* August 2, 1985 (in Hebrew).

Richard, J. M., Jr., and Gottfredson, G. D. Geographic distribution of U.S. psychologists: A human ecological analysis. *American Psychologist,* 34:1–10, 1978.

Riesman, F., and Miller, S. M. Social change versus the "Psychiatric world view." *American Journal of Orthopsychiatry,* 34:29–38, 1964.

Robbins, T. Eastern mysticism and the resocialization of drug users. *Journal for the Scientific Study of Religion,* 8:308–17, 1969.

Robbins, T., and Anthony, D. Getting straight with Meher Baba. *Journal for the Scientific Study of Religion,* 11:122–40, 1972.

Robbins, T., Anthony, D., and Richardson, J. Theory and research on today's "New religions." *Sociological Analysis,* 39:95–122, 1978.

Roberts, F. J. Some psychological factors in religious conversion. *British Journal of Social and Clinical Psychology,* 4:185–87, 1965.

Rochford, E. B., Jr. *Hare Krishna in America.* New Brunswick, N.J.: Rutgers University Press, 1982.

———. Recruitment strategies, ideology, and organization in the Hare Kirshna movement. *Social Problems,* 29:399–410, 1982.

Rokeach, M. *Beliefs, Attitudes, and Values.* San Francisco: Jossey Bass, 1968.

Roman, K. G. *Handwriting—A Key to Personality.* New York: Pantheon, 1952.

Roman, Z. Meditation forever, *Laisha,* June 11, 1979 (in Hebrew).

———. "My son had to die, and he died for a just cause." *Laisha,* September 4, 1983 (in Hebrew).

———. A baby under the sign of Scorpio, *Laisha,* January 9, 1984 (in Hebrew).

Ron-Feder, G. *I Love You Michal.* Tel Aviv: Milo, 1987 (in Hebrew).

Ronen, M. Avrushmi is introverted, uncommunicative, suggestible. *Yediot Aharonot,* January 30, 1984 (in Hebrew).

Rosen, G. M. Self-help treatment books and the commercialization of psychotherapy. *American Psychologist,* 42:46–51, 1987.

Rosen, R. Schechterman, Haifa: The philosophical basis for destruction is here. *Koteret Rashit,* September 19, 1984 (in Hebrew).

Rosenfeld, L. *Numerology—The Wisdom of Numbers.* Jerusalem: Eliahsar, 1984.

Rosenheim, E., and Muchnik, B. Death concerns in differential levels of consciousness as functions of defense strategies and religious belief. *Omega: Journal of Death and Dying,* 15:15–24, 1985.

Rosenthal, M. The common Israeli—figures. *Bamahane,* November 26, 1986 (in Hebrew).

Rosenwald, G. C. Psychodiagnosis and its discontents. *Psychiatry,* 26:222–40, 1963.

Rosenzweig, M. R. Trends in development and status of psychology: An international perspective. *International Journal of Psychology,* 17:117–40, 1982.

Rossman, M. *New Age Blues.* New York: E. P. Dutton, 1979.

Roszak, T. *Unfinished Animal: The Aquarian Frontier and the Revolution of Consciousness.* New York: Harper and Row, 1976.

Roth, P. *Portnoy's Complaint.* New York: Random House, 1967.

Rubin, J. *Growing (Up) at Thirty-Seven.* New York: Evans and Company, 1976.

Rudge, D. Minors developing drink habit, expert says. *The Jerusalem Post,* June 17, 1984.

Rudin, J., and Rudin, M. *Prison Or Paradise.* Philadelphia: Fortress Press, 1980.

Ruitenbeek, H. M. *The New Group Therapies.* New York: Aronson, 1970.

Russell, B. *Why I am not a Christian.* London: Allen and Unwin, 1957.

Ryan, W. *Blaming the Victim.* New York: Random House, 1971.

Salhuv, S. There is anger; where is glory? *Hadashot,* December 11, 1984 (in Hebrew).

Salomon, Z., Noy, S., and Bar-On, R. Who is at risk for a combat stress reaction syndrome? In N. A. Milgram (ed.): *Stress and Coping in Time of War: Generalizations from the Israeli Experience.* New York: Brunner/Mazal, 1986.

Salzman, L. The psychology of religious and ideological conversion. *Psychiatry,* 16:177–87, 1953.

Salpeter, E. A hawkish face in the mirror. *Haaretz,* October 5, 1987 (in Hebrew).

Sarid, Y. Why the celebrations are so sad. *Haaretz.* November 5, 1987 (in Hebrew).

Sarna, Y. Molotov child. *Hadashot,* February 8, 1985a (in Hebrew).

———. On to the Sanhedrin. *Hadashot,* March 22, 1985b (in Hebrew).

Scanlon, R. Adolf Hitler and the technique of mass brainwashing. In D. C. Bryant (ed.): *The Rhetorical Idiom.* New York: Russell and Russell, 1966.

Scheff, T. J. Reevaluation counseling: Social implications. *Journal of Humanistic Psychology,* 12:58–72, 1972.

Schiff, Z. *October Earthquake: Yom Kippur 1973.* Tel-Aviv: University Publishing, 1974.

Schindler, R. The religious framework of mourning and bereavement and its implications for the helping professions in crisis intervention. *Saad,* 19:(4):11–19, 1975 (in Hebrew).

Scholem, G. *Sabbatai Sevi: The Mystical Messiah, 1626–1676.* Princeton, N.J.: Princeton University Press, 1973.

Schofield, W. *Psychotherapy: The Purchase of Friendship.* Englewood Cliffs, N.J.: Prentice Hall, 1964.

Schrag, P. *Mind Control.* New York: Pantheon, 1978.

Schutz, W. My philosophy of psychotherapy. *Journal of Contemporary Psychotherapy,* 6:129–31, 1974.

———. *Here Comes Everybody.* New York: Harper and Row, 1971.

Sedgwick, P. *PsychoPolitics.* London: Pluto Press, 1982.

Selye, H. *The Stress of Life.* New York: McGraw-Hill 1956.

Shaffir, W. Conversion experiences: Newcomers and defectors from Orthodox Judaism. In Z. Sobel and B. Beit-Hallahmi (eds.): *Tradition, Continuity, Conflict: Jewishness and Judaism in Contemporary Israel.* Albany, N.Y.: SUNY Press, 1991.

Shalev, T. She left me, and I am sad. *Haolam Hazeh,* July 1, 1981 (in Hebrew).

Shalit, D. The film man. *Monitin,* November 1984 (in Hebrew).

Shapira, A. From ideology to performance and back. *Haaretz,* September 16, 1983a (in Hebrew).

Shapira, B. From "Divine Intervention" to "Amanda Marga" I. *Yediot Aharonot,* February 21, 1983b (in Hebrew).

———. From "Divine Intervention" to "Amanda Marga" II. *Yediot Aharonot,* February 28, 1983c (in Hebrew).

———. Lucky numbers, *At,* December 1983d (in Hebrew).

Shapiro, H. The missionaries come out. *The Jerusalem Post,* October 20, 1984.

Sharon, U. The massacre in Haifa: Graphologists will try to understand. *Hadashot,* October 28, 1986 (in Hebrew).

Sharot, S. Jewish millenarianism: A comparison of Medieval communities. *Comparative Studies in Society and History,* 22:394–415, 1980.

Shaul, M. *Chirology—Character Analysis by Palm Reading.* Jerusalem: Migdalor, 1986 (in Hebrew).

Sheatsley, P. B., and Feldman, J. The assassination of President Kennedy: Public reaction. *Public Opinion Quarterly,* 28:189–215, 1964.

Shem-Tov, S. Hamtzan survey: Cults or return to Judaism. *Hamtzan,* January 31, 1985 (in Hebrew).

Sherif, M., and Cantril, H. *The Psychology of Ego Involvement.* New York: Wiley, 1947.

Shiffer, S. *Snowball: The Story Behind the Lebanon War.* Tel Aviv: Edanim, 1984 (in Hebrew).

Shipler, D. K. The other Israeli casualties: The mentally scarred. *New York Times,* January 8, 1983.

Shmueli, E. Special Memorandum, January 14, 1982. Ministry of Education and Culture. State of Israel.

Shragai, N. We demonstrate against the Zionist enterprise. *Haaretz,* April 21, 1986 (in Hebrew).

Shye, S. Public attitudes towards religious literature and religious institutions. The Israel Institute of Applied Social Research, Jerusalem, October 1983 (mimeo).

Simmel, G. *Conflict and the Web of Group Affiliations.* Glencoe, Ill.: Free Press, 1964.

Simon, G. C. Psychology, professional practice and the public interest. In B. D. Sales (ed.): *The Professional Psychologist Handbook,* pp. 541–98. New York: Plenum, 1983.

Singer, M. T. Coming out of the cults. *Psychology Today,* January 1979.

Skinner, B. F. *Beyond Freedom and Dignity.* New York: Knopf, 1971.

Sklar, D. *Gods and Beasts.* New York: Crowell, 1977.

Smilansky, S. School adjustment of fatherless orphans. *Megamot,* 22:143–56, 1977 (in Hebrew).

———. The concept of death among Israeli children. In A. Raviv, A. Klingman, and M. Horowitz (eds.): *Children in Situations of Stress and Crisis.* Tel Aviv: Otzar Hamoreh, 1980 (in Hebrew).

Smilanksy, S., and Weisman, T. *A Guide for Rehabilitation Workers: Israel Defense Forces Orphans and their Mothers.* Jerusalem: Henrietta Szold Institute, 1978.

Smolowe, J. The strange world of cults. *Newsweek,* January 16, 1984.

Snow, D. A., Zurcher, L. A., Jr., and Ekland-Olson, S. Social networks and social movements: A microstructural approach to differential recruitment. *American Sociological Review,* 45: 787–801, 1980.

Sobel, Z. *Migrants From the Promised Land.* New Brunswick, N.J.: Transaction Books, 1986.

Soffrin, G., and Yodfat, H. *Cults in Israel.* Confidential Intelligence Report, Intelligence Department, Israel National Police Headquarters, August 22, 1982.

Sohl, J. *The Lemon Eaters.* New York: Simon and Schuster, 1967.

Soliman, P. Confrontation with death. *Israel Annals of Psychiatry and Related Disciplines,* 17:149–64, 1979.

Stallings, R. A. The community context of crisis management. *American Behavioral Scientist,* 16:312–25, 1972.

Starbuck, E. D. *The Psychology of Religion.* New York: Scribner's, 1903.

Stark, R., and Bainbridge, W. S. *The Future of Religion.* Berkeley: University of California Press, 1984.

Stone, R. A. *Social Change in Israel: Attitudes and Events, 1967–1979.* New York: Praeger, 1982.

Strean, H. S. The psychoanalyst: An agent of social change. *Current Issues in Psychoanalytic Practice,* 2:29–37, 1985.

Strier, R. High School seniors speak out. *Koteret Rashit,* December 22, 1982 (in Hebrew).

Szasz, T. S. Psychotherapy: A sociocultural perspective. *Comprehensive Psychiatry,* 7:217–23, 1966.

Talbott, J. A. Radical psychiatry: An examination of the issues. *American Journal of Psychiatry,* 131:121–28, 1974.

Temerlin, M. K., and Temerlin, J. W. Psychotherapy cults: An iatrogenic perversion. *Psychotherapy: Theory, Research and Practice,* 19:131–41, 1982.

Tene, S. When the kibbutz member is searching for meaning. *Yediot Aharonot,* June 15, 1982 (in Hebrew).

———. Parents and children fight the temptation of the cults. *Yediot Aharonot,* March 27, 1983 (in Hebrew).

———. The kibbutz decided: Any alcoholic member will be expelled. *Yediot Aharonot,* August 12, 1986 (in Hebrew).

Thouless, R. H. *An Introduction To The Psychology of Religion.* New York: Macmillan, 1923.

Tiryakian, E. A. Toward the sociology of esoteric culture. *American Journal of Sociology,* 78:491–512, 1972.

Tomer, I. Proposal: Tax on alcohol—for the alcoholics. *Yediot Aharonot,* May 8, 1988 (in Hebrew).

Trevelyan, G. M. *English Social History.* London: Longmans, Green, 1944.

Troeltsch, E. Church and sect. In T. Parsons, E. Shils, K. D. Naegle, and J. R. Pitts (eds.): *Theories of Society.* New York: The Free Press, 1961.

Truzzi, M. Astrology as popular culture. *Journal of Popular Culture,* 8:906–11, 1975.

Tumarkin, T. Who is more frightening, Uri Zohar or Hare Krishna? *Davar,* July 1, 1983 (in Hebrew).

Turner, R. H., and Killian, L. M. *Collective Behavior.* Englewood Cliffs, N.J.: Prentice Hall, 1957.

Tzimuki, T. Gluska to the presidents. *Davar,* November 14, 1986 (in Hebrew).

Tzror, R. The hour of the beast. *Koteret Rashit,* September 21, 1983 (in Hebrew).

Ullman, C. Cognitive and emotional antecedents of religious conversion. *Journal of Personality and Social Psychology,* 43:183–92, 1982.

Ungerleider, J. T., and Wellisch, D. K. Coercive persuasion (brainwashing), religious cults and deprogramming. *American Journal of Psychiatry,* 136:279–82, 1979.

Uziel, M. Talking to the preachers. *Maariv,* March 7, 1985 (in Hebrew).

Vardi, R. Galili never forgave Ben-Gurion. *Yediot Aharonot,* February 14, 1986 (in Hebrew).

Vidal, D. *Le Malheur et son prophète: Inspirés et sectaires en Languedoc calviniste (1685–1725).* Paris: Payot, 1983.

Vonnegut, K., Jr. *Player Piano.* New York: Delacorte, 1965.

Vriend, J., and Dyer, W. W. Schools fail to promote student self-development: The case for deliberate psychological education. *Educational Technology,* 16:7–15, 1976.

Wallace, A. F. C. *Tornado in Worcester: An Exploratory Study of Individual and Community Behavior in an Extreme Situation.* Washington, D.C.: National Academy of Sciences, 1956a.

———. Revitalization movements. *American Anthropologist,* 58:264–81, 1956b.

———. *Religion: An Anthropological View.* New York: Random House, 1966.

———. *The Death and Rebirth of The Seneca,* New York: Knopf, 1970.

Wallace, R. A. A model of change in religious affiliation. *Journal for the Scientific Study of Religion,* 14:345–56, 1975.

Wallfish, A. Jehovah's Witnesses freed from army jails because of MK's intervention. *The Jerusalem Post,* March 2, 1976.

Wallis, N., and Curran, F. Goon's sons and cult of the deadly curse. *Daily Star* (London), October 22, 1981.

Walter, J. "Secret" astrological map delivered personally to Chief of Staff Bureau. *Maariv,* September 5, 1986 (in Hebrew).

Walters, R. Ten years of best sellers. *New York Times,* December 30, 1979.

Warburg, G. A way of life. *Heidim,* July 1983, No. 3 (113) (in Hebrew).

Warner, R. *Recovery from Schizophrenia: Psychiatry and Political Economy.* London: Routledge and Kegan Paul, 1986.

Weber, M. *Economy and Society,* 3 vols. New York: Bedminster, 1968.

Weiner, H. *The Wild Goats of Ein Gedi.* Garden City, N.Y.: Doubleday, 1961.

———. *9½ Mystics.* New York: Holt, Rinehart and Winston, 1969.

Weinstein, F., and Platt, G. M. *Psychoanalytic Sociology: An Essay in the Interpretation of Historical Data and the Phenomena of Collective Behavior.* Baltimore: The Johns Hopkins University, 1973.

Werther, Y. Yaari and Granot are optimistic about the verdict tomorrow. *Hadashot*, January 14, 1986 (in Hebrew).

Wilson, G. D. The Concept of conservatism. In G. D. Wilson (ed.): *The Psychology of Conservatism.* London: Academic Press, 1973.

Wispe, L. G., and Parloff, M. B. Impact of psychotherapy on the productivity of psychologists. *Journal of Abnormal Psychology,* 70:188–93, 1965.

Witztum, E., Greenberg, D., and Buchbinder, J. T. "A very narrow bridge": Diagnosis and management of mental illness among Bratslav hassidim. *Psychotherapy,* 27:124–31, 1990a.

Witztum, E., Greenberg, D., and Dasberg, H. Mental illness and religious change. *British Journal of Medical Psychology,* 63:33–41, 1990b.

Wolfe, T. The "Me" decade. *New York Magazine,* August 23, 1976, pp. 26–40.

Wolfsfeld, G. *The Politics of Provocation,* Albany, N.Y.: SUNY Press, 1988.

Wolfson, R. *A Study in Handwriting Analysis.* New York: Edwards Brothers, 1949.

Wolman, B. B. *Dictionary of Behavioral Science.* New York: Van Nostrand Reinhold, 1970.

Worsely, P. *The Trumpet Shall Sound.* New York: Schocken, 1968.

Wozner, Y. Learning to be parents. *Hed Hahinukh,* February 1982, pp. 16–17 (in Hebrew).

Wulff, W. *Zodiac and Swastika.* London: Athur Barker, 1973.

Yalom, I. *The Theory and Practice of Group Psychotherapy.* New York: Basic Books, 1985.

Yalov, S. The tank in Lebanon and the sunset in Egypt. *Davar,* August 10, 1984 (in Hebrew).

Yeffet, Z. Believers in "Our Lord Jesus" attacked by orthodox. *Haaretz,* October 11, 1977 (in Hebrew).

———. Olmert and Knesset ethics. *Haaretz,* August 10, 1984 (in Hebrew).

Yinger, J. M. Contraculture and subculture. *American Sociological Review,* 25:625–35, 1960.

Yishai, S. "I felt like I was in the cocukoo's nest." *Haolam Hazeh,* May 27, 1981 (in Hebrew).

———. "I am being stifled by loneliness." *Haolam Hazeh,* June 1, 1983 (in Hebrew).

Yizhar, S. We are all partners. *Maariv,* April 15, 1975 (in Hebrew).

Yogev, S. *Graphotherapy.* Tel-Aviv: Masada, 1980.

Young, T. R. A theory of undergrouond structures: Some exploratory theses. No. 46 in the Transforming Sociology Series. The Red Feather Institute, Red Feather, Colorado.

Yudilovich, G. The police suspect: Drunk drivers were involved in recent accidents. *Maariv,* October 27, 1986 (in Hebrew).

Zadock, Y. Michael Lame: Israelis are friendlier than Americans. *Yediot Aharonot,* January 28, 1983 (in Hebrew).

Zaretsky, I. I., and Leone, M. P. (eds.). *Religious Movements in Contemporary America.* Princeton, N.J.: Princeton University Press, 1974.

Zilbergeld, B. *The Shrinking of America.* Boston: Little, Brown, 1983.

Zohar, G. "Emin," "Moonies," etc. *Al Hamishmar,* March 19, 1982 (in Hebrew).

Zohar, U. *Therefore choose life.* Jerusalem: Hamessorah, 1983 (in Hebrew).

Zorea, N. *On Death and Dying.* Tel Aviv: Hakibbutz Hemeuhad, 1975 (in Hebrew).

Zur, Y. A messianic cult in Ashdod removed through pressure from Orthodox. *Hadashot,* November 23, 1984 (in Hebrew).

Zweig, F. *Israel: The Sword and the Harp.* London: Heinemann, 1969.

Index